Thomas Schirrmacher

Indulgences

Cover foto: "Indulgences chest", early 16th century, Used with kind permission by the State of Saxony-Anhalt, "Landesinstitut für Lehrerfortbildung, Lehrerweiterbildung und Unterrichtsforschung von Sachsen-Anhalt (LISA)"

Biblia et symbiotica

Band 9: Bernhard Kaiser. Luther und die Auslegung des Römerbriefes: Eine theologisch-geschichtliche Beurteilung. 1995
Band 11: Jochen Bohn. Der Mensch im calvinischen Staat: Göttliche Weltordnung und politischer Beruf. 1995
Band 12: Thomas Schirrmacher. Galilei-Legenden. 1995.
Band 13: Tobias Jäger. Olavus Petri, Reformator in Schweden und andere skandinavistische Beiträge. 1995
Band 18: Andreas Späth. Luther und die Juden. 2001
Band 19: Thomas Schirrmacher. Beiträge zur Kirchen- und Theologiegeschichte: Heiligenverehrung – Universität Gießen – Reformation / Augustin – Böhl – Spurgeon – Brunner. 2001
Band 20: Reinhold Friedrich. Martin Bucer – ‚Fanatiker der Einheit'?. Seine Stellungnahme zu theologischen Fragen seiner Zeit (Abendmahls- und Kirchenverständnis) insbesondere nach seinem Briefwechsel der Jahre 1524-1541. 2002.

Reihe ab Band 21 getrennt in *Biblia et symbiotica* für Beiträge zur Bibel und die Reihe
Geschichte – Kirchengeschichte – Reformation

Geschichte – Kirchengeschichte – Reformation

Band 24

Band 21: Friedrich Wilhelm Schirrmacher. Briefe und Akten zum Marburger Religionsgespräch (1529) und zum Augsburger Reichstag (1530). 2003
Band 22: Friedrich Wilhelm Schirrmacher. Die Entstehung des Kurfürstenkollegiums. 2003
Band 23: John Warwick Montgomery. Heraldic Aspects of the German Reformation. 2003

Thomas Schirrmacher

Indulgences

A History of Theology and Reality of Indulgences and Purgatory

A Protestant Evaluation

WIPF & STOCK · Eugene, Oregon

Wipf and Stock Publishers
199 W 8th Ave, Suite 3
Eugene, OR 97401

Indulgences
A History of Theology and Reality of Indulgences and
Purgatory: A Protestant Evaluation
By Schirrmacher, Thomas
Copyright©2012 Verlagfur Kultur und Wissenschaft
ISBN 13: 978-1-4982-0628-0
Publication date 9/23/2014

Content

1 Interacting with Roman Catholic Teaching 9
2 Introduction 13
   2.1   A Central Question 13
   2.2   Are Indulgences a Thing of the Past? 13
   2.3   A Preliminary Evaluation and Summary 16
   2.4   Five Components of the Teaching on Indulgences and 18
   2.5   Related Roman Catholic Teachings 18
   2.6   The Teaching of Satisfaction as a Precondition 18
       2.6.1 Sin after Baptism: Mortal Sins and Venial Sins 19
       2.6.2 The Sacrament of Penance 20
       2.6.3 Actions Taken by the Penitent: 1. Confession 21
       2.6.4 Actions Taken by the Penitent: 2. Repentance as
             Contrition of Love or Contrition of Fear 22
       2.6.5 Actions Taken by the Penitent: 3. Penance and
             Satisfaction 23
       2.6.6 Reconciliation with the Roman Catholic Church 24
3 The History of Indulgences and Their Theology from the Time of
Their Inception in the Middle Ages until the Reformation 25
   3.1   Tariff Penance as an Historical Antecedent to Indulgences 25
   3.2   The Indulgence as a Completely New Product of the Middle
       Ages 26
   3.3   Crusade Indulgences 31
   3.4   The Crusades and Indulgences Related There to Bring About
       the Modern Papacy 35
   3.5   Indulgences Began as an Abuse 39
   3.6   The Pope on the Abuses 44
   3.7   Indulgences Heightened the Importance of the Papacy 45
   3.8   Was Money the Mainspring? 47
   3.9   Indulgence Theology Began as a Critique of Indulgences 50
   3.10 Scholasticism Brings About the Theology of Indulgences 52
   3.11 The Meaning of Mendicant Orders for Indulgences 54
   3.12 St. Thomas Aquinas 55
   3.13 Exkursus: Development of a Dogma? 56
   3.14 Purgatory – Also a Completely New Outgrowth of the Twelfth
       Century 60

3.15 The Teaching of the Treasury of the Church – a Completely New Outgrowth of the Thirteenth Century 65
3.16 Indulgences for the Deceased – A Completely New Outgrowth of the Thirteenth and Fourteenth Centuries 68
3.17 Jubilee Indulgences Beginning in 1300 70
3.18 Indulgence Campaigns from 1350-1500 and the 'Ad Instar Indulgences' 71
3.19 The Decline of the Indulgence Campaign from 1500-1517 74

4 The History of Indulgences and Their Theology from the Reformation until the Second Vatican Council 77
 4.1 The Reformation and Indulgences 77
  4.1.1 Martin Luther 77
  4.1.2 Antecedent History and John Tetzel 84
  4.1.3 The Doctrinal Proclamation of Indulgences of 1518 89
  4.1.4 John Calvin 91
  4.1.5 Protestants Favoring Indulgences? The Example of C. S. Lewis 92
 4.2 The Council of Trent 93
 4.3 From the Council of Trent until the Second Vatican Council 96

5 The Reform of the Theology of Indulgences Prior to the Second Vatican Council and Its Failure during the Council and into the Present 99
 5.1 Signs of a Mitigation of Indulgence Theology Prior to 1967 99
 5.2 The Second Vatican Council 102
 5.3 The Abrupt End to Indulgence Theology in 1967 107
 5.4 Orthodox Believers' Response to the Pope's 1967 Apostolic Constitution on Indulgences 111
 5.5 Karl Rahner after 1967 113
 5.6 Schillebeeckx in Light of 1967 115
 5.7 The Modern View of the Treasury of Merit 116
 5.8 The Pope on Indulgences from 1967-2002 117
 5.9 The Apostolic Penitentiary in 2000 121
 5.10 On the Abolishment of Temporal Assignments Relating to Indulgences 124

6 The Dogmatic Debate: Questions and Biblical Justification 129
 6.1 Catholic and Protestant Questions 129
 6.2 Biblical Justification? 132
  6.2.1 The Orthodox Church's View of the Contradiction between the New Testament and the Teaching of Indulgences 132
  6.2.2 Individual Biblical Texts and Topics 134

7 Appendix: The Development of the Papacy and the Final
  Disempowerment of the Council 143
8 Important Literature Regarding Indulgences 151
   8.1.1 Sources 152
   8.1.2 Catholic Literature Prior to the Second Vatican Council
         (chronologically) 152
   8.1.3 Catholic Literature Since the Second Vatican Council
         (alphabetical) 153
   8.1.4 Protestant Writings against Indulgences (chronologically
         and excluding the Reformation) 154
   8.1.5 Historical Presentation from the Pens of Catholics and
         Protestants (chronological) 154
9 Chronology of Indulgences 157

1 Interacting with Roman Catholic Teaching

The Roman Catholic Church and its 1.1 billion members, under the leadership of the Pope, is by far the largest organization in history. It is also the oldest organization to exist without interruption in history, and it has survived massive upheavals since the time of the Roman Empire. The Roman Catholic Church, in the half-millennium since the Reformation, has experienced enormous development and change. One cannot simply cast today's pope into the same pot with the popes of the Crusades and the Inquisition. An honest discussion regarding Roman Catholic teachings always has to be done with respect to the current state of the Roman Catholic Church. One has to soundly research what the official teachings of the Roman Catholic Church and its theologians are today. We see ourselves obligated to truth in a way that requires exhaustive study of the comprehensive literary efforts of the recent popes.

It is not a simple matter of dispensing with all that is Roman Catholic and welcoming everything that is protestant or evangelical, which would be to not listen to the interpretations of others but rather, in an anti-Roman-Catholic reflex, always hold the opposite of papal teaching to be correct. I have come to know the Roman Catholic Church in diverse countries like France, Mexico and China. It is important to note that the 1.1 billion members do not represent a monolithic block.

In my book *Der Papst und das Leiden* (*The Pope and Suffering*), I present the idea that in Protestant theology the theme of suffering and its importance for the body of Christ are all too often completely neglected or forgotten. The Pope reminds us of weighty Bible passages that we may not suppress. I demonstrated with Colossians 1:24, Pope John Paul II. favorite verse, what in my opinion is an incorrect view, that Paul then and the Pope today, with their individual sufferings, make the suffering of Christ more perfect. This is in contrast to the fact that the same verse does not even appear to exist as a general rule in Protestant circles, and furthermore, that the idea of the suffering of the entire body of Christ practically does not even exist as a topic. Even there, where the Pope's interpretation of the Bible is rejected, one still needs to remain open to the critical question of whether we are truer to the Scriptures. To be evangelical means to be self-examining, since we as people are not infallible. It is rather the case that God and his Word are infallible. We as Christians are, and remain until the return of Jesus, threatened by sin, vanity, and self-deception. This is one of the central teachings of the Reformation, and we need to pay attention that we do not preach to others and become condemnable ourselves (1 Corinthians 9:27).

In many questions of faith, the Roman Catholic Church, on the basis of its development over the last 500 years, stands closer to Bible-believing Christians than was the case 500 years ago. Nowadays lay people may read the Bible, and Roman Catholic Bible societies distribute millions of Bibles every year. Home groups, in which the Bible is studied, are also present within the Roman Catholic Church. Granted there may still be too few such groups, but they are welcomed. The Pope is surely still the political leader of a miniature country, but his political and military leadership role from times past has disappeared. It is rather the case that the Pope has consciously relinquished political rights and has even disarmed the remainder of his Swiss Guards, which used to be an effective set of elite troops. Today the Vatican is protected by the Italian State. For more than forty years, worship services have taken place in the vernacular. Latin is only an internal administrative language or the language used in international worship services. In the teaching of grace, the Roman Catholic Church nowadays gives immense priority to grace over merit, which in certain cases cannot always be said about Protestants and Evangelicals. The list of points in which the Roman Catholic Church has changed for the better over the past 500 years could easily be extended.

At the same time, we want to consciously admit that the Roman Catholic Church basically never retracts earlier pronouncements of dogma. Rather, the Roman Catholic Church has its own view of the development of knowledge that allows it to introduce basic changes without officially changing anything. These changes are understood to be elucidations of earlier perspectives, even in cases where *de facto* the opposite is being said. In this manner, the ban on Bible study by lay people has never been repealed, but it has long been replaced by the call to Bible study. This unusual course of action is typically Roman Catholic and is difficult for Protestants to understand, but for the sake of fairness, one should always make sure whether what was once stated as infallible is still to be viewed today as valid or whether it has tacitly been replaced by new, infallible decrees.

Conversely, there are also questions and topics in which the Roman Catholic Church in the past 500 years has distanced itself more from Bible-believing Christians preaching the gospel of the New Testament and the Reformation. The Roman Catholic view of the Virgin Mary at the time of Luther pales in comparison with the present-day view of Mary. In the meantime, Mary, just as Jesus, is not seen to have been born into sin (the immaculate conception). She became sinless just as is Jesus, and she ascended into heaven just as did Jesus. Mary is also *coredemptrix*, or the co-Redeemer. While the Pope has lost and relinquished political and military power, his ecclesiastical and religious power has vastly grown. The Pope is, in the meantime, infallible, and the unanimous decision of the worldwide council of bishops, an authority the Roman Catholic Church repeatedly invoked against Luther, is invalid and fallible today if not confirmed by the Pope.

To simply quote Roman Catholic documents and dogma from the sixteenth century does not suffice for good or for bad. Since my 1982 comments on Roman Catholic Canon Law, I have repeatedly tried, in particular, to address the newest Roman Catholic texts in a matter-of-fact manner. That is not to say that sources from the sixteenth century as well as those which inform us about the Roman Catholic Church's history cannot be of interest to us. Pope Johannes Paul II, as we will see in detail later, called, in his 1998 encyclical, for a Jubilee Indulgence for the Jubilee Year 2000. In doing so, he referred directly and without qualification to the Jubilee bull of his predecessor Boniface VIII in 1300. Such an action clearly demonstrates how important historical continuity is for the Roman Catholic Church, and this, far prior to the Reformation. It also demonstrates how we can practically never understand the teaching of the Roman Catholic Church without at the same time understanding historical developments.

In short, every reader is invited to review the sources and texts presented herein and to come up with his or her own opinion. It is not a matter of winning a discussion, whereby the opponent is put in a worse light than he deserves, or of setting up a straw man, who only imaginarily exists. This has to do with a reliable and comprehensible presentation of the current view of the Roman Catholic Church on the topics found in this book and with a discerning examination in light of Holy Scripture. Both the author and the publisher willingly accept pointers where opposing positions are concerned and where such positions are unintentionally incorrectly presented. These will be accordingly changed in later editions.

Note 1: The many long quotes by the indulgence researcher Nikolaus Paulus are possible because of the fact that rights thereto have lapsed. As his major work was never translated into English, several longer sections from his research are given in full.

Note 2: This translation represents as does the original German book from 2005 the situation under Pope John Paul II. The author is working on a paper on the views on indulgences of Pope Benedicts XVI. which might be added to a later edition.

2 Introduction

2.1 A Central Question

The dispute regarding indulgences goes right to the heart of the difference between Protestant and Roman Catholic faiths, whereby the Orthodox Church also stands in opposition to the Roman Catholic position. We will look at this later in more detail. The pivotal problem is not that in earlier times money was also collected in connection with indulgences and that otherwise indulgences were for hundreds of years associated with abuses also criticized by the Roman Catholic Church. That is perhaps only a typical aftereffect seen up to the time of the Reformation. At the heart of the issue, however, is a central question of theology and belief.

When speaking of the difference between Protestant and Roman Catholic teaching, one should not overlook the fact that not only Protestant confessions (above all, Lutheran, Reformed, Anglican, Baptist, and Pentecostal) but all other Catholic confessions that are non-Roman, that is to say, the Orthodox and Oriental churches, know neither the teachings of indulgences nor of the treasury of merit nor of purgatory.[1]

2.2 Are Indulgences a Thing of the Past?

Many Protestants have the impression that indulgences within Roman Catholicism have taken on less and less meaning and only represent a fringe of Roman Catholic teaching. For this reason, there has only been a limited number of protestant or evangelical treatises on or against indulgences, especially if one ignores shorter articles and other published material.[2] We

---

[1] Comp. Emilianos Timiades. "Zur apostolischen Konstitution über die Neuordnung der Ablässe". pp. 319-349 in: Damaskinos Papandreou (ed.). Stimmen der Orthodoxie: Zu Grundfragen des II. Vatikanums. Wien/Freiburg: Herder, 1969; Johannes N. Karmiris. "Abriss der dogmatischen Lehre der orthodoxen katholischen Kirche", pp. 15-120 in: Panagiotis Bratsiotis (ed.). Die orthodoxe Kirche in griechischer Sicht. 2 Bde./Teile. 1. Teil. Ev. Verlagswerk, 1959[1]; 1970[2] (both parts in one volume). p. 113-117; comp. Andreas Merkt. Das Fegefeuer: Entstehung und Funktion einer Idee. Darmstadt: Wissenschaftliche Buchgesellschaft, 2005. p. 73.

[2] Notable exceptions are, for example, Helmut Echternach. "Korreferat". pp. 39-51 in: Georg Muschalek u. a. Gespräch über den Ablaß. Arbeiten zur kirchlichen Wiedervereinigung – Kirchengeschichtliche Reihe 2. Graz: Verlag Styria, 1965

will see in detail below that indulgences are not only still firmly anchored in popular Roman Catholicism but that they also remained a central concern of the popes in the twentieth century.

Even within Roman Catholic circles there has been a reigning impression that indulgences no longer belong to the central concerns of the Roman Catholic Church and that basic theological changes with respect to indulgences, the treasury of merit, and purgatory have been underway. After all, Pope Paul VI (1963-1978), as we will see, did away with a significant element of indulgences. He namely abolished the connection between concrete services performed and particular periods of time spent in purgatory. Otto Semmelroth, who in 1967 released the papal writing in Germany, was of the opinion in his 1968 "Indulgences – Four Hundred Fifty Years after the Reformation"[3] that so many changes had been made to indulgences that they had lost their *in rem* judicial character and, therefore, for Protestants had nothing more to do with indulgences of the sixteenth century.

Even in 1993 Ottmar Fuchs was able to write: "In spite of new attempts to relay understanding, for a large part of believers the traditional practice of indulgences belongs to the past."[4] Fuchs continued in his comments by mentioning that only conservative Roman Catholic Church groups still hold to it. Back in 1980 Cardinal Joseph Höffner made absolutely no mention of indulgences in his writing on "Repentance and Forgiveness."[5] Up until 1999 the Diocese of Cologne had the following comments regarding indulgences: "One of the reasons why we have difficulty with indulgences is that indulgences raise difficult dogmatic, psychological, and pastoral questions. Indulgences are not monolithic. Indulgences developed with time, and over the course of time, there were accretions that had their meaning at a particular time and in a particular situation and can only be understood within that framework."[6]

---

and Norman L. Geisler, Ralph E. MacKenzie. Roman Catholics and Evangelicals: Agreements and Differences. Baker Books, 1998 (1995). pp. 331-355.

[3] Otto Semmelroth. "Indulgences – Four hundred-fifty Years after the Reformation" (German original "Ablaß – vierhundertfünfzig Jahre nach der Reformation"). pp. 9-27 in: Karl Rahner, Otto Semmelroth (ed.). Theologische Akademie. Bd. 5. Frankfurt a. M.: Josef Knecht, 1968.

[4] Ottmar Fuchs. "Ablaß VI. Praktisch-theologisch". col. 57-58 in: Walter Kasper (ed.). Lexikon für Theologie und Kirche. Bd. 1. Freiburg: Herder, 1993.

[5] Kardinal Joseph Höffner. Fünfzehn Sätze über Buße und Vergebung. Themen und Thesen 3. Köln: Presseamt des Erzbistums Köln, 1980 9th ed.

[6] Johannes Hüttenbügel. Der Ablaß. Zeitfragen 49. Köln: Presseamt des Erzbistums Köln, 1999. p. 7.

Introduction

My earlier critique of indulgence theology was sympathetically received by Roman Catholic authors as late as 2000.[7]

As we will see below, many Protestant and Roman Catholic Christians were all the more astounded that between 1998 and 2000 the entire nature of indulgences was newly brought into the center of attention at several levels around the world by Pope John Paul II.

The proclamation of the Jubilee Indulgence in a "Bull of Proclamation" refers back, without any qualification, to the first Jubilee year over 200 years before the Reformation. In 1300 Pope Boniface VIII made public a bull proclaiming the first Jubilee Indulgence. This proclamation by Pope John Paul II was made as if there had neither been a Reformation nor the Second Vatican Council. Pope John Paul II wrote: "How many historic memories the Jubilee evokes! We can recall the year 1300 when, responding to the wish of the people of Rome, Pope Boniface VIII solemnly inaugurated the first Jubilee in history. Resuming an ancient tradition which offered 'abundant remission and pardon of sins' to those who visited Saint Peter's Basilica in the Eternal City, he wished on that occasion to grant 'a pardon of sins which would be not only more abundant, but complete.' From that time onward, the Church has always celebrated Jubilees as significant steps on her journey toward the fullness of Christ."[8]

This was a new challenge to Protestants. Pierre Bühler, Professor for Systematic Theology in Zurich, wrote a well-informed response to the Roman Catholic indulgence writings from 1999 and 2000.[9] Since that time, however, it has been largely quiet from the Protestant side insofar as indulgences are concerned.

---

[7] E.g., Johannes Grabmeier. Der Ablaß der katholischen Kirche – ein aktuelles Thema im Jahr 2000!? Lecture January 1,2000, Pfarrgemeinde St. Peter, Heidelberg (now on the internet as a pdf file from the author, johannes@grabmeier.net).

[8] Johannes Paul II. Incarnationis mysterium. Verkündigungsbulle des Großen Jubiläums des Jahres 2000. November 29, 1998. Verlautbarungen des Apostolischen Stuhles 136. Bonn: Deutsche Bischofskonferenz, 1998. p. 8. Available in English at http://www.vatican.va/jubilee_2000/docs/documents/hf_jp-ii_doc_30111998_bolla-jubilee_en.html.

[9] Pierre Bühler. Ablass oder Rechtfertigung durch Glauben: Was brauchen wir zum Jubiläumsjahr 2000? Zürich: Pano Verlag, 2000; comp. also Theologischer Ausschuß der Gesellschaft für Innere und Äußere Mission im Sinne der lutherischen Kirche. Ablaß? – Nein danke! Neuendettelsau: Gesellschaft für Innere und Äußere Mission, (Brochure 8 pages) (additional versions of the text please see below).

2.3 A Preliminary Evaluation and Summary

What is an 'indulgence'? The new 1983 Roman Catholic Canon Law, which Pope John Paul II. adopted,[10] defines indulgence very tellingly: "An indulgence is remission before God of temporal punishment for sins whose guilt is already forgiven, which a properly disposed member of the Christian faith gains . . . by the assistance of the Church which as minister of redemption dispenses and applies authoritatively the treasury of the satisfactions of Christ and the saints."[11]

According to Roman Catholic teaching, eternal guilt (including eternal punishment) is forgiven by confession and by the absolution that follows. Temporal punishment, however, remains. In the case of less grievous transgressions, temporal punishment can be satisfied by, e.g., praying the rosary or Hail Mary, but these transgressions must also be atoned for in purgatory. This time of punishment in purgatory can be shortened or cancelled by indulgences. For this the Church uses the so-called treasury of merit or the treasury of Christ's atoning merits. These treasuries contain all surplus good works of Christ and of the Saints and which the Church, or, alternatively, the Pope, administers and can credit to supplicants.

Against this background, one can understand the exact formulation of the quote: "An indulgence is the remission before God of temporal punishment for sins whose guilt is already forgiven." This short statement from 1983 reveals a central problem of Roman Catholic theology, which remains unchanged to this day. It detracts from Christ's death on the cross, which for the Roman Catholic Church only addresses eternal guilt but does not address temporal guilt. Temporal guilt has to be worked off, even in the case where eternal guilt has been forgiven. This also applies where one has good works of the Saints credited to one's account. In such a case, it is simply someone else who works off the temporal penalty. Confession, indulgences, purgatory, and the bloodless repetition of the sacrifice of Jesus

---

[10] Comp. my contributions to discussions of the new Canon Law: "Hat sich die katholische Kirche geändert?" Bibel und Gemeinde 89 (1989) 2: 181-207; "Das neue katholische Kirchenrecht". Licht und Leben 9/1984: 198-200; "Has Roman Catholicism Changed? An Examination of Recent Canon Law". Antithesis: A Review of Reformed/Presbyterian Thought and Practice 1 (1990) 2 (March/April): 23-30.

[11] Johannes Paul II. Codex Iuris Canonici: Codex des kanonischen Rechtes: Lateinisch-deutsche Ausgabe. Verlag Butzon & Bercker: Kevelaer, 1984². Can 992; also quoted in Katechismus der katholischen Kirche. Oldenbourg: München, 1993. p. 401, Nr. 1471. Available in English at http://www.vatican.va/archive/ENG1104/__P3I.HTM.

in the mass reveal that Roman Catholicism has replaced the biblical view where it has least reason to do so: in the question of the meaning of the death of Jesus on the cross.

Even the Old Testament taught, in contrast, that the Messiah is a "Prince of Peace," who at the same time is "Everlasting Father" and "Mighty God" (Isaiah 9:6), not only takes away guilt (Isaiah 53:6). Rather, he was punished for our sins (Isaiah 53:4), and the penalty was placed upon him (Isaiah 53:5) so that we might have peace with God: "The punishment that brought us peace was upon him . . ." (Isaiah 53:5).

Temporal consequences of sin are often mentioned in Scripture as grounds for the continuation of 'temporal punishment' in spite of forgiveness. Specifically, it is 1) the need for redress; 2) the consequences of sin; and 3) the visible punishment of God, which occur in spite of forgiveness.

Regarding 1), a thief, in spite of forgiveness, has to make amends. Other wrongdoings likewise have damages that must be paid. Here, in the first instance, the issue has to do with penalties administered by the state. The Bible indicates that such penalties continue to be so prescribed by the state and not by the church. These are not penalties that the church can set on its own authority and vary as it wishes. They are also penalties that, by the way, cannot simply be absolved. Secondly, reparation is not meant to address one's own punishment but rather the damage that was done to another, and for that reason it simply cannot be absolved.

Regarding 2), remaining earthly consequences of sin, for instance, the case where the murderer's victim is dead or where a divorce has occurred, are mostly, in spite of forgiveness, irreversible. Nothing changes the situation, be it an indulgence or an action on the part of the guilty person.

Regarding 3), God, in particularly severe cases, nevertheless carries out an earthly, visible, and partial punishment in spite of forgiveness. Here as well, no action on the part of the guilty person, that is to say, no indulgence, changes anything. This can least of all effect anything after death. The most famous example often mentioned by Roman Catholics is the case of David, whose adultery and murder (2 Samuel 11), in spite of repentance and forgiveness (Psalm 51; 2 Samuel 12:1-13, particularly 12:13), were punished with the death of the child which resulted from the adulterous relationship (2 Samuel 12: 14-25): "But because by doing this you have made the enemies of the Lord show utter contempt, the son born to you will die" (2 Samuel 12:14). This death has nothing to do with working off guilt, and it was also not able to be avoided by any action. Nowhere is it seen that the prophet Nathan (or later the church) would have had the authority and the power to override such consequences.

2.4 Five Components of the Teaching on Indulgences and

2.5 Related Roman Catholic Teachings

Indulgences consist of five components unique to Roman Catholic theology. These are 1) the teaching of the necessity for human satisfaction for forgiven sins; 2) the intrinsic indulgence; 3) the teaching of the treasuries of merit out of a surplus of good works; 4) the teaching of purgatory; and 5) the teaching that the office of the Pope conveys propitiation and forgiveness, which is the so-called power of the keys.

We will discuss each of these elements as they chronologically appear in indulgence history.

Indulgences as a Roman Catholic teaching, that is to say, a teaching that is completely unknown to all other confessions, stands in close connection not only to these purely Roman Catholic teachings just mentioned. Rather, this teaching is to be seen in the broader context of other basic and purely Roman Catholic teachings, such as papal power of the keys, the understanding of the Roman Catholic Church that sin is also sin against the Church, prayer and mass for the dead, the sacrament of penance, and the view that tradition is revelation from the Holy Spirit to the Church and to popes over the course of time. Using indulgences as a launching pad, one can almost seamlessly explain everything that is proclaimed by confession that differentiates the Roman Catholic Church from other confessions, be they Protestant or Orthodox. Still, we want to limit ourselves to the five issues mentioned, except for other occasional references.

2.6 The Teaching of Satisfaction as a Precondition

In order to understand indulgences, one must understand the broader framework of Roman Catholic teaching on repentance. The individual elements of the teaching on repentance were largely developed before the introduction of indulgences, which were summarily discarded by the Protestant Reformation. Also, viewing these teachings independently demonstrates that Roman Catholic teaching differentiates itself from that of Protestant and Orthodox churches. One can point particularly to the teaching of satisfaction.[12] I will refrain from a presentation of the historical develop-

---

[12] Comp., e.g., Leopold Kopler. Bußsakrament und Ablaß. Linz: Verlag des katholischen Preßvereins, 1931. pp. 176-188; Anton Kurz. Die katholische Lehre

ment. Rather, I will trace the position as it has been quite firmly represented since the time of the Middle Ages, through Scholasticism and the Council of Trent to the Second Vatican Council and the documents from the era of the current Pope, for example in the World Catechism.

2.6.1 Sin after Baptism: Mortal Sins and Venial Sins

According to the Roman Catholic understanding, baptism brings forgiveness for everything prior to baptism, be it temporal punishment or eternal punishment. This means that a person would go directly to heaven after baptism without experiencing purgatory.

The decisive question has to do with sins committed by the Christian after baptism.[13] If one is talking about venial sins, confession, repentance, and forgiveness are required but are not salutary. However, if one is talking about consciously and deliberately committed deadly sins, the Christian forgoes his or her salvation, such that repentance and forgiveness also reinstate salvation. "The Church teaches that when someone commits a grievous sin, the life of grace dies in him; he loses the living relationship to God and is no longer a friend of God. Such a deadly sin has to do with something done out of free will and full awareness (comp. World Catechism 1857-1860). If someone were to die in the state of a deadly sin without remorse for his sins, he would be destined for hell and would remain there forever (comp. World Catechism 1035; 1861). This is what the Roman Catholic Church understands by the term 'eternal punishment for sin.' If, however, someone who has committed a deadly sin confesses or with remorse has the intention to confess sin out of love to God, God forgives the sinner and absolves the sinner from the punishment of hell (comp. World Catechism 1446; 1452)."[14]

How did the differentiation between sins arise, by which a Christian automatically is lost again, as opposed to venial sins, which are wrong but do not affect salvation? "Without doubt this evolution began with the great theologian Anselm of Canterbury, who highlighted the basic difference between a knowingly and an un-knowingly committed sin. In his word *Cur*

---

vom Ablass vor und nach dem Auftreten Luthers. Paderborn: Ferdinand Schöningh, 1900. pp. 12-16 "§1. Die katholische Lehre von der Genugthuung".

[13] See e.g. Bernhard Poschmann. Der Ablass im Licht der Bußgeschichte. op. cit., p. 1.

[14] Peter Christoph Düren. Der Ablass in Lehre und Praxis: Die vollkommenen Ablässe der katholischen Kirche. Buttenwiesen: Stella Maris Verlag, 2000 2nd ed. p. 29 (KKK = Katechismus der katholischen Kirche).

Deus Homo (II, 52, 115), Anselm wrote the following: "The difference between a sin knowingly committed and a sin committed in ignorance is so large that a sin which regardless of its enormity would never have been committed is only a venial sin, because it is committed in ignorance." This basic difference was accepted in the first half of the twelfth century by all the large schools "... The entire theological and moral life was from now on involved in the analysis of intention, oriented toward the question of whether a lapse was knowingly or unknowingly committed ..."[15]

2.6.2 The Sacrament of Penance

Actual forgiveness, above all for mortal sins but also for venial sins, occurs through the sacrament of penance. That is to say, there is repentance, confession, and finally, communion. The sacrament of penance "brings about a healing grace by the operation of godly power."[16] The sacrament of penance does not bring about the same result in the case of guilt for something done knowingly, voluntary, and grievous guilt without repentance,[17] and in the case of excommunication, an additional papal order must be made. The sacrament of penance is one of the seven sacraments of the Roman Catholic Church. Repentance and forgiveness sought in the case of mortal sins are thereby tied to confession in the confessional and the subsequent absolution, such that at the time of the next celebration of the Eucharist, forgiveness becomes effective.[18]

The sacrament of penance means that the Pope, as the representative of Jesus Christ, operatively cancels the obligation. "The necessary jurisdiction for the valid administration of the sacrament of penance is not provided by ordination. Rather, it is directly conferred by Christ upon the Pope, from the Pope to a bishop and from a bishop to a priest."[19]

---

[15] Jacques Le Goff. Die Geburt des Fegefeuers. op. cit., p. 259-260. Anselm in English available at http://www.ccel.org/ccel/anselm/basic_works.pdf?membership_type=4a0da612f3050ff28a6597270e23f503d7a39f6d.
[16] Leopold Kopler. Bußsakrament und Ablaß. op. cit., p. 97.
[17] Details ibid., p. 150.
[18] Johannes Paul II. Codex Iuris Canonici: Codex des kanonischen Rechtes: Lateinisch-deutsche Ausgabe. Verlag Butzon & Bercker: Kevelaer, 1984 2nd ed. Can. 964 § 2; 960.
[19] Leopold Kopler. Bußsakrament und Ablaß. op. Cit., p. 194.

2.6.3 Actions Taken by the Penitent: 1. Confession

What are the "the actions of the penitent?"[20] That is to say, what must be done by the repentant sinner? There is "contrition, confession, and satisfaction."[21]

Let us begin with confession. "Confession to a priest is an essential part of the sacrament of Penance: 'All mortal sins of which penitents, after a diligent self-examination, are conscious must be recounted by them in confession, even if they are most secret and have been committed against the last two precepts of the Decalogue; for these sins sometimes wound the soul more grievously and are more dangerous than those which are committed openly (Council of Trent [1551]: DS 1680 [ND 1626]; comp. 20:17; Deuteronomy 5:21; Matthew 5:28)."[22] The confession developed in the fifth century, when private confession was introduced, in contrast to a general confession by everyone in worship. Private confession of mortal sins became the only way to receive forgiveness. In the seventeenth century, the confessional came into use, in which there is a small screen window at the clergy member's ear level between the bench of the clergy member and the confessing sinner (for this reason in German, there is the term *Ohrenbeichte*, which, translated literally into English, means *ear confession*). Confession before a confessor or clergy member as a method of personal confession of sin was not rejected in the Reformation. Rather, the Reformation dismissed 1) compulsory confession; 2) the punishments imposed (and with them, the indulgences); 3) confession as a sacrament for forgiveness, and 4) particularly the role of the Pope and the priests as agents of

---

[20] Ibid. p. 98; comp. details pp. 98-104.
[21] Ibid. p. 98. Luther aptly describes this in his 'Ein Sermon von Ablaß und Gnade' from 1518 "First you should know that numerous new teachers, such as Peter Lombard, St. Thomas Aquinas, and their successors give repentance three components, namely remorse, confession, and satisfaction. Although according to their opinion this difference is difficult to base upon the Holy Scriptures, if not impossible to be grounded in them, and thus contrived, and while this difference is also not found in the old holy teachers of Christianity, we still want to leave it as is and use their language."
Secondly they say: indulgences do not take away the first or the second part, that is, remorse or confession, but rather the third, namely satisfaction." [Martin Luther. Gesammelte Werke. ed. by Kurt Aland. Digitale Bibliothek Bd. 63. Berlin: Directmedia, 2002 (entspricht Martin Luther: Luther deutsch. Die Werke Martin Luthers in neuer Auswahl für die Gegenwart. 10 Bde. Göttingen: Vandenhoeck und Ruprecht, 1991). p. 1197 (in the book edition vol. 2., p. 83)].
[22] Katechismus der katholischen Kirche. Oldenbourg: München, 1993. pp. 396-397, Nr. 1456.

forgiveness. The Reformation viewed absolution as a mere proclamation of the fulfilled promise of forgiveness.

Confession before a priest became an obligation in 1215 at the 4th Lateran Council. Prior to this time, there was neither compulsory confession nor confession as a sacrament.[23]

2.6.4 Actions Taken by the Penitent: 2. Repentance as Contrition of Love or Contrition of Fear

In addition to confession, contrition plays a large role for the penitent. The Roman Catholic Church differentiates between two types of contrition.[24] Contrition (Old High German *hriuwa*: abomination, grief) is the internal and therefore most important action taken in repentance, which includes the awareness of one's own wrongdoing, loathing for one's own sin, sorrow before God, and the desire to reform. Medieval and Roman Catholic theology differentiates between complete contrition or *contritio* (late Latin, contriteness; also contrition of the heart) and incomplete contrition or *attritio* (repentance out of fear), the latter only happening out of the fear of punishment and not sufficient for forgiveness. "When it arises from a love by which God is loved above all else, contrition is called 'perfect' (contrition of charity). Such contrition remits venial sins; it also obtains forgiveness of mortal sins if it includes the firm resolution to have recourse to sacramental confession as soon as possible [comp. Council of Trent: DS 1677]."[25]

Complete contrition out of love (*contritio*) justifies immediately, that is to say, without a sacrament. However, it includes the desire for a sacrament.[26] Complete contrition is not necessary. Incomplete repentance suffices, albeit only as a result of the sacrament of penance and not on its own.[27]

---

[23] The most important investigation is by Martin Ohst. Pflichtbeichte: Untersuchungen zum Bußwesen im Hohen und späten Mittelalter. Beiträge zur Historischen Theologie 89. Tübingen: J. C. B. Mohr, 1995. In particular., p. 31, 1, 15 Ohst emphasises that confession has only existed in its currect form since 1215. To this end he goes through all relevant sources.

[24] Comp. sources, etc. in Leopold Kopler. Bußsakrament und Ablaß. op. cit., pp. 112-151.

[25] Katechismus der katholischen Kirche. Oldenbourg: München, 1993. pp. 395-396, No. 1452.

[26] Leopold Kopler. Bußsakrament und Ablaß. op. cit., pp. 121-130.

[27] Ibid., pp. 130-150.

2.6.5 Actions Taken by the Penitent: 3. Penance and Satisfaction

Confession follows in the case of repentance out of fear, which demonstrates the rule of penance imposed by the priest on the penitent at confession. "The penance the confessor imposes must take into account the penitent's personal situation and must seek his spiritual good. It must correspond as far as possible to the gravity and nature of the sins committed. It can consist of prayer, an offering, works of mercy, service of neighbor, voluntary self-denial, sacrifices, and, above all, the patient acceptance of the cross the penitent must bear."[28] "These acts of penance imposed by the Church, when viewed from another perspective, have the character of true punishment. Christ took the guilt upon himself, and this guilt is taken away from each person who enters into true, internal, living fellowship with him, the righteous one. But it was not God's intention that those who turn after acquiring personal guilt be excused from temporal punishment. Mankind is able to satisfy such punishment, and righteousness demands that it truly be imposed. For those who have become members of his body by baptism to then defy the commandments of God, and more so to grievously infringe upon these commandments, is, even in the case of reform, truly worthy of punishment and has to be atoned for. The goodness and justice of God are one. If a person voluntarily closes himself to God's forgiving goodness that pulls that person back, he or she will alone sense his justice. Punishments possess the character of being a penalty and at the same time a remedy. According to the type of punishment, the Roman Catholic Church imposes satisfaction in the effectual sense of the word and does so in such a way that it is meant to prevent a relapse, to serve to reinforce the doing of good, and to cultivate the sense of repentance or change of direction in behavior. The merits of Christ cannot be reduced by satisfaction required by the Roman Catholic Church."[29]

That is also the basis of the teaching of satisfaction. The Christian who has confessed and repented out of fear has to make satisfaction on behalf of the temporal punishments of sin. This happened before the Middle Ages via Church punishment and since the Middle Ages by smaller exercises of

---

[28] Katechismus der katholischen Kirche. Oldenbourg: München, 1993. p. 398, No. 1460. Available in English at http://www.usccb.org/catechism/text/pt2sect2chpt2.htm#iv.

[29] P. Thomas Jentzsch. Grundfragen der Ökumene: Die dogmatischen Gegensätze der Katholiken und Protestanten: Nach Johann Adam Möhlers 'Symbolik'. Stuttgart: Priesterbruderschaft St. Pius X., 1992. p. 119.

repentance (e.g., prayers), good works, but above all by indulgences. "The Roman Catholic teaching is that satisfaction brought by the sinner is not to be confused with that which Christ brings. In the final event the works of satisfaction that the church demands have to come from a spirit of penance given by Christ. Only within such a structure do they have their value."[30]

2.6.6 Reconciliation with the Roman Catholic Church

A pivotal thought is also that the Christian does not only have to be repeatedly reconciled to God. It is rather the case that his sins are also turned against the Church, and he therefore has to be reconciled with the Church. This is a reconciliation that therefore ultimately only the Pope, as the representative of the Church, can pronounce and delegate to bishops.

Reconciliation with the Church in the Catechism
"Forgiveness of sins brings reconciliation with God, but also with the Church. Since ancient times the bishop, visible head of a particular Church, has thus rightfully been considered to be the one who principally has the power and ministry of reconciliation: he is the moderator of the penitential discipline [comp. Lumen Gentium 26]."[31] "This sacrament *reconciles us with the Church.* Sin damages or even breaks fraternal communion. The sacrament of Penance repairs or restores it. In this sense it does not simply heal the one restored to ecclesial communion, but has also a revitalizing effect on the life of the Church which suffered from the sin of one of her members. [comp. I Corinthians 12:26]. Re-established or strengthened in the communion of saints, the sinner is made stronger by the exchange of spiritual goods among all the living members of the Body of Christ, whether still on pilgrimage or already in the heavenly homeland [comp. Lumen Gentium 48–50]."[32] "Individual, integral confession and absolution remain the only ordinary way for the faithful to reconcile themselves with God and the Church, unless physical or moral impossibility excuses from this kind of confession" (OP 31).[33]

---

[30] Ibid.
[31] Katechismus der katholischen Kirche. Oldenbourg: München, 1993. pp. 398-399, No. 1462.
[32] Ibid., p. 400, No. 1469.
[33] Ibid., p. 404, No. 1484.

3 The History of Indulgences and Their Theology from the Time of Their Inception in the Middle Ages until the Reformation

3.1 Tariff Penance as an Historical Antecedent to Indulgences

The origins of indulgences can only be understood from looking at the history of how penance was viewed in the early church and the end of this type of penance in the early Middle Ages.[34] The later development that included calculations of days and years for completing acts of penance can only be explained by the fact that Christians seeking repentance had earlier been given certain time frames.[35] Still, first of all, the old way of approaching repentance had to perish.

At the end of the sixth century, Irish monks, and then Scottish monks, brought a new system of penance, one without public penance, to the European continent. This allowed each individual to privately confess to a priest who would announce absolution.[36] This new method was called 'tariff penance.'[37] Its history cannot be reproduced in detail.[38]

"A general precondition for the development of indulgences (in the eleventh century still called absolutio, then relaxatio, retnissio, venia, con-

---

[34] This is discussed by the Catholic author Bernhard Poschmann. Der Ablass im Licht der Bußgeschichte. Peter Hanstein: Bonn, 1948. pp. 99, 101; Paul Anciaux. Das Sakrament der Buße. Mainz: Matthias-Grünewald-Verlag, 1961. pp. 177, 188-189 and often, Georg Muschalek. "Der Ablaß in der heutigen Praxis und Lehre der katholischen Kirche". pp. 13-37 in: Georg Muschalek et al. Gespräch über den Ablaß. Arbeiten zur kirchlichen Wiedervereinigung – Kirchengeschichtliche Reihe 2. Graz: Verlag Styria, 1965. pp. 18-21, die hier stellvertretend für praktisch alle katholischen Autoren stehen.

[35] Particularly Nikolaus Paulus. Geschichte des Ablasses im Mittelalter vom Ursprunge bis zur Mitte des 14. Jahrhunderts. Bd. 1. op. cit., pp. 31-32; Bernhard Poschmann. Der Ablaß im Licht der Bußgeschichte. op. cit., p. 99.

[36] Herbert Vorgrimler. Buße und Krankensalbung. Handbuch der Dogmengeschichte. Bd. IV, Faszikel 3. Herder: Freiburg, 1978 1st ed.; 1978 2nd. ed. pp. 93-94.

[37] Comp. ibid., pp. 93-100.

[38] Ibid., p. 97.

donatio, and since the thirteenth century, indulgentia) is the decline of public and advance of private penance since the eighth century, which (...) began with Irish-Scottish monasticism. While fulfillment of acts of penance was a precondition for re-entry into the church in the case of public penance, in the case of private penance, the believer was already given access to communion after absolution."[39]

There were indeed precursors to indulgences, such as so-called absolutions,[40] but what was new with indulgences was missing completely. What was new was the fact that believers' works did not constitute satisfaction for the temporal punishment of sin. Rather, absolution from the temporal punishment for sin was a jurisdictional and calculable act by which the Pope apportioned a remission of sins to believers that could not be doubted and that came from the works of others.[41]

Basically it is the case, and it is also undisputed among Roman Catholic writers, that the discipline of penance of the old Church and the tariff penance which superseded it were something completely different from the medieval teaching of penance.[42] Nonetheless, these approaches to penance provided the preconditions for penance in the Middle Ages.

3.2 The Indulgence as a Completely New Product of the Middle Ages

The history of indulgences[43], just as the history of the teaching of purgatory and the treasury of merit, is nowadays rather uniformly presented by both Roman Catholic and Protestant historians.[44]

---

[39] Gustav Adolf Benrath. "Ablaß". op. cit., pp. 347-348.
[40] Comp. Bernhard Poschmann. Der Ablass im Licht der Bußgeschichte. op. cit., pp. 15-53.
[41] Comp. Bernhard Poschmann. Buße und letzte Ölung. op. cit., pp.114, 45.
[42] Also Helmut Echternach. "Korreferat". pp. 39-51 in: Georg Muschalek u. a. Gespräch über den Ablaß. Arbeiten zur kirchlichen Wiedervereinigung – Kirchengeschichtliche Reihe 2. Graz: Verlag Styria, 1965. p. 49.
[43] The history of indulgences is dominated by the monumental work of Nikolaus Paulus, which Bernhard Poschmann has updated. An update of the state of research was presented by Thomas Lentes in the introduction to an edition of Paulus's works: Thomas Lentes. "Einleitung zur 2. Auflage: Nikolaus Paulus (1853-1930) und die 'Geschichte des Ablasses im Mittelalter'". p. VII-LXXVIII in: Nikolaus Paulus. Geschichte des Ablasses im Mittelalter. 3 Bde. Bd. 1. Darmstadt: Wissenschaftliche Buchgesellschaft, 2000 2nd. ed. (Literature since Paulus p. XLIX; Literature by Paulus p. LX-LXXVIII – 508 entries).

The History of Indulgences and Their Theology

There is no dispute that these teachings were unknown in the first millennium of Christian timekeeping. In the time period stretching from the end of the tenth until the thirteenth century, these ideas were first found in practice and then later gradually became part of teachings.[45] "The indulgence has been a church practice since the eleventh century, which is before theologians in the twelfth and thirteenth centuries began to give them thought."[46]

The most significant Roman Catholic researcher when it comes to indulgences, Nikolaus Paulus, refers to the fact that research has recognized since the seventeenth century that there were no indulgences prior to the eleventh century.[47] It has been known for a long time that the first indulgence, though not preserved, stems from the year 1029, while the first indulgence preserved in writing stems from the year 1035.[48] At most one could go on to cite, as Adolf Gottlob does, an attested to release from penitent punishment dating from 1011 that was given for helping with church

---

[44] E.g., Herbert Vorgrimler. Buße und Krankensalbung. Handbuch der Dogmengeschichte. Bd. IV, Faszikel 3. Herder: Freiburg, 1978 2nd ed. pp. 203-214; Georg Muschalek. "Der Ablaß in der heutigen Praxis und Lehre der katholischen Kirche". p. 13-37 in: Georg Muschalek et al. Gespräch über den Ablaß. Arbeiten zur kirchlichen Wiedervereinigung – Kirchengeschichtliche Reihe 2. Graz: Verlag Styria, 1965. pp. 18-23; Karl Rahner. "Ablaß". pp. 46-53 in: Josef Höfer, Karl Rahner (ed.). Lexikon für Theologie und Kirche. Bd. 1. Herder: Freiburg: 1986 (Nachdruck von 1957); Gerhard Ludwig Müller. "Ablaß I.-III.". Col. 51-55 in: Walter Kasper (ed.). Lexikon für Theologie und Kirche. Bd. 1. Freiburg: Herder, 1993; Johannes Hüttenbügel. Der Ablaß. Zeitfragen 49. Köln: Presseamt des Erzbistums Köln, 1999. pp. 7-10; P. De Letter. "Indulgences". pp. 436-444 in: New Catholic Encyclopedia. Second edition. Vol. 7. Detroit et al.: Thomson Gale, 2003. pp. 437-438 und die großen Gesamtdarstellungen zur Geschichte des Ablasses aus dem 20. Jh.. A good compilation of the sources leading to indulgences is found in Paul F. Palmer. Sacraments and Forgiveness: History and Doctrinal Development of Penance, Extreme Unction and Indulgences. Sources of Christian Theology 2. Westminster (MD): The Newman Press & London: Darton, Longman & Todd, 1960. pp. 321-368.

[45] See Karl Rahner. "Ablaß". a. a. O. S. 46-53 in: Josef Höfer, Karl Rahner (ed.). Lexikon für Theologie und Kirche. Bd. 1. Herder: Freiburg: 1986 (reprint of 1957 edition). pp. 48-49 and the quoted examples below.

[46] Edward Schillebeeckx. "Der Sinn der katholischen Ablaßpraxis". Lutherische Rundschau 17 (1967): 328-353, p. 328.

[47] Nikolaus Paulus. Geschichte des Ablasses ... Bd. 1. op. cit., p. 96.

[48] Ibid. p. 98.

building (work indulgence) in Spain,[49] where admittedly one's merit still stands in the foreground.[50]

The Roman Catholic Bishop Gerhard Ludwig Müller has written rather classically: "The indulgence has neither a model in the New Testament nor in public church penance found in the first millennium, be it in practice or insofar as theological grounds are concerned. It came as a creative answer to a new constellation in the crossover from old church reconciliatory public penance to sacramental private confession between roughly the sixth and tenth centuries. Originally sacramental absolution from guilt and eternal punishment for sin immediately followed contrition and private confession of sin expressed in the presence of a priest, thereby indicating the completion of the sacramental procedure. Therefore, canonically recognized works of penance, that in more ancient times had been seen as the cause for forgiveness of guilt and punishment by God, were now subsequently imposed and removed from the actual sacrament of penance. They required a quasi extra-sacramental initiative of the ecclesiastical service of healing. This was the place for the indulgence."[51]

The presence of indulgences cannot be verified before the eleventh century.[52] There are precursors such as the absolutions on behalf of the dead,[53] but there is nothing that one could rightly call an indulgence. The first

---

[49] Adolf Gottlob. Kreuzablass und Almosenablass. op. cit., pp. 204-205.

[50] Ibid., pp. 196-202 advances the theory that did not hold sway, namely, that indulgences developed out of a situation where those excommunicated were allowed to return to church sooner if they helped with the building or renovation of the church.

[51] Gerhard Ludwig Müller. "Ablaß I.-III.". Col. 51-55 in: Walter Kasper (ed.). Lexikon für Theologie und Kirche. Bd. 1. Freiburg: Herder, 1993. Sp. 52 (Abkürzungen ausgeschrieben). According to a Zenit press report: "Indulgences Are Not Invention of Medieval Age." from September 17, 1999, on www.ewtn.com/library/theology/zindulg.htm (May 13, 2004). Bischof Dario Rezza, Vatican canon law specialist, communicated that silence on the topic of indulgences and research regarding their abuse in the Middle Ages goes far back. He maintained that indulgences were not a creation of the Middle Ages. The theologian of the Vatican's 'Apostolic Penitentiary' Ivan Fucek answers the question as to whether the teaching of indulgences can already be found in St. Thomas Aquinas and communicates, in addition, that indulgences were implicitly a part of church teaching from the beginning. Such statements contradict all the results of indulgence research conducted by Catholic historians.

[52] Bernhard Poschmann. Der Ablass im Licht der Bußgeschichte. op. cit., pp. 59, 100.

[53] Comp. with this antecedent history Bernhard Poschmann. Der Ablass im Licht der Bußgeschichte. op. cit., pp. 9-42.

proven indulgences stem from the Bishop of Urgel for San Pedro de Portella in the year 1035.[54] Indulgence historians have explicitly rejected all alleged records of indulgences prior to the eleventh century. "The actual practice of indulgences was introduced into the Latin church in the eleventh century. Still, there was much confusion between the different forms of absolution into the twelfth century. Only as a systematic theology of the sacrament of penance was developed did the distinctions between the different forms of relief and absolution emerge in the church."[55]

Martin Ohst has documented that the particular thing about indulgences is that they constitute a blanket benefit of service. This means that the individual does not have to render any special service based on his or her situation. Rather, it is the blanket determination as made by the Pope that counts.[56] Vorgrimler has written in this vein: "The distinctive novelty with regard to the indulgence, to which church practice made a transition in the eleventh century without a corresponding theory at its base, consists in the presumed otherworldly effect of absolution when the assessment of earthly and ecclesiastical penance is considered and correspondingly reduced. And so absolution, formerly prayer, became the formal release of church punishment relating to penance and at the same time a jurisdictional act. Indulgences were not merely a type of earnest money for a period of time after death. Indulgences were also an extremely welcomed release during earthly life. It was this aspect that ensured their quick proliferation. From the point of view of the bishops, it is without dispute that the promise of revenues from people's acclimatization to indulgences and concomitant proliferation of the same also played a role."[57]

Before we turn our attention to a detailed history, it can be underscored on the basis of further examples from Roman Catholic authors that indulgences are considered a practice that developed very late in church history and developed in a labyrinthine manner. The teaching on indulgences made a subsequent appearance. Johannes Hüttenbügel, commissioned by the Archbishopric of Cologne, wrote: "Indulgences are not a figure made from

---

[54] Bernhard Poschmann. Der Ablass im Licht der Bußgeschichte. op. cit.,, pp. 44-45; Texte: Paul F. Palmer. Sacraments and Forgiveness. op. cit., p. 329-333; comp. for discussion Bernhard Poschmann. Der Ablass im Licht der Bußgeschichte. op. cit.,pp. 43-62 "6. Die ersten Ablässe".

[55] Paul Anciaux. Das Sakrament der Buße. Mainz: Matthias-Grünewald-Verlag, 1961. p. 182.

[56] Martin Ohst. Pflichtbeichte: Untersuchungen zum Bußwesen im Hohen und späten Mittelalter. Beiträge zur Historischen Theologie 89. Tübingen: J. C. B. Mohr, 1995. pp. 104-107.

[57] Herbert Vorgrimler. Buße und Krankensalbung. op. cit., pp. 204-205.

the same mould. The practice developed over the course of history. On the long path of their development, there were various elements of accretion which had their meanings in particular periods of time and situations and can only be understood in those contexts. In order to understand indulgences, one basically has to know the history of the theology surrounding repentance and the practice of penance. Regarding this, I have several pointers. The teaching and practice of indulgences have their roots in the early church's practice of penance and its requirement that the sinner, through a long and difficult period of penance, demonstrate tangible proofs of a new life upon which absolution was then conferred. The church claimed Matthew 18:18 for itself ('I tell you the truth, whatever you bind on earth will be bound in heaven, and whatever you loose on earth will be loosed in heaven . . .') as a way to impose works of penance and at the same time to stand in solidarity with the penitent with prayers of intercession. For further understanding indulgences and the accretions that occurred in the period of transition from public to private penance (sixth to tenth centuries), it can be noted that original strict punishments lasting a considerable period of time were replaced by other works of penance that the church sanctioned. The church also allowed others to representatively do penance and conduct works of penance for the sinner. The thought that the efforts of penance comprised the actual factor that paid for sin remained, even as a gradual transition from public to private penance occurred."[58]

The ecumenical church historian Gustav Adolf Benrath has also written similarly on this point: "The easing of and dispensing with efforts required for penance by church officers is as old as the fixing of such requirements within the church. Indulgences in their developed form were really a way of dealing with penance that was different from that in the ancient church. It constituted a new feature in the occidental church of the Middle Ages and up until today represents a distinctive feature of the Roman Catholic theory and practice of penance. In the early Middle Ages, indulgences grew out of various roots of religious thought and practice. In the Scholastic period, indulgences were thought through theoretically, though not unanimously set down and clarified in every detail. In the late Middle Ages, indulgences came to possess significant importance in church life in Western Christianity. The antagonism of the Protestant churches against the mistakes they pointed out, in particular against the legalism, in rem and patronizing manner of addressing Christian salvation was not without ef-

---

[58] Johannes Hüttenbügel. Der Ablaß. Zeitfragen 49. Köln: Presseamt des Erzbistums Köln, 1999. p. 7.

fect. However, the reformation of Roman Catholic teaching and piety has always revitalized indulgences. Even though in their present theoretical and practical meaning they are appearing to retreat and experience a guarded theological evaluation, indulgences in their relation to the sacrament of penance belong as an integral part of Roman Catholic teaching that has not been abandoned."[59]

3.3 Crusade Indulgences

"In the first half of the eleventh century, indulgences were only seldom granted. While the papal practice of indulgences was guarded, bishops granted frequent and large-scale indulgences."[60] How did it come to be, then, that indulgences became a hallmark of the papacy?

The proliferation of indulgences did not just have local dimensions. Rather, it was a striking hallmark of the catholic, 'universal' church, and this has much do to with the tragedy of the crusades.[61] **The Pope used indulgences in order to finance the crusades and to increase enthusiasm for them. Indulgences were also used to directly tie Christianity to the global papacy. This is to say that out of the combination of the papacy, papal wars in various places in the world, and the papal authority to grant indulgences, the papacy developed into the religious and political epicenter of the occidental world.**

When the Pope used indulgences to fuel participation in the crusades, indulgences had only recently arisen, and a theoretical basis for them was still 100 years away. Crusade indulgences were, by the way, originally granted by overzealous crusade preachers without consent. However, because of the great effect they had, the Pope followed suit.[62]

---

[59] Gustav Adolf Benrath. "Ablaß". op. cit., p. 347
[60] Herbert Vorgrimler. Buße und Krankensalbung. op. cit., p. 205.
[61] Comp. Christoph Auffarth. Irdische Wege und himmlischer Lohn: Kreuzzug, Jerusalem und Fegefeuer in religionswissenschaftlicher Perspektive. Veröffentlichungen des Max-Planck-Instituts für Geschichte 144. Göttingen: Vandenhoeck & Ruprecht, 2002.
[62] Nikolaus Paulus. Geschichte des Ablasses im Mittelalter vom Ursprunge bis zur Mitte des 14. Jahrhunderts. Bd. 2. op. cit., pp. 166-169.

While the first crusade indulgences[63] were given in 1063 by Alexander II for Spain,[64] their actual history begins with the celebrated Synod of Clermont in 1095. It was there that Urban II called the world to join in crusades.[65] Benrath writes: "A remission of all temporal punishment for sin was granted by Alexander II in 1063 for those fighting against the Saracens, and the same was granted in 1095 by Urban II.[66] The popes were of the opinion that the services required were so extreme that in return, full canonical penance could be offered. With this the practice of the 'plenary indulgence' (indulgentia plenaria) began. It is in contrast to the 'partial' indulgence with a fixed time frame."[67] "In contrast to the numerically limited and so-called partial indulgence, in 1095 Urban II offered the well-known 'plenary indulgence' (indulgentia plenaria). This indulgence was offered for participation in the crusades (...) out of a pious intention pro omni poenitentia, and the reward was seen as appropriate. It was not only understood as a comprehensive redemption of all church punishments. It promised simultaneously the forgiveness of all sins (remissio omnium peccatorum) and the annulment of temporal punishment imposed by God."[68]

Given the extensive crusade indulgences, made in connection with general calls to participate in crusades (specifically in 1063, 1095, 1187, and 1215), the crusades and the triumph of the idea of indulgences are inseparably tied to one another.[69] The age of the crusades and of the persecution

---

[63] Comp. for discussion Nikolaus Paulus. Geschichte des Ablasses ... Bd. 1. op. cit., pp. 134-144 "Die ältesten Kreuzzugsablässe"; Par Jean Richard. "Urbain II, la prédication de la croisade et la définition de l' indulgence". pp. 129-135 in: Ernst-Dieter Hehl et al. (ed.). Deus qui mutat tempora: Festschrift für Alfons Becker zu seinem fünfundsechzigsten Geburtstag. Sigmaringen: Jan Thorbecke, 1987 und Adolf Gottlob. Kreuzablass und Almosenablass. op. cit.

[64] Nikolaus Paulus. Geschichte des Ablasses ... Bd. 1. op. cit., p. 134.

[65] Ibid., p. 135.

[66] Lat. Texts: Walther Köhler. Dokumente zum Ablassstreit 1517. Tübingen: Mohr, 1934 2nd. ed. p. 7.

[67] Herbert Vorgrimler. Buße und Krankensalbung. op. cit., p. 205.

[68] Gustav Adolf Benrath. "Ablaß". op. cit., p. 348.

[69] The history of Crusade indulgences over the centuries can be found in Nikolaus Paulus. Geschichte des Ablasses ... Bd. 1. op. cit., pp. 134-144; Nikolaus Paulus. Geschichte des Ablasses ... Bd. 2. op. cit., pp. 25-60; Nikolaus Paulus. Geschichte des Ablasses ... Bd. 3. op. cit., pp. 166-188 und in der älteren Darstellung Adolf Gottlob. Kreuzablass und Almosenablass: Eine Studie über die Frühzeit des Ablasswesens. Stuttgart: Ferdinand Enke, 1906; Nachdruck: Amsterdam: P. Schippers, 1965. Part., pp. 37-194.

of the Jews (1096-1270) was the age of the development and rapid proliferation of indulgences.[70]
While the thought of religious wars was foreign to the ancient church,[71] in 853 Pope Leo IV for the first time promised heavenly rewards, even if in a very vague form, to those participating in religious wars.[72] Adolf Gottlob surmises that this thought came from Islam.[73] Let us briefly follow his presentation of the development of this thinking. The first attempts to amass an army using indulgences at the beginning of the eleventh century are not easy for historians to identify.[74] They are found explicitly in 1053 for the first time with Leo IX.[75] The decision of the Council of Clermont at the end of 1095 was a first consequence of the development.[76] Gradually the crusade indulgence changed the understanding of penance itself, and penitents and non-penitents were more and more placed on the same footing.[77] This is blamed on the "use of penance for another purpose, namely for amassing an army."[78] Still, at this point, indulgences had to do with the remission of earthly punishments relating to penance and not of those that were otherworldly.[79] In 1145 Pope Eugene III (1145-1153), for the first time and in clearly recognizable form, granted crusade indulgences that remitted not only earthly punishment relating to penance but also remission of otherworldly punishment in purgatory as well. The result was that the Second Crusade was justified by the transcendental effect of indulgences.[80] In 1145/1146 Eugene III, for the first time, authorized collections for indulgences to be taken by orders related to the crusade, namely via the Knights Templar. In 1199, on the basis of a papal bull, collection boxes in which crusade indulgences could be placed were set up in all churches in Europe.[81]

---

[70] Comp. Nikolaus Paulus. Geschichte des Ablasses im Mittelalter vom Ursprunge bis zur Mitte des 14. Jahrhunderts. Bd. 1. op. cit., p. 194-211. Texte bei Paul F. Palmer. Sacraments and Forgiveness. op. cit., p. 333-338 (Kreuzzugsablässe von Alexander II. 1063, von Urban II. 1095 mit zwei Ablasspredigten Urbans II. und Laterankonzil 1215).
[71] Comp. Adolf Gottlob. Kreuzablass und Almosenablass. op. cit., pp. 13-17.
[72] Ibid., pp. 18-22.
[73] Ibid., p. 20.
[74] Comp. details at ibid., pp. 37-43.
[75] Ibid., pp. 40-42.
[76] Ibid., p. 63.
[77] See details at ibid., pp. 85-88.
[78] Ibid., p. 87.
[79] Ibid., p. 91.
[80] Ibid., pp. 105-115.
[81] Ibid., p. 186.

Later the popes extended indulgences to include those who financed crusades. This developed into a significant source of financing for the crusades by noblemen and others who did not want to participate, or could not participate, in crusades. "A century later Gregory VIII bestowed indulgences upon those who directed funds toward the Crusades without participating in them (1187). It is understandable that in such cases the connection with the sense of penance could be lost."[82]

Finally, in 1275 the 4th Lateran Council, in its 71st Constitution, confirmed crusade indulgences for all time,[83] even when in the 62nd Constitution it wanted to prevent the abuse and hinted at the (apparent) mitigation of indulgences granted by papal action. This council took place during the crusades against the heretic Albigensians and Catharists in the middle of Europe, and Pope Innocence III (1198-1216) saw to it with crusade indulgences that sanction was given to the controversial crusades against the Catharists.

The crusades were in this manner repeatedly undertaken against new foes, at first pagans and Jews, and then against the schismatics and heretics[84] (e.g., 1420 and 1421 against the Hussites;[85] 1487 against the Waldensians[86]); and finally against all political enemies of the Pope, even among Christian princes.[87] "Crusades were conducted throughout the entire Middle Ages. There was rarely a pope who would not issue indulgences in order to promote such ventures, against the Turks and Tartars in the East, against the Moors in the West, against the heretics or other opponents of the apostolic chair. Of the numerous crusade indulgences which were issued from the middle of the fourteenth century until the time of Luther, only the most important can be mentioned here."[88] Crusades financed with indulgences included those against the Moors in Spain and Portugal (12th-15th centuries), pagan peoples in the Baltic region, the Wendens (1147), the Estonians (beginning in 1171), the Liven (beginning in 1198), the Pruzzen (beginning in 1230), the Finns and Karelians (beginning in 1157 and 1256, respectively), the heretics and schismatics such as the southern French Catharists and Albigensians (1170, 1209-1229), the Greeks (beginning in

---

[82] Gustav Adolf Benrath. "Ablaß". op. cit., p. 348
[83] Lat. Texts: Der Kreuzzugsablass Innocenz' III. 1215 Walther Köhler. Dokumente zum Ablassstreit 1517. Tübingen: Mohr, 1934 2nd.ed. pp. 10-11.
[84] Nikolaus Paulus. Geschichte des Ablasses ... Bd. 3. Op. cit., pp. 166-178.
[85] Ibid., pp. 166-167.
[86] Ibid., pp. 177-178.
[87] Nikolaus Paulus. Geschichte des Ablasses ... Bd. 2. Op. cit., p. S. 21.
[88] Nikolaus Paulus. Geschichte des Ablasses ... Bd. 3. Op. cit., p. 166.

1204), the Stedingers (1230-1234), and the Colonna in Italy (beginning in 1290) and the Hussites in Bohemia (1420-1431). Swedes made an armed pilgrimage with the support of St. Birgitta against Orthodox Russians (1348-1351), and even the Finns, who had not been Christianized a long time, undertook something similar (1496) under the authorization of Pope Alexander VI. Finally, crusaders fought in 'political crusades.' These were nothing more than crusades against heretics upon the behest of the popes against the Reichstruchseß Markward von Annweiler in Sicily; against 'alius Saladinus' (1199-1202); against the Caesar Friedrich, his sons and successors and party supporters (1240-1268); and lastly, against King Peter III of Aragon (1284)."[89]

Money played a central role in these events. In 1240 the Pope allowed people to buy their non-participation in crusades – the official justification was simply the lack of funds of the western members of the Roman Empire at Constantinople.[90] At the end of the twelfth century, the business of crusade indulgences really gained momentum, and Paulus states the following with regard to the thirteenth century: "Crusade sermons were henceforth almost more directed at amassing money than in recruiting teams of participants."[91] Beginning with the third crusade, this was, at any rate, the case.[92]

Crusade indulgences thereby exercised influence directly upon the theology of indulgences and their expansion. It is indisputable that indulgences for the dead were dispensed without the approval of the Pope in connection with the crusades. However, the Pope soon seized upon them and thereby was able to considerably boost their financial benefits. The first official papal indulgence for the dead was dispensed in 1457 in the crusade against the Spanish Moors.[93]

3.4 The Crusades and Indulgences Related There to Bring About the Modern Papacy

Rainer Christoph Schwinges, in his *Handbook of European History*, has provided a fascinating synopsis of the reasons that led to the movement

---

[89] Rainer Christoph Schwinges. "Die Kreuzzugsbewegung". Op. cit., p. 192.
[90] Nikolaus Paulus. Geschichte des Ablasses ... Bd. 2. Op. cit., p. 27.
[91] Ibid., p. 25. Comp. Adolf Gottlob. Kreuzablass und Almosenablass. Op. cit., p. 165-194 "Die Erniedrigung des Kreuzablasses zu einem Mittel des Gelderwerbs".
[92] As at Ibid., p. 166.
[93] Bernhard Poschmann. Buße und letzte Ölung. Op. cit., p. 121.

known as the crusades.⁹⁴ He refers to the fact that since the eighteenth century, the concept of crusades has increasingly been found to not be solely used with respect to the crusades in the East against Islam.⁹⁵ In fact "the view is becoming prevalent that Crusades not related to the East are included, and that in the Crusades the Roman papal church sees a universal attempt to accomplish its global interests against all external as well as internal enemies."⁹⁶ Crusades are seen to begin in 1045⁹⁷ within the scope of the reconquest of Islamic portions of Spain and to last until the actual recapture of Spain, the conquest of Middle and Latin America, and the wars of the Turks of the sixteenth and seventeenth centuries.

Schwinges describes the social readiness for the crusades as well as widespread eschatological expectations.⁹⁸ Pilgrimages, which were also instruments of penance, were the starting point for the idea of crusades. Crusades were actually just 'armed pilgrimages.' From there, what unfolded was the idea of indulgences as indulgences for a pilgrimage. "'The Crusade was a consequence of the enhancement of the idea of pilgrimage' (H.E. Mayer). Here lay the deeper reason that the church never seriously prevented anyone from participating in the taking of the cross (excepting monks). In 1095 there was a readiness for pilgrimage, and there had already been a readiness for war for a long time. No one would have gone to fight against the Muslims in the East, who were considered pagans, had Europe's Christians not already fought against pagan peoples, Vikings, Slavs, Hungarians or Arabs, for a long time. The teaching of the church father Augustine regarding just war for the defense or rescue of Christian legal interests was automatically associated with war against pagans. After all, no one would have thought about making an armed pilgrimage to Palestine had this not been built upon a case of defense and rescue according to Augustinian doctrine."⁹⁹

The connection between the idea of crusades and the papacy is to be understood within the context of prevailing feudalism. In such a context, the Pope was in the position of liege lord with 'militia Dei' or 'militia Christiana' and called for military service.¹⁰⁰ "Just as the siege lord with

---

⁹⁴ Rainer Christoph Schwinges. "Die Kreuzzugsbewegung". pp. 178-198 in: Theodor Schieder (ed.). Handbuch der europäischen Geschichte. Bd. 2. Stuttgart: Klett-Cotta, 1987.
⁹⁵ Ibid., pp. 180-181.
⁹⁶ Ibid., p. 181.
⁹⁷ Ibid., pp. 181-183.
⁹⁸ Ibid., pp. 185-187.
⁹⁹ Ibid., p. 187.
¹⁰⁰ Ibid., p. 188.

his armed following, Christ protects and rewards his crusaders. In theory, God's militia was not fighting for an earthly booty, but rather for remuneration from God, expecting forgiveness of sin, eternal life, and, in the case of death on the battlefield, a martyr's crown. Among all the privileges... the crusade indulgence was for the medieval mentality the most sought-after personal reward. This was to give the crusade movement its own supreme dynamic, but it was built upon a misconception. The Pope had only thought about a remission of temporal punishments for sin when he spoke of remissio peccatorum. The crusaders, however, thought about complete satisfaction for guilt and related penalties. They had taken the rather imprecise terminology found in the teaching on indulgences and made it their own. In so doing, however, one can see proof for just how seriously spiritual reward was taken, even if there were unavoidably conspicuous material incentives. The church had to finally bow to the popular interpretation and sanction it in the end. Bernhard von Clairvaux, who summarized the experiences of the first half-century of the history of the crusades, specifically highlighted this motif of spiritual deservingness within crusades. He brought it down to a simple and lucid (advertising) formula: A clever businessman does not let a favorable opportunity to do good business slip away. The time of a crusade was simply the tempus acceptable to perform penance. In exchange for wearing the marginally valuable cloth cross on the shoulder, participants bore the cross to achieve salvation. Stripped of its salvific-eschatalogical dimensions, the Bernhardinian notion found its way into the papal crusade bulls under Alexander III and came to completely dominate preaching and propaganda beginning with the time of the Third Crusade (1189-1192)."[101]

The crusades and the crusade indulgences are closely tied to the ascent of the papacy in a worldly as well as a spiritual manner. "A final motif of the cultural readiness for armed pilgrimages as God's horsemen was indispensible: the conviction that the Pope (sic) possessed the legitimate authority to conduct war and to lead the movement of the crusades. It would have certainly never come to this decision – independent of Urban's initiative – had the papal reform of the eleventh century not won the moral and political authority that secured its claim to universal rule for at least the next two centuries... This theory, to be sure, developed gradually during the twelfth century, yet from the beginning, the leading role of the Pope stood fixed in the field of vision of the crusaders because of the presence of crusade legates. From the time when Eugene III issued the first crusade bull (quantum praedecessores), with a clear reference to the authority of his

---

[101] Ibid., pp. 188-189.

predecessor Urban, it became increasingly normative over time to appeal to the claim of papal leadership. This was most clearly demonstrated under Innocence III and his successors in the thirteenth century, when one learned to use a crusade as a political instrument of papal world domination. Without authorization by the Pope, there were no crusades, and without the belief in the legitimacy of a papal call, no one would have take up the cross."[102]

Without the Pope, then, there was no crusade. This was because "the crusade was a pope's war."[103] Crusades took place upon the initiative of the Pope. "The Pope stoked the readiness, preached, solicited, organized, offered privileges, and conducted financing."[104] The most important link between the crusaders and the Pope was the crusader's oath, such that church legal authorities treated all questions regarding the crusades under the *de voto* (from the oath) rubric.[105]

Even if the idea of the crusades lasted for hundreds of years, in reality the times during which there were no crusades were much longer and the disinterest rather significant. The crusades had to be put into motion by the popes again and again. In particular, the crusades against heretics and the political crusades of the thirteenth century were very unpopular.[106] For the vast majority of the population it could not be understood why crusades against Christians were just as worthy of indulgences as were others. In Spain there were no clear fronts but rather Moorish and Christian princes who banded together against common enemies. This was even the case with the hero of the Reconquista, Ridrigo Diaz (el Cid). The situation in the Baltic States was similarly convoluted, and even after 1099, in the Holy Land. The crusades were an affair relating to the visible and worldly rule of the Pope and its byproduct, indulgences, which related to the invisible rule of the Pope over people's souls. "Employing crusades in oriental and European arenas in the service of papal worldly rule and the close succession of expeditions forced the creation of increasingly tight organizations. This began with Innocent III. In addition to intensive recruiting and the rising number of privileges offered (including Ehedispense), the financing of equipment, transportation, fresh supplies, and salaries became the major management tasks of the popes and other members of church administration. As fewer participants demonstrated a tendency to make a pilgrimage

---

[102] Ibid., p. 189.
[103] Ibid., p. 189.
[104] Ibid., p. 189.
[105] Ibid., pp. 189-190.
[106] Ibid., p. 190.

suis expensis,[107] the more such administration was necessary . . . All these papal efforts always had the same reason and same aim: the global defense, restoration or expansion (mission) of the domain of the Roman papal church."[108]

3.5 Indulgences Began as an Abuse

Also from the point of view of Roman Catholic theologians, indulgences began as an abuse and as a way of profiteering from the faith.[109]

The Dutch Roman Catholic theologian Edward Schillebeeckx attributes the combination of the purchase of indulgences and the indulgence itself to the earlier system of penance and writes: "Even before there was the practice or theory of indulgences, in the system itself . . . the fact of misuse was a given."[110] Gustav Adolf Benrath writes similarly: "The practice of indulgences was from the beginning accompanied by grave abuses. 'The proliferation of indulgences, and, above all, their use as a source of funds to finance all sorts of church projects, the crude exaggerations of untrained indulgence gatherers (quaestores, quaestuarii, stationarii), who in part conducted their business professionally and in return received a portion of the revenues (praedicatores mercenarii), the deceit with contrived or fictitious authorization, the embezzlement, the shifting and misappropriation of collected funds, the rival efforts of different church and secular entities to receive portions of the profits, the occasional leasing of the indulgence business to lay people against up-front, one-time, lump-sum payments (compositio), and other factors contributed to the well-known secularization of the Occidental Church that was continually lamented but was never effectively combated."[111]

In Benrath's opinion, this is not something that was happening on the fringes. "It is not a case of individual occasions of excrescence or infringement but rather of an official church practice that caused damage be-

---

[107] At their own cost.
[108] Ibid., pp. 191-192.
[109] Paul Anciaux. Das Sakrament der Buße. Mainz: Matthias-Grünewald-Verlag, 1961. p. 72 and the authors he quote agree with my view; comp. W. H. Kent. "Indulgences". Catholic Encyclopedia (1908). pp. 9-10. www.newadvent.org/cathen/07783a.htm (January 3, 2004) (aus Charles G. Herbermann [ed.]. The Catholic Encyclopedia. 15 vol.. New York: Appleton, 1907-1912).
[110] Edward Schillebeeckx. "Der Sinn der katholischen Ablaßpraxis". Lutherische Rundschau 17 (1967): 328-353, p. 334.
[111] Herbert Vorgrimler. Buße und Krankensalbung. Op. cit., p. 209.

cause of other peculiarities of the character of indulgences. This included the proliferation of indulgences beyond conceivable dimensions, by displacing popular, older indulgences with newly dictated and erratically difficult works of indulgence for the same amount of pardon, by interfering in the life of the local church with indulgence preachers, etc. Such a deplorable state of affairs led to intense and, in part, completely repudiating critiques of the essence of indulgences (alongside these critiques there were others found, particularly in circles that were influenced by mysticism as well as a spirituality that simply no longer acknowledged the essence of indulgences and other excessive religious practices)."[112]

Already at the time of the Lateran Council in 1215, when the indulgence had first been theologically justified, there were strong words voiced against the widespread abuse.[113] For this reason, indulgences were limited to a one-year shortening of the time in purgatory. The widespread abuse by bishops should have been stemmed by this action, since papal approval was required.[114] Additional papal writings against the misuse of indulgences, for example by Pope Clement V (1305-1314) in 1312[115] or from the Council of Constance in 1418,[116] were without effect. However, they indicate the concern caused in the highest circles of the church by the misuse of indulgences.

The Council of Trent was dealing with similar abuses 350 years later.[117] In the particular case of the Council of Trent, however, it had to do with making the case for indulgences to Protestants rather than demonstrating their necessity to members of the Roman Catholic faith. "The Council desires that indulgences be granted in a restrained manner, that abuse should be suppressed and any profiteering therefrom prevented ... This does not

---

[112] Ibid.
[113] The text of the decree can be found in "Innocenz' III. gegen den Ablassunfug" von 1215 bei Walther Köhler. Dokumente zum Ablassstreit 1517. Tübingen: Mohr, 1934 2nd. ed. p. 9 und bei Heinrich Denzinger, Peter Hünermann (ed.). Enchiridion symbolorum definitionum et declarationum de rebus fidei et morum: Kompendium der Glaubensbekenntnisse und kirchlichen Lehrentscheidungen: Lateinisch-Deutsch. Herder: Freiburg, 1991 37th ed. p. 367, Randnr. 819.
[114] Comp. Gustav Adolf Benrath. "Ablaß". Op. cit., pp. 349-350.
[115] Text in Walther Köhler. Dokumente zum Ablassstreit 1517. Tübingen: Mohr, 1934 2nd. ed. pp. 33-34.
[116] Text in Neuner, Heinrich Roos. Der Glaube der Kirche in den Urkunden der Lehrverkündigung. Op. cit., p. 433; comp. Karlheinz Frankl. "Papstschisma und Frömmigkeit: Die 'ad instar-Ablässe'". Römische Quartalschrift für christliche Altertumskunde und Kirchengeschichte 72 (1977): 57-124; 184-247, p. 231.
[117] Extract of the text in bei Neuner, Heinrich Roos. Der Glaube der Kirche in den Urkunden der Lehrverkündigung. Op. cit., pp. 434-435.

The Crusades and Indulgences

have to do with a dogmatic definition, but rather with a decree of reform."[118] "Out of a desire that indulgences be modestly issued, so that the church does not suffer by acting too loosely, the decree generally sets down that dishonorable lucre be excluded."[119]

Nikolaus Paulus has shown that during the Middle Ages, indulgences, because they were associated with significant money flows, were a central cultural factor.[120] Indulgences were not only responsible for financing the crusades, hospitals, and building of churches, they also were behind more secular societal activities such as the building of bridges and dams, canalization, and guilds.[121] As positively as Paulus presents this, he also furnishes comprehensive evidence for the fact that the financial aspect of indulgences was not an occasional fringe occurrence. Rather, indulgences were a fact that significantly determined the church and culture. Little is changed by the indication that one could obtain indulgences by conducting other good works besides financial donations.[122]

Other Roman Catholic authors go further than the Pope. James Akin maintains that indulgences were never sold. Rather, the money was employed for the sake of church buildings and the poor. Besides, according to the Council of Trent, to receive indulgences in exchange for such gifts was forbidden.[123]

Roman Catholic historians, such as the monumental works from Paulus[124] and Poschmann, are of a very different opinion at this point. They provide many details for the disastrous combination of indulgences with politics and business. According to them, the abuse of indulgences was in

---

[118] Herbert Vorgrimler. Buße und Krankensalbung. Op. cit., pp. 210-211.
[119] Johannes Hüttenbügel. Der Ablaß. Zeitfragen 49. Köln: Presseamt des Erzbistums Köln, 1999. p. 9.
[120] Nikolaus Paulus. Der Ablaß im Mittelalter als Kulturfaktor. Görres-Gesellschaft ... Erste Vereinsschrift 1920. Köln, J. P. Bachem. 1920; ähnlich Nikolaus Paulus. Geschichte des Ablasses im Mittelalter vom Ursprunge bis zur Mitte des 14. Jahrhunderts. Bd. 2. Op. cit., pp. 175-205 und 226-264. Comp. also Nikolaus Paulus. Geschichte des Ablasses ... Bd. 3. Op. cit. "Der Ablaß als Geldquelle" 379-394.
[121] P. De Letter. "Indulgences". pp. 436-444 in: New Catholic Encyclopedia. 2. Aufl. Bd. 7. Detroit et al.: Thomson Gale, 2003. p. 438 assumes that in the Middle Ages a large portion of cathedrals, monasteries, schools, universities and hospitals were paid for with indulgence revenues.
[122] E.g., Bernhard Poschmann. Buße und letzte Ölung. Op. cit., p. 116.
[123] James Akin. "How to Explain Purgatory to Protestants" (13 S.). www.cin.org/users/james/files/how2purg.htm (January 3, 2004), p. 2; also www.ewtn.com/library/answers/how2purg.htm, p. 2 (January 3, 2004).
[124] Part. Nikolaus Paulus. Geschichte des Ablasses ... Bd. 3. Op. cit., pp. 395-420 "Mißbräuche in der Ablaßpraxis".

place before there ever was a theology of indulgences. **It was through their abuse that indulgences became a big affair in the first place.** The first theological statements we have relating to indulgences are from bishops and theologians in the eleventh and twelfth centuries, who rejected indulgences because of their abuse. Poschmann writes: "For this reason one cannot generalize and exaggerate the allegation of unrestrained handling of indulgences out of a profiteering mindset, in spite of how regard for indulgences' material returns played a role in their proliferation and their becoming a standard part of civil life."[125]

Paulus thoroughly describes that all measures taken by popes and councils to combat the situation were unsuccessful, in particular because the popes themselves or their successors did not hold to conditions.[126] At several parliamentary gatherings, there were complaints that the Pope misused indulgences relating to crusades for other purposes.[127] Around 1502, Ferdinand and Isabella of Spain warned the King of England about transferring crusade funds to Pope Alexander VI (1492-1503), since the King of England had given his son significant portions of such funds for local wars.[128] Leo X (1513-1521), who was the Pope at the beginning of the Reformation, gave funds received from indulgences to his sister.[129]

So how did things look after the Reformation and after the Council of Trent? The Council of Trent, which confirmed indulgences in its dispute with Luther, called for indulgences to be issued in a moderate manner in order not to debilitate church order in 1563.[130] This did little to influence practice, however. Paulus writes: "Since, however, the old abuses associated with indulgence collections arose again, Pius V decided to go at this misuse at the roots. In his bull 'Etsi dominici gregis', dated February 8, 1567, he revoked all indulgences for which a monetary amount was paid (pro quibus consequendis manus sunt porrigendae adiutrices). Without specific permission from the Apostolic See, no future collections in connection with already issued indulgences or indulgences still to be issued were allowed to be made."[131]

---

[125] Bernhard Poschmann. Buße und letzte Ölung. Op. cit., p. 116.
[126] Nikolaus Paulus. Geschichte des Ablasses ... Bd. 3. Op. cit., p. 411.
[127] Ibid., p. 391.
[128] Ibid., p. 392.
[129] Ibid., pp. 392-393.
[130] Text: Josef Neuner, Heinrich Roos. Der Glaube der Kirche in den Urkunden der Lehrverkündigung. Op. cit., pp. 434-435.
[131] Nikolaus Paulus. Geschichte des Ablasses ... Bd. 3. Op. cit., p. 419.

From the point of view of Roman Catholic researchers, Pius V's 1567 bull entitled 'Etsi Dominici gregis'[132] is also the evidence for the fact that the reforms Trent installed had no effect.[133] The pious but rather politically interested Pope again set an end to the contributions relating to indulgences, only to again act inconsistently when it came to the financing of crusades in Spain!

As a result, it was the same pope who immediately made an exception to the rule. "Such permission was given five years later by Pius V himself. On March 12, 1572, completely in line with the Medieval pattern, Pius promised a complete indulgence for contributions to the War against the Turks."[134] Another large exception was officially directed at the Muslims. "Another much more important exception had already been made prior to that for Spain's benefit. Following Philipp II's demand, Pius approved a crusade, admittedly with different and meaningful limitations. As a result, the King sent the bull back to the Pope with the request to extend it. Pius V resolutely rejected the request. He was even less inclined to again approve a conventional crusade in the old form, because he had heard of the objectionable ways indulgences had been promoted in Spain. Philipp, who at that time (1569) required substantial funds in order to put down the insurgence of the Moors, sought a way to replace missing crusade funds. He authorized Spanish bishops, who had been called together, to approve larger, partial indulgences with all kinds of faculties. When Pius V heard of this, he moved quickly to issue the bull 'Quam plenum sit' on January 2, 1570, in order to send the bishops a strong censure and to annul the indulgences that had been granted. The impending danger from the Turks necessitated that the Pope call upon the help of Spain shortly thereafter. In order to move the king to unite his battle fleet with the papal and Venetian galleys for a large concerted venture against the Turks, he approved the desired Cruciata on May 21, 1571. There were, however, conditions. No pressure was allowed to be exerted upon believers, and the objectionable and market-like manner in which indulgences had earlier been promoted had to be avoided. This condition was actually met, as attested to by the Venetian envoy L. Donato (sic-come e stato fatto). Admittedly, receipts were half what they had earlier been. From that time on, the Spanish Crusade was repeatedly renewed. In the long run there were some changes, namely one to twelve years, which came about with Benedict XV's bull *Ut praesens periculum* from August 12, 1915. The net amount of alms contributed for

---

[132] Text: Paul F. Palmer. Sacraments and Forgiveness. Op. cit., p. 366.
[133] E.g., ibid. and Nikolaus Paulus. Geschichte des Ablasses ... Bd. 3. Op. cit., p. 419.
[134] Ibid.

indulgences and the assigned privileges were to be used to defray the dioceses of Spain's operating costs after a deduction of a portion for the apostolic chamber. An entirely similar bull had been issued by Benedict XV on December 31, 1914, for ten years for Portugal's benefit."[135]

3.6 The Pope on the Abuses

Mention of abuse can also be linked to the popes, who not only were the originators of indulgences but were also often the ones disapproving them. Pope Paul VI (1963-1978) wrote in 1967 about this undesirable development. His view was that "the practice of indulgences has at times been improperly used." Further, he referred to the Church's response: "The Church, in deploring and correcting these improper uses . . ."[136] In the case of doubt everyone is guilty, that is, anyone but the Church and the Pope, because the entire context is as follows: "... Unfortunately, the practice of indulgences has at times been improperly used either through 'untimely and superfluous indulgences,' by which the power of the keys was humiliated and penitential satisfaction weakened, or through the collection of 'illicit profits,' by which indulgences were blasphemously defamed. But the Church, in deploring and correcting these improper uses 'teaches and establishes that the use of indulgences must be preserved, because it is supremely salutary for the Christian people and authoritatively approved by the sacred councils; and it condemns with anathema those who maintain the uselessness of indulgences or deny the power of the Church to grant them.'"[137]

And so it is that the Pope could not get around speaking about abuses. Indulgences had admittedly "at times been improperly used." The Church had responded by "deploring and correcting these improper uses," which is why the Church condemns each person who declares indulgences as futile.

In this the Pope follows an old Roman Catholic apologetic method. Anton Kurz wrote in 1900, in defense of the Catholic Church: "When abuses crept in, [the Church] is assuredly not guilty. The Church always pursued

---

[135] Ibid., pp. 419-420.
[136] Papst Paul VI. "Apostolische Konstitution über die Neuordnung des Ablasswesens 1967" (Latin/German). pp. 72-127 in: Akten Papst Paul VI. Apostolische Konstitution 'Paenitemini'. Trier: Paulinus-Verlag, 1967. p. 111.
[137] Ibid. Available in English at http://www.vatican.va/holy_father/paul_vi/apost_con stitutions/documents/hf_p-vi_apc_19670101_indulgentiarum-doctrina_en.html.

solid instruction for the people regarding indulgences . . ."[138] Abuses, yes, but guilt, no. This is, however, in spite of the fact that indulgences became significant as crusade indulgences. Furthermore, it is also in spite of the fact that Johann Tetzel operated on the basis of a papal bull and that without exception, all indulgences were granted by the Pope or so authorized.

If one considers that the Church in the Middle Ages at times financed itself largely by indulgences, that St. Peter's Basilica was built with funds from indulgences, that indulgences and their abuse are connected with the crusades, and if one furthermore assumes, with Benrath and indulgence historian Vorgrimler, that indulgences materially contributed to the well-recognized secularization of the Church in the Middle Ages,[139] and finally, if one thinks about the Reformation of the sixteenth century, the position of the Pope is an unbelievable belittlement of historical truth.

3.7 Indulgences Heightened the Importance of the Papacy

The Pope is also not in a position to respond as if the abuses relating to indulgences had nothing to do with the papacy. Indulgences were a substantial element in enhancing the spiritual and worldly meaning of the papacy.[140] Adolf Gottlob wrote in 1900: "Indulgences stood in the center of ecclesiastical and political life in the last three centuries of the Middle Ages. Whether one occupies himself with the internal or external questions of life, or with the activity of the papacy with regard to mass, or with political actions taken, or whether one explores and addresses internal questions of ecclesiastical reform, one cannot avoid indulgences. One encounters indulgences daily and hourly."[141] "In front of the historically oriented eye, indulgences are initially a means of papal political power. Here we see how, on the one hand, wars against unbelievers were supported, and on the other hand, how wars were fought against recalcitrant Christian kings, princes, and people groups. Church building, bridge building, and the like were advanced everywhere with indulgences. Indulgences are therefore not something to look at from the bottom up, that is to say, from the standpoint

---

[138] Anton Kurz. Die katholische Lehre vom Ablass vor und nach dem Auftreten Luthers. Paderborn: Ferdinand Schöningh, 1900. p. 9.
[139] Gustav Adolf Benrath. "Ablaß". Op. cit., p. 351; Herbert Vorgrimler. Buße und Krankensalbung. Op. cit., p. 209 quoted above).
[140] Comp. Nikolaus Paulus. Geschichte des Ablasses ... Bd. 2. Op. cit., pp. 1-18 "Päpstliche Ablässe für Almosen und Kirchenbesuch von 1216 bis 1350".
[141] Adolf Gottlob. Kreuzablass und Almosenablass. Op. cit., p. 1.

of a pastor. No, they are rather to be seen from the top, from the standpoint of politics and social welfare in the Middle Ages, from the standpoint of popes in Rome who mishandled them. With this understanding, a researcher gains externally, as well as internally, a freer and much clearer position. It also becomes obvious that with the impetus for the Reformation, not only the so-called indulgence abuses were at issue, and that the problem was not solved with the admission of such abuses. Unfortunately not. The evil of which is spoken, and it can be said in advance, sits much deeper."[142]

One of the leading current researchers in the area of indulgences has written: "The institutional aspect of indulgences is not able to be limited to what is in turn the transcendental extent of the corpus mysticum. Moreover, as a legal instrument, indulgences were potentially the largest possible push toward an attachment of the individual to the institution of the church and the papacy. It is not by accident that a pope such as Boniface VIII, a lawyer who deliberately looked to strengthen the papacy, via the Jubilee Indulgence of 1300 gained his first large sense of popularity and, at the same time, was nothing less than surprised by its acceptance by flocks of pilgrims. In addition Karlheinz Frankl has . . . shown how toward the end of the fourteenth century the actual success of the so-called Portiuncula Indulgence was connected with the expansion of the office of the Pope to a highly organized set of expedition-oriented authorities, operating in inventory and public record archives over highly varied and wide stretches of land. So much as the development of the institution of the office of the Pope advanced indulgences, it was conversely the case that this should lead to an increased attachment to the institution. The legal instrument, with which the relationship of the individual and transcendence was to be regulated, at the same time was a medium of religio-social integration as well as a stabilizing factor for the institution. With this the increasing focus on the central office of the Pope can hardly be overlooked. With any permission for bishops and cardinals to grant their own indulgences, these were increasingly limited by the papal keys of authority. Whoever acquired an indulgence – in whatever manner – necessarily placed himself or herself under papal authority. Even within the liturgy relating to the granting of an indulgence, this could be demonstrated by the fact that the papal crest with the cross of Christ were always set up together in the sanctuary . . ."[143]

---

[142] bid., p. 2.
[143] Thomas Lentes. "Einleitung zur 2. Auflage: Nikolaus Paulus (1853-1930) und die 'Geschichte des Ablasses im Mittelalter'". S. VII-LXXVIII in: Nikolaus Paulus. Geschichte des Ablasses im Mittelalter. 3 Bde. Bd. 1. Darmstadt: Wissenschaft-

One could well live with the facts if Pope John Paul II would have distanced himself from the history of indulgences. The crusades have not been wheedled by the Pope for a long time now, and there have been apologies made to Muslims and non-Catholics. Why is the same not possible with regard to indulgences? Why can it not be admitted that indulgences were the cause of a terrible secularization of the Church? Why, of all things, does one have to make the first Jubilee Indulgence at the time of the Crusades (1300) the starting point for the considerations made with respect to the Jubilee Year 2000?

3.8 Was Money the Mainspring?

Already at the time of the Crusades we have seen that the financial prospects indulgences offered very soon started to play a central role. In time, the question also obviously arose about how to increase revenues. At least up until the time of the Reformation, concerns surrounding increased revenues played an important role in the development of indulgences and of their theology.[144] The weighting assigned to financial receipts, as opposed to spiritual concerns, varied widely over the course of history according to each particular pope. For example, popes range from Boniface IX (1389-1404), who was in office during the time of the great occidental schism and about whom we only know of political, military, and financial interests, to the Pope John Paul II. and Benedict XVI. who are little, if at all, influenced by financial or other aspects relating to indulgences.

In a report in 1414 Oxford University demanded restrictions on papal indulgences, because the impression had arisen that what one was dealing with was not the healing of souls but profit.[145] For this reason, in 1418 Pope Martin V (1417-1431) revoked all the plenary indulgences of his predecessors from 1378 onward.[146] Pope Sixtus IV (1471-1484) was, how-

---

liche Buchgesellschaft, 2000 2nd. ed. S. XXXIII-XXXIV. Comp. concerning the use of Luther's coat of arms in thesis 79 of his 95 theses: " To say that the cross, emblazoned with the papal arms, which is set up [by the preachers of indulgences], is of equal worth with the Cross of Christ, is blasphemy" (Martin Luther. Gesammelte Werke. Digitale Bibliothek. Op. cit., p. 1186).

[144] Comp. Georg Muschalek. "Der Ablaß in der heutigen Praxis und Lehre der katholischen Kirche". pp. 13-37 in: Georg Muschalek et al. Gespräch über den Ablaß. Arbeiten zur kirchlichen Wiedervereinigung – Kirchengeschichtliche Reihe 2. Graz: Verlag Styria, 1965. p. 22.

[145] Nikolaus Paulus. Geschichte des Ablasses ... Bd. 3. Op. cit., p. 135.

[146] Ibid., p. 136.

ever, more lavish with indulgences than were all his predecessors.[147] Even the Roman Catholic theologian Bernhard Poschmann sees the Pope, with his famous indulgence of 1476 for the Saintes Cathedral, dangerously close to the adage, "As soon as the coin in the coffer rings, the soul from purgatory springs."[148]

Let us listen again to the Roman Catholic researcher on indulgences Nikolaus Paulus, for whom basically an indulgence, when viewed as alms, is not a problem:[149] "Church leaders could feel all the more disposed to grant general remission from penance when the opportunity was offered to make these remissions serviceable for special ecclesiastical or public service institutions and ventures. One has maintained that the thought of 'always expediently using gratuitous penance remission from that time on' was 'actually the driving one.' 'One can confidently say that the outer appearance of the reason for the origination of indulgences was in the expedient use of services of penance for the temporal interests of the church. In contrast stood the interest of the penitent, and insofar as the gravity of the penalty of penance was a reason for the origination of the indulgences, this took a secondary position.' 'One cannot see this interest (namely the financial interest) simply as an accompanying symptom. Rather, it was the actual mainspring, of course, not in the sense of the later selling of indulgences.' Why had one first thought in the eleventh century of such utilization of what used to be remission from penance offered without any charge? 'The transition to indulgences (i.e., the expedient use of conventional general absolution) had to be more determined by external circumstances and requirements, and these arose.' Did 'external requirements' not arise until the eleventh century? Were there not churches and establishments requiring support before that time? Indeed one refers to the advent of 'Stolgebühren' (charges for services of the church such as baptism, marriages, etc.). 'General remissions of all public penance' – that would be general absolutions – had existed before. 'What was still missing was that a quasi gift in the Church's interest was required in return. At a time in which the church required compensation for all services offered, the latter would not arouse misgivings anymore.' In this context one refers to the required 'Stolgebühren.' In the period of time in which a general alms indulgence emerged and spread to a large extent, that is, in the eleventh and until the end of the twelfth century, synods forbade any requirement of fees

---

[147] Ibid., p. 144.
[148] Bernhard Poschmann. Buße und letzte Ölung. Op. cit., pp. 121-122.
[149] Nikolaus Paulus. Geschichte des Ablasses ... Bd. 1. Op. cit., p. 21.

('Stolgebühren'). In contrast, alms indulgences during this time were never forbidden by any synods."[150]

Let us hear a few more statements from Paulus on the relationship between indulgences and financial proceeds. "In the late Middle Ages there was no purpose for which popes and bishops granted so many indulgences as for the erection and decoration of buildings of worship. For the innumerable church building projects that were undertaken in the fifteenth century, the indulgence played a more or less important role almost everywhere. Indulgences were granted not only for financial contributions but for efforts of personal labor as well."[151]

"There is nothing objectionable about the custom of granting indulgences to promoters of charitable work and in this way to connect financial contributions with indulgences. If the support one confers upon charitable works is a good and laudable deed, one may be rewarded with spiritual grace by church leaders. Unfortunately this custom gave rise to grave abuses over the course of time. It led, namely, to a situation where indulgences, which were primarily a spiritual means intended for the pastoral care of people, were made into a useful source of funds. 'The financial contributions for good purposes that were auxiliary in nature turned out to be the main issue. In this way indulgences moved from their position as a lofty ideal and were debased to a financial operation. Receiving spiritual grace was no longer the actual reason to ask for and be granted indulgences. Rather, it was the need for funds.' Indulgences were first of all a source of funds for the Curia, or papal court, for two reasons: firstly, on account of charges that were made for the issuance of letters of indulgence and thereafter, because for more significant indulgences, part of the revenue had to be paid to the papal chambers."[152]

"It would be an error to assume that, apart from the papal portion of revenues, the revenues from indulgences and the authority relating thereto came to the good of those to whom indulgences were granted. Large amounts were used simply to finance business operations. Commissioners, preachers, fathers taking confession, and others who helped to make indulgences known and to dispense them in one way or another had to be compensated for their efforts. The required printed materials led to expenses that were not insignificant. For these reasons, in 1501 the Empire's regiment determined that Cardinal Peraudi should receive a third of revenues generated by indulgences to cover these costs. After Peraudi, Nikolaus von

---

[150] Ibid., p. 20.
[151] Nikolaus Paulus. Geschichte des Ablasses ... Bd. 3. Op. cit., p. 365.
[152] Ibid., p. 379.

Cues also received a third of the revenues in 1451 for the same purposes. Oftentimes it was necessary to give a portion of revenues to princes and city authorities, since they otherwise would not have allowed promulgation of indulgences."[153]

3.9 Indulgence Theology Began as a Critique of Indulgences

In the beginning the practice of indulgences occurred without a theological basis.[154] "As is so often the case in life, so it was with indulgences. Practice preceded theory."[155] Theory followed practice, as had also been the case with "various institutions in the Catholic Church."[156]

The beginning of indulgence theology was a critique of the practice of indulgences. The first substantial theology that addressed the topic[157] was by Peter Abelard (1079-1142), who rejected indulgences.[158] This was the first theological treatment of indulgences, and the topic was thereby introduced into theological literature.[159] In Abelard's work, one can already

---

[153] Ibid., p. 389.
[154] According to Ludwig Hödl. Die Geschichte der scholastischen Literatur und der Theologie der Schlüsselgewalt. 1. Teil. Beiträge zur Geschichte der Philosophie und Theologie des Mittelalters XXXVIII/4. Münster: Aschendorffsche Verlagsbuchhandlung, 1960. p. 385 Very early in history 'usus' (convention) ist taken to be the justification for indulgences.
[155] Bernhard Poschmann. Buße und letzte Ölung. Op. Cit., p. 116.
[156] Nikolaus Paulus. Geschichte des Ablasses ... Bd. 1. Op. Cit., p. 145.
[157] Text extract in Latin: Walther Köhler. Dokumente zum Ablassstreit 1517. Tübingen: Mohr, 1934 2nd. ed. pp. 8-9 und pp. 11-15; English texts relating to the first theologians addressing indulgences in Paul F. Palmer. Sacraments and Forgiveness. Op. Cit., pp. 338-343.
[158] Gustav Adolf Benrath. "Ablaß". Op. Cit., p. 349; Nikolaus Paulus. Geschichte des Ablasses ... Bd. 1. Op. Cit., pp. 145-149; Bernhard Poschmann turns against Paulus. Der Ablass im Licht der Bußgeschichte. Op. Cit., pp. 63-68, who menas that Abelard only turned against normal and episcopal indulgences and not against the papal crusade indulgences. Actually Abelard does not address the latter. Whether he does this because he was in favor of them or because his refutation of indulgences also applies to these, or whether it has to do with his not wanting to expressly turn against the Pope, remains an open issue.
[159] Adolf Gottlob particularly emphasizes this. Kreuzablass und Almosenablass. Op. cit., pp. 99-101, and he also sees in Abelard the initiation of a separation between temporal and eternal punishments.

find essential arguments against indulgences having to do with the greed with which they were associated.[160]

The Roman Catholic dogmatic historian Ludwig Hödel has written the following:
"Over against the practice of indulgences one finds that theologians were collectively very critically disposed. From Peter Abelard to Courson, theologians strove against all too liberal and lavish indulgences."[161] Herbert Vorgrimler writes: "The first theological utterance regarding indulgences is the fierce critique leveled by Abelard between 1125 and 1138 (Ethica 26). Abelard did not only express theological doubts regarding indulgences. He also severely criticized the shameless greed of the bishops which manifested itself in the practice of indulgences. Specifically, because the bishops arbitrarily invoked their full authority, Abelard contested their very possession of the keys of authority within the Church. An example of where, on a theological basis, Abelard's views have been taken to task is not known. Peter Lombard does not mention it, and in Gratian's Decree there is no reference to it. From Abelard to Robert de Courson, theologians commented upon indulgences and spoke out against the practice (in particular against indulgences that were too liberal). Simon of Tournai, Radulfus Ardens, and others emphatically argued that by accumulating partial indulgences, the entire penance for sin's penalty could not be produced. Waldensians also argued against the possibility of satisfying the entirety of penance by a collection of indulgences. They, as well, denounced the disproportionate relationship between remission achieved through a long period of penance and a financial contribution. Church practice and teaching about indulgences have been defended by Alain von Lille, admittedly with a special teaching that did not tie in to later theology."[162]

Included among the opponents of indulgences is, according to Adolf Gottlob, the greatest Pope and "most important man of the entire epoch," Gregory VII (1073-1085).[163]

---

[160] Comp. The Latin text in Walther Köhler. Dokumente zum Ablassstreit 1517. Op. cit., pp. 8-9.
[161] Ludwig Hödl. Die Geschichte der scholastischen Literatur und der Theologie der Schlüsselgewalt. 1. Teil. Beiträge zur Geschichte der Philosophie und Theologie des Mittelalters XXXVIII/4. Münster: Aschendorffsche Verlagsbuchhandlung, 1960. p. 386, regarding Abelard's general theology comp. pp. 78-114.
[162] Herbert Vorgrimler. Buße und Krankensalbung. Op. cit., p. 206.
[163] See details in Adolf Gottlob. Kreuzablass und Almosenablass. Op. cit., pp. 47-57, 240-241.

Just about 100 years lie between what was self-evident criticism of the practice of indulgences by the great theologians in the middle of the twelfth century and the almost final formulation of indulgence theology by St. Thomas Aquinas (1225-1274).

Since that time, the rejection of indulgences (and appended teachings such as purgatory) by Catharists, Waldensians, and followers of Wycliffe and Hus[164] has been seen as heresy and became a standard allegation against other churches and movements.

3.10 Scholasticism Brings About the Theology of Indulgences

Ludwig Hödl writes in his classic study on the papal keys of authority: "The scholastic teaching of the keys of authority have their provenance in the theology of sentence commentaries at the beginning of the twelfth century. This era became fateful like no other for Catholic theology."[165] The same also applies for indulgence theology.

In the second half of the twelfth century, indulgence theology was gradually and systematically expanded. In the thirteenth century, it became increasingly uniform in its formulation, and with that, the otherworldly values of indulgences moved to the center of the teaching on indulgences. That indulgence theology proper developed with the prominent theologians of the twelfth and thirteenth centuries is not a disputed fact.[166] Poschmann writes: "It is to the merit of High Scholasticism that out of the confusion of opinions, questions, and doubts, a reasonably uniform conception was developed."[167] The Catholic opinion that theory and theology followed established practice can also be seen here.[168]

---

[164] Comp. Nikolaus Paulus. Geschichte des Ablasses ... Bd. 2. Op. cit., p. 267-273 und pp. 339-349 ("Gegner des Ablasses") and Gustav Adolf Benrath. "Ablaß". Op. cit., pp. 351-352 as well as in relation to purgatory "Waldenser und Wiedergänger: Das Fegefeuer im Inquisitionsregister des Bischofs Fournier von Pamiers (1317-1326)". pp. 125-134 in: Peter Jezler. "Himmel Hölle Fegefeuer: Das Jenseits im Mittelalter. Zürich: Verlag Neue Zürcher Zeitung, 1994 2nd. ed.

[165] Ludwig Hödl. Die Geschichte der scholastischen Literatur und der Theologie der Schlüsselgewalt. 1. Teil. Beiträge zur Geschichte der Philosophie und Theologie des Mittelalters XXXVIII/4. Münster: Aschendorffsche Verlagsbuchhandlung, 1960. p. 376.

[166] Comp. Nikolaus Paulus. Geschichte des Ablasses ... Bd. 1. Op. cit., pp. 268-316.

[167] Bernhard Poschmann. Buße und letzte Ölung. Op. cit., p. 118.

[168] E.g., Nikolaus Paulus. Geschichte des Ablasses ... Bd. 1. Op. cit., p. 212.

Indulgences became an object of remission of temporal penalty for sin in purgatory, as formulated for the first time by Albert the Great.[169] "In contrast to teachings up until that time, it came to be understood that the Church's interaction with regard to 'otherworldly penalty' no longer was only intercessory in nature and that a positive outcome to such intercession rested with God. Rather, the Church acted in a magisterial role that had remission of 'otherworldly penalty' at its disposal. This new teaching was of particular relevance with regard to 'plenary indulgences,' which assured the remission of all penalties of sin."[170]

The first recognition of indulgences can be found with Petrus Cantor (+1197) and his student, the Archbishop of Canterbury, Stephan Langton.[171] Still, there is much uncertainty among historians.[172] The teaching of the treasury of the church is something that arose as an appendage for the first time in 1230 with Heinrich von Susa or Albertus Magnus.[173]

Admittedly, there is one thing to note about "indulgence theory": "For practical church life it played a subordinate role. Practice always preceded theory, such that the practice of indulgences oftentimes deviated from the official teaching of the Church."[174]

Chronologically, an additional development during the Scholastic period can be mentioned. It indeed does not have to do directly with indulgence theology, but it is still closely related to the practice of indulgences. As we have already seen at the beginning, confession before a priest became a requirement in 1215 at the Fourth Lateran Council. Prior thereto, confession was neither compulsory nor was confession a sacrament.[175]

---

[169] Comp. to his teaching on indulgences Nikolaus Paulus. Geschichte des Ablasses ... Bd. 1. Op. cit., pp. 272-279.
[170] Herbert Vorgrimler. Buße und Krankensalbung. Op. cit., p. 207.
[171] According to Ludwig Hödl. Die Geschichte der scholastischen Literatur und der Theologie der Schlüsselgewalt. ... p. 385 Langton is the first person to try to make a biblical justification by using 2 Corinthians 2:10.
[172] According to Bernhard Poschmann. Der Ablass im Licht der Bußgeschichte. Op. cit., pp. 71-74.
[173] According to Nikolaus Paulus. Geschichte des Ablasses ... Bd. 2. Op. cit., p. 184-206, part. pp. 192, 197-198.
[174] Christine Neuhausen. Das Ablasswesen der Stadt Köln ... Op. cit., p. 17.
[175] The most important investigation in this regard is Martin Ohst. Pflichtbeichte: Untersuchungen zum Bußwesen im Hohen und späten Mittelalter. Beiträge zur Historischen Theologie 89. Tübingen: J. C. B. Mohr, 1995. Bes. pp. 31, 1, 15 Ohst emphasizes that confession in its present form has existed only since 1215. He addresses all relevant sources.

3.11 The Meaning of Mendicant Orders for Indulgences

"In the thirteenth century, popes and bishops exploited the apparent advantages of indulgences for the purposes of targeted support and promotion of local establishments of mendicant orders and their female counterparts, and likewise the establishment of White Women and Cistercians."[176] The background to this is a fundamental change of papal policy. In the same way that poverty movements had been fought as heretical, now mendicant orders were supported and became the most effective tool against these poverty movements. Innocent III freed the ideal of poverty from its heretical blemish,[177] and Franciscans and Dominicans became the Pope's 'track hounds.' This was closely connected with indulgences, since mendicant orders received the largest concessions for promulgating indulgences, which in turn contributed to their financing.[178]

It was not accidental, then, that it was the great theologians of the mendicant orders, foremost the Dominicans, who classically developed the indulgence and theologically formulated it.[179] St. Thomas Aquinas was a Dominican. "The breakthrough in indulgence theology occurred in the time of High Scholasticism and became largely possible due to the teaching by Hugo of St. Cher, developed regarding the treasury of the church."[180] Hugo of St. Cher, as well, was not only accidentally a Dominican and papal legate and as such issued indulgences in Cologne.[181] Johann Tetzel, Luther's adversary, was also a Dominican.

Nikolaus Paulus has discussed in detail who specifically formulated classic indulgence theology for the first time. His results: in 1248/1249 the Dominican Albert the Great (1200-1280) began the formulation, followed by the Franciscan Bonaventura (1221-1274), and concluded by the Dominican St. Thomas of Aquinas (1225-1274) from 1253-1255.[182] It is not accidental that all three theologians mentioned belonged to mendicant orders.

---

[176] Ibid., p. 19.
[177] Comp. ibid., pp. 20, 28.
[178] Comp. ibid., pp. 18-38.
[179] Comp. details in Adolf Gottlob. Kreuzablass und Almosenablass. Op. cit., pp. 257-296.
[180] Christine Neuhausen. Das Ablasswesen der Stadt Köln ... Op. cit., p. 16.
[181] Ibid., p. 38.
[182] Nikolaus Paulus. Geschichte des Ablasses ... Bd. 1. Op. cit., p. 191 and pp. 189-191.

3.12 St. Thomas Aquinas

St. Thomas Aquinas (1225-1274), the most important theologian of the Middle Ages and the primary Scholastic theologian, formulated the final indulgence teaching as a student of Albert the Great in his commentary on sentences of 1253-1255.[183] "Not until St. Thomas Aquinas does one find a fully orbed and positive theory on indulgences."[184] What was new in St. Thomas's writings was that the effect of an indulgence lies in the treasury of the Church and no longer in the merit of the recipient.[185] It is to be noted, however, that most commentators did not follow Aquinas in this aspect of his teaching.[186] "Thomas Aquinas detached indulgences from the practice of penance and associated them with a jurisdictional power. The indulgence became a legal act."[187] "Actually, after Aquinas there was no additional material building block to indulgence theology. The only thing added[188] is that much later the Pope, as we shall see, officially confirmed the teaching of the treasury of the Church.

Let us look more closely at Aquinas' teaching. Vorgimler summarizes Aquinas' teaching well and names his sources: "A particularly influential representative of the new teaching was Thomas Aquinas (S. th. Suppl. q. 25 a. 1). According to his view an 'indulgentia omnium peccatorum' [indulgence for all sins] granted by the pope extended to cover the 'universitas poenarum' [entirety of penalties], such that a dying person with this type of indulgence and without anything else is transferred into heavenly blessedness (Quodl. II q. 8 a. 2)... Thomas gave the new theory radical consequences. While Albertus Magnus (IV Sent. d. 20 a. 17) and Bonaventure (IV Sent. d. 20 p. 2 a. 1 q. 6) had taught, subsequent to earlier theologians, that an indulgence was only valid if a iusta aestimatio [deserved correspondence] between the work of indulgence and the extent of the

---

[183] Latin Text extracts: Walther Köhler. Dokumente zum Ablassstreit 1517. Tübingen: Mohr, 1934 2nd ed. pp. 15-18, 34-35. Comp. Aquinas' teaching on indulgences in Nikolaus Paulus. Geschichte des Ablasses ... Bd. 1. Op. cit. pp. 205-217; specifically regarding purgatory: Jacques Le Goff. Die Geburt des Fegefeuers: Vom Wandel des Weltbildes im Mittelalter. München: dtv, 1990. p. 322-337; Texts in English in: Paul F. Palmer. Sacraments and Forgiveness. Op. cit., pp. 343-349.
[184] Gustav Adolf Benrath. "Ablaß". Op. cit., p. 349.
[185] Above all in Bernhard Poschmann. Der Ablass im Licht der Bußgeschichte. Op. cit., p. 95.
[186] According to ibid., p. 97.
[187] Christine Neuhausen. Das Ablasswesen der Stadt Köln ... Op. cit., p. 17.
[188] Also according to Bernhard Poschmann. Buße und letzte Ölung. Op. cit., p. 122.

remission of penalty existed, Thomas reduced the work of indulgence from a causa effectiva [effective cause] to a causa motiva [stimulating cause]. The work had the point of associating the penitent with the intention of the saints and of moving the upper ecclesiastical members to dispense from the treasury of the church. The dispenser could procure a discretionary penalty remission ... (Suppl. q. 25 a. 2 und ad 1) ... Bonaventure (IV Sent. d. 20 p. 2 a. 1 q. 3) and Thomas (Suppl. q. 26 a. 1 und 2) rejected the earlier reigning notion that the power of indulgences was connected with the sacramental authority of penance and that the priest could grant indulgences (this rejection had to do with mendicants' claims on penance, they wanted and needed to assure themselves of the support of the Pope). Rather, both theologians taught that the administration of the thesaurus Ecclesiae [treasury of the Church] was reserved for the Pope and bishops by the power vested in them (also non-ordained bishops). According to Thomas Aquinas, the authority regarding indulgences is concentrated in the Pope ... (S.th. Suppl. q. 26 a. 3, comp. also a. 2). With respect to the recipient of indulgences, Thomas Aquinas radicalized the theory that had been handed down. Albert the Great (IV Sent. d. 20 a. 18) and Bonaventure (IV Sent. d. 20 p. 2 a. 1 q. 4) had taught that indulgences were for worldly inclined Christians, not for the zealously inclined (who served their own penance). St. Thomas turned against this view and taught that everyone was in need of 'merita aliorum' [merits of others] in the face of daily unavoidable sins (Suppl. q. 27 a. 2). His view was that the status of grace and the performance of a work of indulgence (ibid. a. 1 und 3) were required for receipt of an indulgence."[189]

3.13 Exkursus: Development of a Dogma?

For Protestants it is a basic problem when such a foundational teaching, having to do with questions of salvation, is not anchored in the Holy Scriptures. Furthermore, it is a problem when such a teaching is not even mentioned in the early church but rather first appears in the High Middle Ages.

As we have seen, the view that indulgences appeared late is an undisputed fact among Catholic theologians. Bernhard Poschmann writes that indulgences "first appeared in the eleventh century not only within the

---

[189] Herbert Vorgrimler. Buße und Krankensalbung. Op. cit., p. 208. The translations in brackets have been added.

The Crusades and Indulgences

Church, but also from God."[190] Otto Semmelroth refers to Pope Paul VI's Apostolic Constitution on Indulgences in 1967. The Pope "does not maintain" that indulgences in this form are to be inferred as the expressed revealed word and endowment of Christ's will."[191] Nevertheless, Semmelroth sees in indulgences a legitimate "development,"[192] that is to say, "on the whole a legitimate progression from the beginnings of church teaching and practice of penance, which have not really been changed, but rather have unfolded and developed."[193]

The theology of indulgences has, according to the Catholic understanding, not been taken from the Scriptures. Rather, over a thousand years later, it was taught by the Holy Spirit with the same revelatory quality. In this connection, Benrath uses a quote from Valentin Gröne from the year 1863: "The Catholic Church understands divine logic – since God's Spirit is also its spirit – better than to not take up a truth that so clearly carries the character of catholicity into its cycle of teaching."[194] In 1863 Gröne was convinced from the start of his book: "Indulgences are as old as the Church, the ecclesiastical penal power."[195] When Paul decreed that after penance the Corinthians were absolved of their church discipline, the authority of indulgences was already in force.[196] That the Pope had for hundreds of years not used his authority over indulgences to address temporal penalties of sin, or had used it differently, was, according to Gröne, not evidence that the Church had not possessed it. Luther and the Protestants are accused by him of not being aware of the practice of the ancient church. All of that was written before Catholic historians, foremost among them Nikolaus Paulus, documented in detail that prior to the eleventh century, indulgences were completely unknown in both theory and practice. This is true even in the case where indulgences grew out of the ancient church's discipline of penance, which was of a completely different nature. However, as long as it has been known that there are indulgences, which is only since the eleventh century, nothing other than what Gröne says holds: Indulgences are a

---

[190] E.g., Bernhard Poschmann. Der Ablass im Licht der Bußgeschichte. Op. cit., p. 100 und Nikolaus Paulus. Geschichte des Ablasses im Mittelalter vom Ursprunge bis zur Mitte des 14. Jahrhunderts. Bd. 1. Op. cit., pp. 132, 24, 31.
[191] Otto Semmelroth. "Zur Theologie des Ablasses". Op. cit., p. 53.
[192] Ibid., p. 65.
[193] Ibid.
[194] Gustav Adolf Benrath. "Ablaß". Op. cit., p. 355 zitiert Valentine Gröne. Der Ablass, seine Geschichte und Bedeutung in der Heilsökonomie. Regensburg: Georg Joseph Manz, 1863. p. 28)
[195] Ibid., p. 1.
[196] Ibid., pp. 1-2.

revelation of the Spirit of God to the Church and have developed out of the apostolic authority of the New Testament. The Roman Catholic understanding of tradition says something completely different[197] from the Protestant view (tradition as that which has always been held) or the Orthodox view (tradition as the oral tradition or transmission at the time of the Apostles and their successors). Tradition for the Catholic Church is not that which is old, even though it might look like that in cases where tradition is based on decisions and developments from the first centuries of Christianity. Tradition is instead all godly revelation since the closure of the New Testament. In the same way that the Holy Spirit revealed himself infallibly to the Apostles, so the Holy Spirit has revealed himself for centuries to the successors of the Apostles, that is to say, to the bishops and, in particular, to the Pope as Peter's successor. For this reason, Roman Catholic 'tradition' also includes teachings that were revealed and declared in this century and for which there is no traditional line, for example, the 1950 teaching of Mary's ascension, which goes back to a dream the Pope had. Tradition is therefore progressive revelation and, in the final event, not a preserving concept (old = good). Rather, it is a very flexible and even rather toppling concept.

Orthodox churches understand something completely different with the word *tradition*.[198] Tradition is not what has accreted over the course of history. Rather, it is the oral tradition of the Apostles. The New Testament is the written legacy of the Apostles. Tradition is the oral legacy which was discreetly given to the bishops and from then on passed through the centuries to their respective successors. With the Greek-speaking church fathers, oral tradition is the most easily palpable. The Orthodox concept of tradition does not include the idea that things came along in the course of history or that an old age confers correctness. The error of the Orthodox churches is that oral tradition has the same significance as does the Bible and, at the same time, cannot be examined to see whether what the bishops passed on orally is actually how the Apostles saw it. To call upon the church fathers, as little as I can gather from the evangelical ignorance of the church fathers, is a difficult undertaking. This is the case since among the church fathers there were very

---

[197] Comp. Johannes Beumer. Die mündliche Überlieferung als Glaubensquelle. Handbuch der Dogmengeschichte Bd. I: Das Dasein im Glauben, Faszikel 4. Freiburg: Herder, 1962; Georg Söll. Dogma und Dogmenentwicklung. Handbuch der Dogmengeschichte Bd. I: Das Dasein im Glauben, Faszikel 5. Freiburg: Herder, 1971.

[198] Comp. Daniel B. Clendenin. "Orthodoxy and Tradition: A Comparison with Reformed and Catholic Perspectives". Westminster Theological Journal 57 (1995) 2: 383-402.

different views and also heresies. There are even heresies that the Orthodox Church condemned such that with all that one can learn from the church fathers, there is no required guideline for judging the church fathers. Incidentally, there are a number of questions regarding tradition in which the Orthodox churches are at odds. Some say that the Apocrypha belong to the Bible, while others deny this. Why is this the case? Because the church fathers were already at odds in the past.

The most important church fathers, also those of the Catholic Church, including Augustine, did not, by the way, see tradition in the sense of the later Catholic view (teachings that were revealed to the church in the course of the centuries). The same applies to the important Orthodox church fathers (teachings that were orally proclaimed by Jesus or the Apostles and passed on to the bishops). Rather, the correct legacy of scriptural interpretation appears to be the apostolic point of view, i.e., that tradition is the Holy Scriptures aided with the understanding found among early Christians.[199] This notion appears to me to be the correct one.

The equal footing on which the Bible, tradition, and the papal see are placed according to the Catechism of the Catholic Church

"Sacred Tradition and Sacred Scripture, then, are bound closely together and communicate one with the other. For both of them, flowing out from the same divine well-spring, come together in some fashion to form one thing and move toward the same goal" (DV 9).[200]

As a result, the Church, to which the transmission and interpretation of revelation are entrusted, "does not derive her certainty about all revealed truths from the Holy Scriptures alone. Both Scripture and tradition must be accepted and honored with equal sentiments of devotion and reverence" (DV 9).[201]

"The task of giving an authentic interpretation of the Word of God, whether in its written form or in the form of tradition, has been entrusted to the living, teaching office of the Church alone. Its authority in this matter is exercised in the name of Jesus Christ." This means that the task of interpre-

---

[199] Part. also Alister E. McGrath. Der Weg der christlichen Theologie. C. H. Beck: München, 1997. pp. 34-35.

[200] Katechismus der katholischen Kirche. Oldenbourg: München, 1993. p. 60, No. 80. Available in English at http://www.usccb.org/catechism/text/pt1sect1chpt2.htm.

[201] Ibid., p. 60, No. 82. Available in English at http://www.usccb.org/catechism/text/pt1sect1chpt2.htm.

tation has been entrusted to the bishops in communion with the successor of Peter, the Bishop of Rome (DV 10)."[202]

"It is clear, therefore, that in the supremely wise arrangement of God, Sacred tradition, Sacred Scripture, and the Magisterium of the Church are so connected and associated that one of them cannot stand without the others. Working together, each in its own way, under the action of the one Holy Spirit, they all contribute effectively to the salvation of souls (DV 10, 3)."[203]

The Church "continues to be taught, sanctified, and guided by the Apostles until Christ's return, through their successors in pastoral office: the college of bishops, 'assisted by priests, in union with the successor of Peter, the Church's supreme pastor'" (AG 5).[204]

3.14 Purgatory – Also a Completely New Outgrowth of the Twelfth Century

In the Harenberg Lexicon of Religions, I described purgatory as follows: "Purgatory [also a state of purification, purgatorium (from Latin, meaning place of purification)] is only known within the Roman Catholic Church. Purgatory is the teaching that there is an intermediate state between earthly life and eternal life in which a person atones in order to attain eternal life. This teaching is rejected by Protestant and Orthodox churches. Purgatory is closely tied to the teaching of indulgences, by which the time in purgatory for oneself or for another can be shortened. Purgatory is for those who are basically saved, that is to say, those who have received forgiveness for their eternal guilt and have eternal life. They still have to atone for their venial sins before heaven is open to them. On All Souls Day, the Roman Catholic Church commemorates these people in purgatory, who in common parlance are called 'poor souls.' Purgatory was declared dogma at the Council of Florence in 1439."[205]

---

[202] Ibid., p. 61, No. 85. Available in English at http://www.usccb.org/catechism/text/pt1sect1chpt2.htm.

[203] Ibid., p. 63, No. 95. Available in English at http://www.usccb.org/catechism/text/pt1sect1chpt2.htm.

[204] Ibid., pp. 254-255, No. 857. Available in English at http://www.usccb.org/catechism/text/pt1sect2chpt3art9p3.htm.

[205] Thomas Schirrmacher. "Lexikon des Christentums" etc., pp. 8-267 in: Thomas Schirrmacher, Christine Schirrmacher u. a. Harenberg Lexikon der Religionen. Harenberg Verlag: Düsseldorf, 2002. p. 138.

The Catechism of the Catholic Church defines the teaching of purgatory in the following manner: "All who die in God's grace and friendship, but still imperfectly purified, are indeed assured of their eternal salvation; but after death they undergo purification, so as to achieve the holiness necessary to enter the joy of heaven."[206] Heinrich Ott explains: "Behind the Catholic teaching of purgatory is the thought that the believer, while indeed justified at the time of death, is at the same time normally not holy and refined enough that he or she can appear before God's face. For this reason, a shorter or longer period of purification has to be passed through in which a disagreeable remainder of earthly life has to be removed. The living can come to the aid of the dead with intercession and indulgences."[207]

The teaching of purgatory was also a new outgrowth of Scholastic theology and, as such, was indeed a supplement to the teaching of indulgences. The standard work on the history of purgatory and its use from the time of the Middle Ages until today is Jacques Le Goff's famous book *Die Geburt des Fegefeuers: Vom Wandel des Weltbildes im Mittelalter (The Birth of Purgatory: The Modification of the Middle Age Worldview).*[208] Jacques Le Goff shows that up until the end of the twelfth century, there was neither the concept 'purgatorium' in the sense of purgatory nor anything of a similar type or teaching.[209] Le Goff discusses the question of dating and comes to the distinct conclusion that the concept and matter of purgatory came up at the end of the twelfth century with Cantor (+ 1197) for the first time[210] and that there was no evidence of it prior to

---

[206] Katechismus der katholischen Kirche. Oldenbourg: München, 1993. p. 294, Section 1030.
[207] Heinrich Ott. Die Antwort des Glaubens: Systematische Theologie in 50 Artikel. Berlin: Kreuz Verlag, 1973². pp. 462-463.
[208] Jacques Le Goff. Die Geburt des Fegefeuers: Vom Wandel des Weltbildes im Mittelalter. München: dtv, 1990. Comp. also with the newest literature of Susanne Wegmann. Auf dem Weg zum Himmel: Das Fegefeuer in der deutschen Kunst des Mittelalters. Köln: Böhlau, 2003 ; as well as Peter Jezler. "Himmel Hölle Fegefeuer: Das Jenseits im Mittelalter. Zürich: Verlag Neue Zürcher Zeitung, 1994 2nd. ed., therein part. Brigitte Rotach. "Der Durst der Toten und die zwischenzeitliche Erquickung (Refirgerium Interim)". p. 33-40; Christa Oechslin. "Der Himmel der Seeligen". pp. 41-46; Martina Wehrli-Johns. "'Tuo daz guote und lá daz übele': Das Fegefeuer als Sozialidee". pp. 47-58; Martin Illi. "Begräbnis, Verdammung und Erlösung". p. 59-68; Susan Martin, Daniela Mondini. "'Ich manen dich der brüsten min, Das du dem sünder wellest milte sin!': Marienbrüste und Marienmilch im Heilsgeschehen". pp. 79-90.
[209] Jacques Le Goff. Die Geburt des Fegefeuers. Op. cit., part. p. 11.
[210] Ibid., pp. 200-203.

1170.[211] "The first theologians addressing purgatory were Peter Cantor and Simon of Tournai".[212] The establishment of the teaching followed shortly thereafter by Pope Innocent III (1198-1216),[213] which teaching was then adopted everywhere between 1250 and 1350.[214] Visions played a central role here, which in general at this time were often the motor of theological development.[215]

The oldest declaration[216] regarding purgatory handed down to us comes from 1231, and it is a deliberate demarcation to the Greek Orthodox Church and its rejection of purgatory. Purgatory quickly became a central topic in the question of the splitting of the Church.[217] In 1254 the first papal definition of purgatory was expressly made against the Eastern Greek churches,[218] and in 1274 the Council of Lyon decided upon the teaching of purgatory against the Greek Church.[219] In 1300, within the framework of the bull proclaiming the first Jubilee Indulgence, the teachings of indulgences and purgatory conflated.[220]

The teaching of purgatory and indulgences had already been, for a quarter of a millennium prior to the Reformation, an expressly anti-ecumenical teaching and one for which a church break and the splitting of the global church was accepted. It is not accidental that the teachings of purgatory and indulgences became one of the central arguments against each type of alleged or actual heresy, as well as against all pre-Reformation movements such as the Waldensians or Hussites. Le Goff writes, "The fight against heresy cannot be ignored as a sort of third front. A string of church authors, who at the turn of the thirteenth century contributed to the birth of purgatory, were also marked by their involvement in the fight against heresy and made use of the new idea of purgatory in this battle. Purgatory emerged, as is the case with many other beliefs, not only as a result of positive tendencies and out of the reflection of intellectuals and pressure from the masses, but rather out of negative impulses as well, out of the battle against those who did not believe in it. With this it becomes clear that there was a lot at stake when it came to purgatory. The

---

[211] Ibid., pp. 187-200.
[212] Ibid., pp. 200-203 (section heading).
[213] Ibid., pp. 211-213.
[214] Ibid., pp. 211-253; comp. p. 14.
[215] According to Ibid., pp. 133-149.
[216] Ibid., pp. 341-342.
[217] Ibid., pp. 340-343.
[218] Ibid., pp. 343-349.
[219] Ibid., pp. 344-349.
[220] Ibid., pp. 401-403.

Roman Church formulated the doctrine of purgatory against heretics in the twelfth and thirteenth centuries, against the Greeks from the thirteenth until the fifteenth centuries, and against the Protestants in the sixteenth and seventeenth centuries. It is significant that the opponents of the official Roman Church repeatedly attacked the belief in purgatory and were consistently convinced that the destiny of people in the afterlife was dependent upon their merits and the will of God and that, therefore, at the time of death, all dice had been cast. People who have died go directly (or after the judgment) to paradise or to hell, but between death and resurrection there is no possibility for sins to be forgiven. And as a result, there is no purgatory. It is therefore also futile to pray for the dead. This gave the heretics, who, of course, did not like the church, an opportunity to deny the church any relevancy after death and to refuse to let the church extend its power over people."[221]

One of the most severe critics of Le Goff,[222] Christoph Auffarth, still comes to results that only differ in the details. Surely when it comes to these details, Auffarth can demonstrate that there are errors with Le Goff, as well as some thoughts that count as harbingers. Le Goff's socialistic and atheistic leanings also bother him, but Auffarth cannot prove that the teaching of purgatory had been formulated anywhere anytime earlier.

In recent times Andreas Merkt has basically contradicted Le Goff.[223] He confined himself to church fathers and writers from North Africa, by which he meant primarily Tertullian and Cyprian, as proof for having found an early understanding of purgatory. At the same time, he assumed that purgatory did not develop in antiquity or in pagan religions but rather in Christianity on the basis of a stimulus coming from a Jewish influence. What he proves, in my opinion, is that in Northern Africa in the second and third centuries, there was the idea that prayers of the living helped the dead, in particular, Christians who had died and awaited the resurrection. There was also the thought that Christians would somehow be refined in their state of waiting or that they would be refined immediately after the judgment. Here we have a number of points of departure for the later development of purgatory but not for the Scholastic teaching of purgatory.

---

[221] Ibid., p. 205.
[222] Christoph Auffarth. Irdische Wege und himmlischer Lohn: Kreuzzug, Jerusalem und Fegefeuer in religionswissenschaftlicher Perspektive. Göttingen: Vandenhoeck & Ruprecht, 2002. pp. 151-158.
[223] Andreas Merkt. Das Fegefeuer: Entstehung und Funktion einer Idee. Darmstadt: Wissenschaftliche Buchgesellschaft, 2005.

The teaching of purgatory has something in common with the teaching of indulgences and the teaching of the treasury of the Church. This commonality lies in the fact that the teaching of purgatory was not known in the first millennium of the Christian era and that it was not until the Middle Ages that it crept in. Additionally, it arose 100 years after the teaching of indulgences and remained in its details a very disputed topic among theologians. As with the other two dogmas, purgatory was (and is) rejected by many theologians, by pre-Reformers and Reformers, but from all other confessions as well, that is to say, also by the Orthodox and Oriental churches.[224]

In order to make room for the teaching of 'purgatorium,' the teaching of 'refrigerium' from the first millennium had to be displaced. 'Refrigerium' referred to a pre-paradise, to 'Abraham's bosom' as a resting place for believers who had not yet been resurrected (Luke 16:19-26). Everywhere that we come across the church fathers, a teaching of purgatory is unthinkable. However, Le Goff mentions Clement of Alexandria (+ 215) and Origen (+ 253/4) as fathers of purgatory,[225] since they took the notion from the Greek philosophers that punishment by the gods was always instructional. Augustine[226] is also viewed as a father of the teaching, since in his view there were certain sins for which remission after death is thinkable. As significant as all this might be for understanding the history of ideas, the teaching of purgatory is nowhere to be found.[227]

Central passages relating to purgatory were 2 Maccabees 12:41-46[228] and I Corinthians 3:11-15[229], whereby the history of the interpretation of the latter text is closely tied to the emergence of the notion of purgatory. These texts will be more closely examined below.

Le Goff makes it clear that the teaching of purgatory brought with it some far-reaching changes to the thinking of the early church. "Only very seldom can the developmental history of a faith be precisely followed, even where, as in the case of purgatory, elements from that dark, unidenti-

---

[224] Comp. Jacques Le Goff. Die Geburt des Fegefeuers. Op. cit., part. pp. 337-343, 403-406.
[225] Ibid., pp. 72-78.
[226] Ibid., pp. 84-107.
[227] James Akin. "Purgatory" (1996). www.ewtn.com/library/answers/purgatory.htm (January 3, 2004) cites voices of the Church Fathers in favour of purgatory. In the best case they have to do with items documenting prayer for the dead, and often times not even that. In no case do they have to do with items documenting the teaching of purgatory.
[228] Ibid., pp. 59-60.
[229] Ibid., pp. 61-62.

fiable time come together, in which the source of most religions seems to arise. Purgatory is not a minor point. It is not an unimportant little insertion into the original structure of the Christian faith, not something which simply developed in the Middle Ages and in the following centuries in the form of Roman Catholicism. The afterlife looms on the grand horizon of religions as well as of societies. The belief that the die has not been cast when death occurs changes the life of believers. The appearance of purgatory over the centuries has to do with a substantial change in the way Christians orient themselves within their framework of space and time. The conceptions of space and time are the scaffolding for the ways of thought and life in a society."[230]

3.15 The Teaching of the Treasury of the Church – a Completely New Outgrowth of the Thirteenth Century

In the thirteenth century, along with the deliberations given to indulgences, there arose the teaching of the treasury of the Church.[231] This term was initially formulated in 1230 by Hugo of St. Cher.[232] In his view, the treasury of the Church is limited to the surplus good works of Christ and the martyrs. It was not until his successors that the treasury of the Church assimilated the surplus works of all Christians. Thomas Aquinas expanded the teaching, but it was never propagated by a pope. It was only mentioned in 1343.[233] The idea of the treasury of the Church first became an official teaching through Leo X in 1520, but then again with Pious VI in 1794. Both popes, however, only taught the doctrine by condemning the rejection of the treasury of the Church.[234]

Pierre Bühler writes the following regarding the history of the teaching of the treasury of the Church:[235] "Initially the remission of believers' pun-

---

[230] Jacques Le Goff. Die Geburt des Fegefeuers. Op. cit., p. 9.
[231] According to, e.g., Georg Muschalek. "Der Ablaß in der heutigen Praxis und Lehre der katholischen Kirche". pp. 13-37 in: Georg Muschalek et al. Gespräch über den Ablaß. Arbeiten zur kirchlichen Wiedervereinigung – Kirchengeschichtliche Reihe 2. Graz: Verlag Styria, 1965. p. 21.
[232] Nikolaus Paulus. Geschichte des Ablasses ... Bd. 2. Op. cit., p. 152.
[233] Ibid., p. 155-157; Textauszug in Heinrich Denzinger, Peter Hünermann (ed.). Enchiridion symbolorum ... Op. Cit., pp. 412-413, margin no. 1025-1027.
[234] Nikolaus Paulus. Geschichte des Ablasses ... Bd. 2. Op. cit., pp. 157-158.
[235] Comp. in detail Nikolaus Paulus. Geschichte des Ablasses ... Bd. 2. Op. cit., pp. 141-158.

ishments rested upon the Church's intercession. This mediation was gradually replaced by a legal principle: God's justice requires that all punishment has to be served. For this reason, there has to be compensation with each remission. So it was that in the thirteenth century that the idea of a treasury of works of expiation, from which the Church can draw in order to distribute its remission from punishment. This has to do with the treasury of supererogatory merit (i.e., excessive or collateral merit), which Jesus Christ and the saints had acquired throughout the centuries. These merits had value as compensation: they serve to balance out the partial works of expiation of other members of the mystical body of Jesus Christ. It is incumbent upon the Church to administer this treasury of merit, and the Church can for that reason share it with believers."[236] Johannes Hüttenbügel adds: "The teaching of the treasury of merit was introduced for the first time in 1230 by the Dominican Cardinal Hugo of St. Cher in Paris. It can be found in the canonist Henry of Susa (+ 1271), where it is expressed with the following picture: The superabundant blood of Christ, which was shed for us, as well as the blood of the martyrs, is placed within the Church as a shrine. The Church has the key to this shrine. At its discretion, the Church can open this shrine and in issuing indulgences distribute from its store to whom it wishes. This conception of a treasury, likened to a storehouse that stands ready and from which the Church takes what it needs for indulgences, leads to the danger of reification. Grace and remission of punishment are understood as the distribution of something that is taken from the depot."[237]

In the papal bull of 1343, the following was stated: "He left behind this treasury ... to distribute healing among believers by the blessed Peter and his successors, his representatives on earth, and for the purpose of merciful benefit for all those who truly experience contrition and have confessed for right and sensible reasons, and who shortly thereafter seek a plenary remission or a partial remission, generally or specifically, with respect to temporal punishments (depending on what they recognize as appropriate before God). To the excess of this treasury belong, as is generally known, the merits of the blessed Mother of God and all the chosen from the first righteous one to the last righteous one; the depletion and reduction of this treasury, respectively, are not to be feared in the least, due to the unlimited merits of Christ (as was mentioned before) as well as due to the fact that the

---

[236] Pierre Bühler. Ablass oder Rechtfertigung durch Glauben: Was brauchen wir zum Jubiläumsjahr 2000? Zürich: Pano Verlag, 2000. p. 12.
[237] Johannes Hüttenbügel. Der Ablaß. Op. cit., pp. 16-17.

excess of merits grows all the more as more (people) who, on the basis of its benefits, are drawn toward righteousness."[238]

Max Lackmann goes on the assumption that the treasury of merit was never declared to be an infallible teaching on the part of the Roman Catholic Church, nor was it more precisely defined.[239] The treasury of merit is a side effect of the teaching on indulgences[240] since the Jubilee Bull of 1343, which secured the treasury of merit an 'in rem' understanding.[241] When Luther also placed the treasury of merit in question within the framework of the 95 Theses,[242] his opponent Cajetan (Thomas de Vio, 1469-1534) referred solely to this bull in his 1518 interrogation of Luther as a papal envoy[243] – at that time there was simply no more justification for the teaching of the treasury of merit than that. In his commentary to Thesis 62, Luther argued among other things against the treasury of merit by saying that we are all unworthy servants according to Luke 17:10. We never do enough good. "Luther, in his Thesis 62 regarding indulgences, said everything necessary on the topic: 'The true treasure of the church is the holy gospel of the glory and the grace of God' (Thesis 62).[244] Furthermore, in Thesis 37 Luther held that every Christian, without indulgences, had participation in all the goods that Christ and the church possess and that these did not have to be acquired.[245]

---

[238] Heinrich Denzinger, Peter Hünermann (ed.). Enchiridion symbolorum ... Op. cit., p. 413, No. 1026-1027.
[239] Max Lackmann. "Überlegungen zur Lehre vom 'Schatz der Kirche'". p. 75-157 in: Georg Muschalek et al. Gespräch über den Ablaß. Arbeiten zur kirchlichen Wiedervereinigung – Kirchengeschichtliche Reihe 2. Graz: Verlag Styria, 1965. p. 75.
[240] Ibid., p. 77.
[241] Ibid., pp. 90-33.
[242] Theses 56-66, Literature description see above. Comp. to Luther's view of the treasury of the Church in Max Lackmann. "Überlegungen zur Lehre vom 'Schatz der Kirche'". Op. cit., pp. 94-131.
[243] Ibid., p. 113.
[244] Theological committee of the society for internal and external missions for the Lutheran Church (Theologischer Ausschuß der Gesellschaft für Innere und Äußere Mission im Sinne der lutherischen Kirche). Ablaß? – Nein danke! Op. cit.; Comp. Per Erik Persson. "Der wahre Schatz der Kirche". Lutherische Rundschau 17 (1967): 315-327, p. 318. Protestant and biblical arguments against the teaching oft he treasury of the Church can be found in Norman L. Geisler, Ralph E. MacKenzie. Roman Catholics and Evangelicals: Agreements and Differences. Baker Books, 1998 (1995). pp. 340-347.
[245] Martin Luther. Gesammelte Werke. Digitale Bibliothek. Op. cit., p. 1151.

3.16 Indulgences for the Deceased – A Completely New Outgrowth of the Thirteenth and Fourteenth Centuries

The single classic building block of teaching today, as far as indulgences are concerned and which was missing among the great Scholastics, is the matter of indulgences for the deceased.[246] This is the case even if one basically finds them in Thomas Aquinas' thought.[247] We have already seen that indulgences arose during the crusades and that here the practice preceded the theory.[248] Indulgences were proclaimed without authorization by preachers of the crusades[249] but were, however, still largely rejected by theologians in the thirteenth century.[250] It was not until after 1350 that the teaching of indulgences expanded on a large scale.[251] Even then it was not seen as an official teaching of the Catholic Church, which demonstrates that up until the time of the Reformation, it was still rejected by a large number of theologians.[252] As we have seen, it was not until 1476 that indulgences for the deceased were proclaimed within the framework of new crusades, and this by Pope Sixtus IV.[253] The first time indulgences were proclaimed by a pope for the deceased was in 1457,[254] and they were declared indubitable and infallible teaching at the Council of Trent.

The development of indulgences was driven forward by a practice whereby theory and theology came subsequently. This is the case for the

---

[246] Comp. Nikolaus Paulus. Geschichte des Ablasses ... Bd. 2. Op. cit., pp. 114-120 "Die Anfänge des Sterbeablasses" und pp. 121-140 "Der Ablaß für Verstorbene".
[247] Text extract in Walther Köhler. Dokumente zum Ablassstreit 1517. Tübingen: Mohr, 1934². pp. 34-35.
[248] Part. in Nikolaus Paulus. Geschichte des Ablasses ... Bd. 2. Op. cit., p. 126.
[249] Nikolaus Paulus. Geschichte des Ablasses ... Bd. 2. Op. cit., pp. 166-169. According to p. 163-165 there were isolated prior representative acts of penance for the dead which were not to be taken as actual indulgences.
[250] Supporting documents in ibid., pp. 170-182.
[251] Ibid., p. 183.
[252] According to Nikolaus Paulus. Geschichte des Ablasses ... Bd. 2. Op. cit., p. 132 und Bd. 3. Op. cit., pp. 316-324.
[253] Latin Text in Walther Köhler. Dokumente zum Ablassstreit 1517. Tübingen: Mohr, 1934 2nd. ed. pp. 37-38; Engl. in Paul F. Palmer. Sacraments and Forgiveness. Op. cit., pp. 350-352.
[254] Text in Walther Köhler. Dokumente zum Ablassstreit 1517. Tübingen: Mohr, 1934 2nd ed. p. 37.

innovation that had the farthest reaching consequences,[255] the practice of relatives predominantly being the donors of indulgences for the deceased. "From the middle of the thirteenth century onward, it became in many cases common church practice that indulgences for 'souls in purgatory' were donated without official explanation or without a supportive theological theory. After Hugo of St. Cher and Hostiensis rejected this practice, Raimund of Pellafort declared such indulgences to be efficacious in cases where donations to the deceased were pronounced as such when granted. Albert the Great, Bonaventure, and Thomas Aquinas all granted the possibility of donating indulgences to the deceased, while on the other hand, this possibility was still being contested toward the end of the fifteenth century. The first certain attestation of papal approval of indulgences for the deceased (there are numerous falsified documents) comes from Calixtus III (+ 1458). From the fifteenth century onward, it was taught repeatedly (R. Peraudi, and later, F. de Suárez, among others) that the state of grace of the donor of indulgences for the deceased was an expendable issue. At the same time, this view was just as strongly contradicted (at the Sorbonne, among other places) as the opinion that arose in the fifteenth century that the Pope could empty purgatory if he only wanted to."[256] Since that time, nothing has changed in this notion, and the Catechism of the Catholic Church correspondingly embeds indulgences for the deceased in general intercession:[257] This teaching is also based on the practice of prayer for the dead, already mentioned in sacred Scripture: "Therefore [Judas Maccabeus] made atonement for the dead, that they might be delivered from their sin. From the beginning the Church has honored the memory of the dead and offered prayers in suffrage for them, above all the Eucharistic sacrifice [comp. DS 856], so that thus purified, they may attain the beatific vision of God. The Church also commends almsgiving, indulgences, and works of penance undertaken on behalf of the dead."[258]

---

[255] Part. according to Bernd Moeller. "Die letzten Ablaßkampagnen". Op. cit., pp. 59-64.
[256] Herbert Vorgrimler. Buße und Krankensalbung. Op. cit., pp. 208-209.
[257] Protestant an biblical arguments against prying towards dead saints and dead people in general can be found in Norman L. Geisler, Ralph E. MacKenzie. Roman Catholics and Evangelicals: Agreements and Differences. Baker Books, 1998 (1995). pp. 347-350, 353-355.
[258] Katechismus der katholischen Kirche. Oldenbourg: München, 1993. p. 294, Section 1032.

3.17 Jubilee Indulgences Beginning in 1300

Within the framework of growing papal centralization and the increasing significance that finances had in the Vatican, the substantial components of the theory of indulgences, that had with few exceptions almost been completely laid out by Thomas Aquinas, were expanded and finalized in the fourteenth century.

The introduction of the year of jubilee, in connection with the Jubilee Indulgence,[259] signaled the beginning. Up to our day, this steers large numbers of pilgrims to Rome.

The unfounded rumor of a Jubilee Indulgence at the end of 1299 and the beginning of 1300 brought an unbelievable number of pilgrims to Rome. "A concrete reason is not known. The physical presence of believers, as well as the high expectations and hopes, forced the Pope to act."[260] Only after Pope Boniface VIII (1294-1303) saw the crowds[261] did he include a complete indulgence in his February 22, 1300, bull entitled 'Antiquorum habet' for all visitors of the prominent basilicas in Rome.[262] This action represented the first time that a plenary indulgence was granted for something other than participation in crusades.[263] *Once again practice had coerced theory and theology.*

The unbelievable stream of pilgrims to Rome – reputable estimates[264] assume two million pilgrims, and that in the year 1300! – had naturally, desired or undesired, enormous financial bearing on the Vatican. The same is true today – desired or undesired – because the numbers of pilgrims arising in the jubilee years of 1983 and 2000 from the actions of Pope John Paul II – particularly the indulgences for a visit at one of the seven papal churches in Rome – are enormous even until today and are therefore a significant source of income for the papal state.

---

[259] Comp. to the history of the Jubilee indulgence in Nikolaus Paulus. Geschichte des Ablasses ... Bd. 2. Op. cit., pp. 78-94; Nikolaus Paulus. Geschichte des Ablasses ... Bd. 3. Op. cit., pp. 155-165 (Jubiläumsablässe 1390 bis 1500).

[260] Christine Neuhausen. Das Ablasswesen der Stadt Köln ... Op. cit., p. 103.

[261] Nikolaus Paulus. Geschichte des Ablasses ... Bd. 2. Op. cit., p. 80.

[262] Comp. to the Bull dated 1300 in Nikolaus Paulus. Geschichte des Ablasses ... Bd. 2. Op. cit., p. 110-114, part. 103-105. Latin text of Bonifatius VIII's Jubilee indulgence in 1300 in Walther Köhler. Dokumente zum Ablassstreit 1517. Tübingen: Mohr, 1934 2nd. ed. p. 18-19; by Clemens VI in 1343 ibid., p. 19-21; by Urban VI in 1389 ibid., pp. 21-22.

[263] Nikolaus Paulus. Geschichte des Ablasses ... Bd. 2. Op. cit., p. 82.

[264] Ibid., p. 85; comp. Christine Neuhausen. Das Ablasswesen der Stadt Köln ... Op. cit., pp. 101-103.

This becomes particularly clear with the second Jubilee Indulgence. "With a memory of the income achieved in 1300, the Romans – clerics as well as lay people – were interested to soon again have a holy year pronounced, against the instructions of Boniface VIII."[265] Since the Pope and the papal court (Curia) were at that time residing in Avignon and Rome was having financial problems, Romans sent a delegation to Avignon in 1342 with the wish for a new Jubilee Indulgence.[266] This is the reason the Pope, in Avignon, proclaimed a Jubilee Indulgence for Rome in 1350.[267] In 1350 the Pope himself remained the entire year in Avignon.

As far as the development of the teaching of indulgences is concerned, the bull of 1300 is particularly significant. This is due to the fact that it was the first time that a Pope referred to purgatory,[268] and this bull formed the basis from which purgatory elsewhere is addressed.

On January 25, 1343, Pope Clement VI prematurely proclaimed the next jubilee year in his jubilee bull 'Unigenitus Dei Filius.'[269] As far as the development of the teaching of indulgences is concerned, it carried significant meaning. The penultimate missing element was therein taught by the Church, that is, the teaching of the treasury of merit ('thesaurus meritorum Christi per Ecclesiam dispensandam'), over which the successors of Peter could freely dispose. Admittedly, this teaching was not more precisely substantiated. Rather, it was simply applied, and the teaching of the treasury of merit did not receive infallible status. "What one was dealing with here was an official, and not an infallible, declaration."[270]

3.18 Indulgence Campaigns from 1350-1500 and the 'Ad Instar Indulgences'

Boniface IX (1389-1404), perhaps the Pope who was least concerned with spiritual matters and who most strongly engaged himself in politics, war,

---

[265] Christine Neuhausen. Das Ablasswesen der Stadt Köln ... Op. cit., p. 104.
[266] Nikolaus Paulus. Geschichte des Ablasses ... Bd. 2. Op. cit., p. 87.
[267] According to Bernhard Schimmelpfennig. "Die Anfänge des Heiligen Jahres von Santiago de Compostela im Mittelalter". Journal of Medieval History 4 (1978): 285-303, p. 296 und Nikolaus Paulus. Geschichte des Ablasses ... Bd. 2. Op. cit., pp. 114-123.
[268] Comp. Jacques Le Goff. Die Geburt des Fegefeuers: Vom Wandel des Weltbildes im Mittelalter. München: dtv, 1990. pp. 401-403.
[269] Nikolaus Paulus. Geschichte des Ablasses ... Bd. 2. Op. cit., p. 87; Paul F. Palmer. Sacraments and Forgiveness. Op. cit., pp. 349-350.
[270] Herbert Vorgrimler. Buße und Krankensalbung. Op. cit., p. 208.

and finances, found himself in great need of funds during the Papal Schism. It was for this reason that he prematurely ordered a jubilee year in 1390 and for the first time took indulgence revenues which had heretofore been left with the churches from the cathedrals in Rome for the Vatican. In order to increase indulgence revenues, he invented the notion of bestowing Jubilee Indulgences on cities such as Milan and Munich, which occurred up until 1397. Since this was much more lucrative, he denied Rome its upcoming Jubilee Indulgences in 1400.[271] In time, instead of this practice, Jubilee Indulgences were eventually given to entire territories.

The grave of St. James in Santiago de Compostela in Spain, which in any event was, next to Rome, the greatest site of pilgrimage in the Middle Ages already, in this way became the most important site of pilgrimage for those people seeking indulgences. This continued through the time of the Reformation and beyond, even when the indulgence of 1500 was shown to be a falsification.[272]

This was the perfected form of the so-called 'ad instar' indulgences,[273] indulgences 'of the kind of.' This is to say the receipt of indulgence grace occurred as if one had been at another location. Bernd Moeller names two innovations in indulgences as the real impact of Boniface IX. These were the "conveyance of the jubilee to other locations in Europe" and "the immense popularization of the so-called 'ad instar indulgences.'"[274] He emphasized that of all places *Wittenberg* had become the most important center of these and similar indulgences.[275]

Luther's adversary Johannes Tetzel was therefore able to correctly proclaim in his indulgence sermons in Germany: "Here is Rome."[276] The Reformation was an upshot of such a "Rome," because "the Portuncula indul-

---

[271] Comp. details of indulgence policy of this Pope in Karlheinz Frankl. "Papstschisma und Frömmigkeit: Die 'ad instar-Ablässe'". Römische Quartalschrift für christliche Altertumskunde und Kirchengeschichte 72 (1977): 57-124; 184-247, pp. 70-73 und Bernd Moeller. "Die letzten Ablaßkampagnen". Op. cit., p. 57.

[272] See details in Bernhard Schimmelpfennig. "Die Anfänge des Heiligen Jahres von Santiago de Compostela im Mittelalter". Journal of Medieval History 4 (1978): 285-303.

[273] Comp. part. Bernhard Schimmelpfennig. "Die Anfänge des Heiligen Jahres von Santiago de Compostela im Mittelalter". Journal of Medieval History 4 (1978): 285-303; Karlheinz Frankl. "Papstschisma und Frömmigkeit". Op. cit. (all). Nikolaus Paulus does not address these indulgences.

[274] All ibid.

[275] Ibid., pp. 57-58.

[276] According to Martin Brecht. Martin Luther: Sein Weg zur Reformation 1483-1521. Op. cit., p. 180.

gence was also granted to the Wittenberg Castle Church for All Saints Day."[277]

The output of indulgence letters in 1401 and 1402 was higher than ever before.[278] However, to the alarm of many princes and believers in all of Europe, at the end of 1402, Boniface IX repealed all indulgences and 'ad instar' indulgences,[279] only to proclaim new indulgences on a grand scale 14 days later.[280] In principle, this required all indulgences to be reacquired, while in fact, intentionally or unknowingly, the indulgences that had become invalid were nonetheless still proclaimed.[281]

In the second half of the fourteenth century, up until the high point in 1500, the number of indulgences continued to grow enormously because of an intense spread of piety and fear of not possessing salvation.[282]

In addition to the 'ad instar' indulgences and the large Europe-wide indulgence campaign, the spread of the Toties Quoties Indulgence also played a role.[283] It was so called because it was valid as often as one liked, as long as certain actions were performed. It approximated a rosary. These were partial indulgences that increased in popularity in the fifteenth century. Today they are the formative outline for indulgences, of which Poschmann can say the following: "The current practice is primarily characterized by the clustering of indulgences. Every believer can obtain not only the most varied and partial indulgences. Rather, the opportunity exists to obtain a number of plenary indulgences . . ."[284]

It is still to be mentioned that the large indulgence campaigns were significantly influenced by the invention of printing and the spread of single-sheet printing. It was not only as a result of Luther's 95 Theses that the

---

[277] Ibid., p. 175.
[278] Also in Karlheinz Frankl. "Papstschisma und Frömmigkeit". Op. cit., p. 72.
[279] Ibid., p. 60 and pp. 221-224.
[280] Ibid., pp. 229-230.
[281] Ibid., p. 231.
[282] Comp. Christine Neuhausen. Das Ablasswesen der Stadt Köln ... Op. cit., p. 51 (Table), especially the literature named in footnote 3 as well as Bernd Moeller. "Die letzten Ablaßkampagnen ...". Op. cit. (all) and Wilhelm Ernst Winterhager. "Ablaßkritik als Indikator historischen Wandels". Archiv für Reformationsgeschichte 90 (1999): 6-69.
[283] Comp. e. g. Christine Neuhausen. Das Ablasswesen der Stadt Köln ... Op. cit., pp. 52-53 (Table). Strangely enough Nikolaus Paulus completely skips over this type of indulgence.
[284] Bernhard Poschmann. Der Ablass im Licht der Bußgeschichte. Op. cit., p. 113.

topic of indulgences was associated with the history of printing.[285] Rather, it is the case that printing, in particular, single-page printing, was used prior to that time for the distribution of bulls announcing and requesting indulgences. The oldest preserved printed version of an indulgence letter dates from 1454. For the first time since the Jubilee Indulgence of 1475, the invention of printing made the distribution of papal bulls and letters relating to confession possible in large numbers in Europe, and the thinking relating to indulgences could spread in a way that had not been seen up to that time.[286]

3.19 The Decline of the Indulgence Campaign from 1500-1517

In his seminal work 'A Critique of Indulgences as an Indication of Historical Change' Wilhelm Ernst Winterhager points out in the archives of Reformation history that prior to Luther, the critique of indulgences had already gained enormous steam and that the revenues from indulgences had dramatically declined.[287] In the fifteenth century, indulgences were increasingly in the center of what was happening in the church. This was primarily because of the large indulgence campaigns beginning in the middle of the fifteenth century. The financial aspect took on increased importance, because "long ago the service of penance had given way to a mere payment of money..."[288] "The situation was brought to an extreme by the Holy See, when in 1476 it sanctioned the possibility of using indulgences for the deceased. This provided an advantage to the church treasury, since it opened up a completely new market for indulgences."[289] The culmination of indulgences[290] was reached around the year 1480, and with it, the high point of financial success as measured against the geographic spread of indulgence campaigns.[291]

---

[285] Comp. the great importance of letters of indulgence and documents relating to indulgences for the art of printing in Nikolaus Paulus. Geschichte des Ablasses ... Bd. 3. S. Op. cit. IX-X.
[286] Comp. the text examples in Wilhelm Ernst Winterhager. "Ablaßkritik als Indikator historischen Wandels". Op. cit. pp. 41-42 and 45.
[287] Wilhelm Ernst Winterhager. "Ablaßkritik als Indikator historischen Wandels". Archiv für Reformationsgeschichte 90 (1999): 6-69.
[288] Ibid., p. 8.
[289] Ibid., pp. 8-9.
[290] Ibid., p. 22.
[291] In Walther Köhler. Dokumente zum Ablassstreit 1517. Tübingen: Mohr, 1934 2nd ed. the following important indulgence texts in Latin are found from the time prior

It is no miracle that reflection about whether a person could derive amends only by making a payment of money increased and that indulgences became "the embodiment of a church that was hardened fiscally and spiritually astray."[292] Luther himself declared that he had taken up an already present and widespread criticism of indulgences.[293] Luther's success, according to Winterhager, can only be explained by the fact that already, between 1501 and 1503, there was "an effect of erosion and a loss of credibility"[294] that led to a decrease in revenues. There were hardly any revenues generated with the indulgence campaign in Trier in 1515-1516 to make the campaign worthwhile.[295] Winterhagen estimates that from 1500 to 1517, revenues from indulgences fell dramatically.[296] The misappropriation of indulgence moneys by princes, but also by the Pope, were widely known, and men such as Luther's priest Johann Staupitz, who was authorized to hear confessions, openly criticized the indulgence campaign.[297] A significant reason was also the fact that with each indulgence campaign, the indulgence letters from prior campaigns were at least declared temporarily invalid, since otherwise many people would have not acquired a new indulgence.[298]

Because of a lack of success, the indulgence campaign by the Archbishop of Mainz and Magdeburg that was criticized by Luther in 1517 was ended in 1518. Not only Luther was responsible for this result. When in September 1518 the parliament (Reichstag) met, the thought of a crusade indulgence against the Turks arose. This was immediately rejected, since the weariness with indulgences would have made it unsuccessful. When in 1518 indulgences were to be introduced in the diocese of Breslau, the chapter simply opposed this move on the basis of the rejection people indicated toward it.[299] Still, the Pope had forced the Archbishop of Mainz

---

[292] to the Reformation: p. 50-83: Johannes v. Paltz, Coelifodina, Erfurt 1502, a classic portrayal of the teachings and practice of indulgences; p. 83-94 the indulgence bull issued by Leos X in 1515; pp. 23-24 Pope Paul II's Jubilee Indulgence of 1470 and p. 24-26 Alexanders VI's Jubilee Indulgence in 1500.
Wilhelm Ernst Winterhager. "Ablaßkritik als Indikator historischen Wandels". Op. cit., p. 9.
[293] Examples see ibid., pp. 12-21.
[294] Ibid., p. 24.
[295] Ibid., p. 25.
[296] Ibid., pp. 22-34.
[297] Comp. Martin Brecht. Martin Luther: Sein Weg zur Reformation 1483-1521. p. 185; additional examples ibid., pp. 34-43.
[298] Comp. details ibid., pp. 38-39.
[299] According to ibid., p. 10.

to conduct the indulgence campaign while the Archbishop himself and his court held this for senseless. The Franciscans, who were supposed to have organized this indulgence, successfully refused.[300] If this had never happened, the Dominican Johann Tetzel would never have gone into action.

---

[300] According to ibid, pp. 40-42.

4 The History of Indulgences and Their Theology from the Reformation until the Second Vatican Council

4.1 The Reformation and Indulgences

4.1.1 Martin Luther

"The proclamation of the Peter's Indulgence was the last big campaign of Europe-wide dimensions."[301] It was the formal reason for the Reformation.

The Reformation began with Martin Luther's critiquing the practice of indulgences in his 95 Theses. His focus was not primarily the scandalous financial side but rather the theological foundations. Martin Luther initially published his 95 Theses for academic discussion,[302] after, however, he had preached from the pulpit against indulgences in 1514.[303] When the 95 Theses were printed against his wishes and distributed, Luther composed a Sermon in German entitled 'Sermon about Indulgences and Grace'[304] in 1518, which was broadly understandable, as well as an academic defense of the theses entitled 'Resolutiones disputationum de indulgentiarum virtute.'[305]

Luther himself was surprised by the course of things. Regardless of whether the nailing of the theses is historically provable or not, Luther did not want – and this finds consensus among historians – to start a large

---

[301] Christine Neuhausen. Das Ablasswesen der Stadt Köln . . . Op. cit., p. 167.
[302] Easily accessible editions: Martin Luther. Martin Luthers 95 Thesen nebst dem Sermon von Ablaß und Gnade 1517. Kleine Texte für Vorlesungen und Übungen 142. Walter de Gruyter: Berlin, 1983 3rd. ed; Martin Luther. Ausgewählte Schriften. Bd. 1. Insel-Verlag: Frankfurt, 1983 2nd. ed. pp. 26-37; Martin Luther. Glaube und Kirchenreform. Martin Luther Taschenausgabe Bd. 2. Evangelische Verlagsanstalt: Berlin, 1984. pp. 24-33.
[303] Supporting documents in Martin Brecht. Martin Luther: Sein Weg zur Reformation 1483-1521. Op. cit., p. 182; Latin example texts in Walther Köhler. Dokumente zum Ablassstreit 1517. Tübingen: Mohr, 1934 2nd ed. pp. 94-104.
[304] Text as example in Martin Luther. Ausgewählte Schriften. Bd. 1. Op. cit., p. 35-40 and together with most of the noted editions of the 95 Theses.
[305] Martin Luther. Gesammelte Werke. ed. by Kurt Aland. Digitale Bibliothek Bd. 63. Berlin: Directmedia, 2002 (entspricht Martin Luther: Luther deutsch. Die Werke Martin Luthers in neuer Auswahl für die Gegenwart. 10 Bde. Göttingen: Vandenhoeck und Ruprecht, 1991). pp. 1114-1195.

movement against indulgences with his theses.[306] Even the close tie between indulgences and other Catholic teachings, such as penance, purgatory, and the office of the Pope, only became gradually clearer. Luther's actual written "Repudiation of Purgatory," for example, did not follow until 1530.[307] This notwithstanding, the literary dispute regarding indulgences surged with many writings for and against them from 1517 onward.[308]

Luther's letter to the Archbishop Albrecht of Mainz, dated October 31, 1517, as well as his May 1518 letter to Pope Leo X, make it clear that Luther's initial intention was directed only at a reform of indulgences and not at the papacy.[309] In his letter to the Pope, Luther wrote: "I have heard evil reports about myself, most blessed Father, by which I know that certain friends have put my name in very bad odor with you and yours, saying that I have attempted to belittle the power of the keys and of the Supreme Pontiff."[310] In his 41st thesis, Luther suggests that indulgences only be proclaimed with caution, and in the 39th thesis, he states that he understands them only as a notification of remission by God[311] and wants it to be respected as such.[312]

"In his 95 Wittenberg Theses, Luther did not reject indulgences per se; he accepted them as an act of the keys of authority (Thesis 61) by which canonically laid out penance was eased (Thesis 5,20). However, indulgences did not lead to the remission of all temporal penalties for sin as required by God's righteousness (Thesis 21,23). Above all, Luther rejected the teaching of the treasury of merit, namely that with indulgences the merits of Christ and the saints could be allocated to recipients (Thesis 58). He

---

[306] Such is found in Wilhelm Ernst Winterhager. "Ablaßkritik als Indikator historischen Wandels vor 1517". Archiv für Reformationsgeschichte 90 (1999): 6-71, p. 7.

[307] Comp. Julius Köstlin. Luthers Theologie in ihrer geschichtlichen Entwicklung und ihrem inneren Zusammenhange dargestellt. 1. Bd. J. F. Steinkopf: Stuttgart, 1901 2nd ed. pp. 373-376.

[308] Walther Köhler. Dokumente zum Ablassstreit 1517. Tübingen: Mohr, 1934 2nd ed.

[309] Latin Text: Walther Köhler. Dokumente zum Ablassstreit 1517. Tübingen: Mohr, 1934 2nd ed. pp. 143-145.

[310] Martin Luther. Gesammelte Werke. ed. by Kurt Aland. Digitale Bibliothek Bd. 63. Berlin: Directmedia, 2002 (entspricht Martin Luther: Luther deutsch. Die Werke Martin Luthers in neuer Auswahl für die Gegenwart. 10 Bde. Göttingen: Vandenhoeck und Ruprecht, 1991). p. 1207 (in the book edition vol. 2. p. 88). Also available in English at http://www.iclnet.org/pub/resources/text/wittenberg/luther/nine5-pope.txt.

[311] Ibid., p. 1153.

[312] Ibid., p. 1154.

held that recipients had a share in these merits without any action on the part of the Pope (Thesis 37). This notion held by Luther regarding indulgences did not contradict any defined teaching of belief. Rather, it contradicted the prevailing teaching of theologians, who for their part followed the practice of indulgences and tried to justify them. Luther's intention was directed at the disastrous consequences of what were doubtful theological formulas (such as the remission of guilt and penalties) or to effectively denounce the explicit false propaganda relating to indulgences (such as acquiring indulgences with a certain effect on the poor souls without repentance and confession in the afterlife). His intention also extended to denouncing the appalling error that a person could be freed from sin without an internal dissociation of sin and that with financial donations poor souls could definitely be delivered from purgatory. What weighed on Luther was the disregard for the remaining true works of penance and love (Theses 41-48) and a backing away from the proclamation of the gospel to make room for preaching on indulgences (Theses 52-55). No one can argue today that these concerns Luther had were true and well founded."[313] So writes a Catholic historian of the Council of Trent. He continues: "Luther was not the first and the only person who came out against existing grievances relating to indulgences. But in turn he was right when he charged the Pope and the bishops with neglect in their supervisory duties (Theses 69-74, 80). There can be no doubt about the fact that the embarrassing and sarcastic questions of educated lay people, which Luther expresses in theses 81-90, were truly asked or at least could have been asked. His attack on the practice of indulgences was largely justified, and his teaching on indulgences, on which it was based and to which it was geared, was to remove the floor upon which indulgences stood. It was not until the disputation in Leipzig that Luther called indulgences a pious deceit."[314]

In 1523 Luther's opponent Johannes Eck still saw the exaggerated practice of indulgences and the absence of a willingness to change this, in particular, with regard to the St. Peter's Indulgence, as the cause of the Reformation.[315]

---

[313] Hubert Jedin. Geschichte des Konzils von Trient. Bd. 3. Op. cit., p. 77.
[314] Ibid. Available in English at http://www.ccel.org/s/schaff/history/7_ch06.htm.
[315] I am following Wilhelm Ernst Winterhager. "Ablaßkritik als Indikator historischen Wandels". Op. cit., p. 26. According to Martin Brecht. Martin Luther: Sein Weg zur Reformation 1483-1521. Op. cit., p. 332 Eck was competent in legal matters and required from the Pope a benefice in Ingolstadt for the office of the inquisitor in Eastern Germany.

It was not until the Church's reaction that it did not need to give reasons for its stance and that it could rather refer, without discussion, to the papal office that the question of indulgences became a fundamental issue concerning the Church. With this reaction, the Church tried to designate Luther's actions as primarily an act of disobedience toward the Pope.[316] Tetzel and Eck immediately turned the theses against the abuse of indulgences into an attack on the authority of the Pope.[317] This meant that in 1519/1520, Luther finally had to occupy himself with the history of papal primacy, and at the famous disputation in Leipzig in 1520 between Luther and Eck, the topic was almost exclusively the papacy. This was of "epic importance,"[318] because there had never been such a conflict regarding the primacy of the papacy.

There has been an embittered scholarly dispute as to whether Luther actually nailed his theses in Wittenberg on October 31, 1517, or whether he did this later or not at all. The dispute initially led to the denial that Luther nailed the theses in Wittenberg, but in the meantime, there has been a return to the idea that there is a certain likelihood that he did. What is certain is that Luther himself held October 31, 1517, to be the defining date. He thought this not due to nailing the theses, but rather because on this day his letter against indulgences was sent to Archbishop Albrecht of Mainz,[319] the

---

[316] Luther wrote in retrospect: "If from the beginning the one from Mainz, when I warned him, and if the Pope, who condemned me before listening to me and then raged in his bull, had come to the conclusion which Karl (von Miltitz) reached – too late of course – and had immediately suppressed Tetzel's rage, then in my opinion things would not have become so tumultuous. The one from Mainz carries the entire guilt" [translator's rendition]., Martin Luther. Gesammelte Werke. ed. by Kurt Aland. Digitale Bibliothek Bd. 63. Berlin: Directmedia, 2002 (entspricht Martin Luther: Luther deutsch. Die Werke Martin Luthers in neuer Auswahl für die Gegenwart. 10 Bde. Göttingen: Vandenhoeck und Ruprecht, 1991). p. 1080-81 (in the book edition, vol. 2, p. 18-19).

[317] E.g., Martin Brecht. Martin Luther: Sein Weg zur Reformation 1483-1521. Op. cit., pp. 194, 204.

[318] Ibid., p. 302.

[319] Martin Brecht. Martin Luther: Sein Weg zur Reformation 1483-1521. Op. cit., p. 187; Text: Kurt Aland. Die 95 Thesen Martin Luthers und die Anfänge der Reformation. Op. cit., pp. 71-73. In 1545 in retrospect Luther saw his letters of October 31, 1517 as the decisive date and only wanted them published when there was no reaction: Martin Luther. Gesammelte Werke. ed. by Kurt Aland. Digitale Bibliothek Bd. 63. Berlin: Directmedia, 2002 (entspricht Martin Luther: Luther deutsch. Die Werke Martin Luthers in neuer Auswahl für die Gegenwart. 10 Bde. Göttingen: Vandenhoeck und Ruprecht, 1991). p. 1071 (in the book version vol. 2. p. 13).

local bishop, and others. Melanchthon first mentioned the nailing of the theses on October 31, 1517, in his preface to Luther's Latin works in 1546.[320] I certainly agree with Kurt Aland that nailing academic theses was a common occurrence at that time. There is also an independent eye witness by Agricola on October 31, 1517.[321] This would have been meaningless if Luther, on the one hand, had written to church authorities[322] and, on the other hand, the Theses had not been printed immediately in Latin and German and distributed. The existence of the Theses in Merseburg and Dresden, as well as in Hamburg and Nuremberg, can be verified as early as November 1517.[323]

Admittedly, one can draw the conclusion from all of this that Luther was never really completely against indulgences and think, rather, that he was only against their abuse. This can, however, only be said at the outset. Luther's statements against indulgences became increasingly categorical and radical,[324] and the Protestant movement, in all of its various branches, did not even adopt hints of notions such as indulgences, a treasury of merit, or purgatory. Two statements by Luther should suffice as examples: "We know of no other indulgence than the one the Son of God secured for us unworthy ones and so richly and freely dispensed out of his graces..."[325] "Whoever depends upon and consoles himself with an indulgence and so dies or lives in such a state and relinquishes his hold on Jesus Christ has denied him and has forgotten him and can have no comfort in him. If any-

---

[320] Martin Brecht. Martin Luther: Sein Weg zur Reformation 1483-1521. Op. cit., pp. 196-197; Text: Kurt Aland. Die 95 Thesen Martin Luthers und die Anfänge der Reformation. Op. cit., p. 55.

[321] See discussion of handwritten evidence in Kurt Aland. Die 95 Thesen Martin Luthers und die Anfänge der Reformation. Op. cit., p. 103-109; comp. additional arguments, ibid., pp. 113-135.

[322] Kurt Aland. Die 95 Thesen Martin Luthers und die Anfänge der Reformation. Op. cit., p. 18.

[323] Kurt Aland. Die 95 Thesen Martin Luthers und die Anfänge der Reformation. Op. cit., p. 15; comp. Martin Brecht. Martin Luther: Sein Weg zur Reformation 1483-1521. Op. cit., pp. 199-200.

[324] Comp. Pierre Bühler. Ablass oder Rechtfertigung durch Glauben: Was brauchen wir zum Jubiläumsjahr 2000? Zürich: Pano Verlag, 2000. p. 29-48 und die Sammlung der Äußerungen Luthers zum Ablassstreit und seiner Geschichte: Kurt Aland. Die 95 Thesen Martin Luthers und die Anfänge der Reformation. Gütersloh: Gütersloher Verlagshaus, 1983.

[325] Quoted from Martin Luther. Sämtliche Schriften. ed. by Johann Georg Walch. Bd. 23. Verlag der Lutherischen Buchhandlung: Groß Oesingen, 1986 (1910 reprint[2]). Col. 12. (also there Col. 10-14 numerous additional quotes from Luther regarding indulgences).

one sets his source of comfort on anything besides Jesus Christ, he can have no comfort in Jesus Christ."[326]

One needs to specifically point out that the actual Reformational discovery took place after the 95 Theses and, admittedly, prior to the time that their academic elucidation ('Resolutionen') took place. I agree with Martin Brecht, that the dispute surrounding indulgences would have remained an isolated episode[327] had there not been a basic volte-face in March/April 1518.[328] The first proof for a Reformational discovery is a sermon dated March 28, 1518,[329] while against Spalatin, an older notion was represented by Luther on February 15, 1518.[330]

There commenced in the nineteenth and at the beginning of the twentieth centuries a discussion as to whether there were tendencies prior to Luther to intermingle indulgences and the sacrament of penance, whereby indulgences were granted not only for temporal punishment, but also for eternal punishment and guilt.[331] This allegation has, in the meantime, been refuted. Investigations by Nikolaus Paulus significantly contributed to understanding how the Middle Age formula "indulgence from guilt and punishment" is to be understood.[332] Indulgences at the time of the Reformation, for example, entitled two confessions with a subsequent discharge,

---

[326] Quoted according to Kurt Aland (ed.). Lutherlexikon. Vandenhoeck & Ruprecht: Göttingen, 1989 (1983 reprint 4th ed). p. 11

[327] Martin Brecht. Martin Luther: Sein Weg zur Reformation 1483-1521. Op. cit., p. 174.

[328] Comp. the discussion regarding the date on in Martin Brecht. Martin Luther: Sein Weg zur Reformation 1483-1521. Op. cit., p. 215-230. Luther himself, in retrospect, dated the insight into Romans 1:17 after the publication of the 95 Theses: Martin Luther. Gesammelte Werke. ed. by Kurt Aland. Digitale Bibliothek Bd. 63. Berlin: Directmedia, 2002 (entspricht Martin Luther: Luther deutsch. Die Werke Martin Luthers in neuer Auswahl für die Gegenwart. 10 Bde. Göttingen: Vandenhoeck und Ruprecht, 1991). p. 1083-1084, 1072 (in the book version, vol. 2. 20-21, 13).

[329] Ibid., p. 222.

[330] So in ibid, p. 216.

[331] Comp. the historical development in Karlheinz Frankl. "Papstschisma und Frömmigkeit: Die 'ad instar-Ablässe'". Römische Quartalschrift für christliche Altertumskunde und Kirchengeschichte 72 (1977): 57-124; 184-247, pp. 206-214.

[332] Comp. Nikolaus Paulus. Geschichte des Ablasses ... Bd. 2. Op. cit., p. 105-113 "Die Anfänge des Ablasses von Schuld und Strafe"; Nikolaus Paulus. Geschichte des Ablasses ... Bd. 3. Op. cit., pp. 277-296 "Der sogenannte Ablaß von Schuld und Strafe" and p. 297-315 in connection with the sacrament of penance; and Anton Kurz. Die katholische Lehre vom Ablass vor und nach dem Auftreten Luthers. Paderborn: Ferdinand Schöningh, 1900. pp. 33-34.

one being immediate and the other in the hour of death. With this came the "remission of guilt and punishment,"[333] namely remission of guilt by confession and remission of punishment via the indulgence.

Martin Brecht rightly noticed that the instructions regarding indulgences according to Albrecht of Mainz were theologically correct but added: "It is unmistakable that the reigning interest was large financial proceeds."[334]

Conversely, one has to protect Luther against the allegation that he wrongly maintained that the teaching was that indulgences provided salvation. On the basis of theses 32-34 in his 95 Theses, it is beyond question that Luther himself precisely knew that indulgences only related to temporal punishment. Thesis 34 reads as follows: "For the grace conveyed by these indulgences relates simply to the penalties of the sacramental satisfactions decreed merely by man."[335] Where Luther saw the danger that people believed they purchased salvation with indulgences was with the simple listeners. In the Academic Resolutions, Luther wrote as follows: "They had heard this, as they said, from the indulgence preachers, or (to be fair) at least understood it as such. I do not want to judge this here. Since I did not hear the indulgence preachers, I am not entitled to say."[336] In Thesis 81, Luther assumed that the indulgence preachers often exceeded the Church's teaching: "This unbridled preaching of indulgences makes it difficult for learned men to guard the respect due to the Pope against false accusations or at least from the keen criticisms of the laity."[337] He added: "One should teach Christians. If the Pope knew how the indulgence preachers extort money, he would rather burn St. Peter's Basilica to ashes than to build it with the skin, flesh, and bones of his sheep."[338]

---

[333] Martin Brecht. Martin Luther: Sein Weg zur Reformation 1483-1521. Op. cit., p. 175.
[334] Martin Brecht. Martin Luther: Sein Weg zur Reformation 1483-1521. Op. cit., p. 179.
[335] Martin Luther. Gesammelte Werke. Digitale Bibliothek. Op. cit., p. 1151.
[336] Ibid., p. 1146.
[337] Ibid., p. 1186.
[338] Ibid., p. 1155.

4.1.2 Antecedent History and John Tetzel

Let us turn to the history prior to Luther's critique of indulgences.[339] The big business[340] with St. Peter's Indulgences was set into motion by Archbishop Albrecht von Brandenburg. This Archbishop was more a politician and prince than a church leader and shepherd of souls, and the business with St. Peter's Indulgences was legitimated by Pope Julius II (1503-1513) via the bull 'Liquet omnibus.'[341] Big business with St. Peter's Indulgences was the historical cause of Luther's sermons and theses regarding the question of indulgences and with it the Reformation. The 24-year-old Archbishop Albrecht von Brandenburg had large debts with the Fuggers, because, in particular, of all the money he borrowed for his elevation to a second archbishopric (against canon law). In connection with this achievement, Archbishop Albrecht von Brandenburg had to pay the Vatican and others. One-half of the revenues from indulgence activities had to be paid to the Fuggers while the other half went directly to the Pope. (The funds were never amassed, in part because the indulgence revenues, as early as 1510, were overestimated and in part because of the consequences of the 95 Theses.) It was already shown that the Pope forced the Archbishop into this course of action and that the Franciscans successfully refused to carry out the indulgence.

---

[339] Comp. the useful summary of the state of research in: Bernd Moeller. "Die letzten Ablaßkampagnen: Der Widerspruch Luthers gegen den Ablaß in seinem geschichtlichen Zusammenhang". p. 539-567 in: Hartmut Boockmann, Bernd Moeller, Karl Stackmann (ed.). Lebenslehren und Weltentwürfe im Übergang vom Mittelalter zur Neuzeit. Abhandlungen der Akademie der Wissenschaften zu Göttingen. Phil.-hist. Klasse 3, Folge 179. Göttingen: Vandenhoeck & Ruprecht, 1989 = Bernd Moeller. "Die letzten Ablaßkampagnen: Der Widerspruch Luthers gegen den Ablaß in seinem geschichtlichen Zusammenhang". p. 53-72 in: ders. Die Reformation und das Mittelalter: Kirchenhistorische Aufsätze. Göttingen: Vandenhoeck & Ruprecht, 1991. A useful and comprehensive compilation of texts for and against indulgences from the time immediately prior to and at the beginning of the Reformation can be found in Martin Luther. Sämtliche Schriften. hrsg. von Johann Georg Walch. Bd. 15. Groß Oesingen: Verlag der Lutherischen Buchhandlung, 1987 (1880-1910 reprint 2nd ed.). P. 1-381 prior to and after Luther 1300-1532, p. 381-418 Luther und die Diskussionen 1517/1518, thereunder also numerous otherwise difficult to locate letters of indulgence.

[340] Comp. Nikolaus Paulus. Geschichte des Ablasses ... Bd. 3. Op. cit., p. 150.

[341] Comp. the translated text in: Paul F. Palmer. Sacraments and Forgiveness. Op. cit., pp. 354-355.

The History of Indulgences and Their Theology 85

Martin Brecht summarizes the details well: "Just how much indulgences could become or had become a scandalous business mixed with political and economic interests is demonstrated by the plenary indulgence issued by Pope Leo X on March 31, 1515, with which Julius II's new construction of St. Peter's Basilica in Rome was to be financed. This ignited protests by Luther leading to the Reformation and, by the way, also ignited Ulrich Zwingli in 1518 in Switzerland. The occasion for this indulgence in the Church provinces of Mainz and Magdeburg, and thereby in large parts of Germany, arose because of a particular constellation, which indicated something of the difficult and serious deficiencies existing at the time in the leadership system of the Church. The Archbishop of Mainz, which was the largest within Christendom and which was also the seat of the Archchancellor of Germany, had changed three times between 1504 and 1514. This meant that the fees for confirming the new archbishop and for conferring the pallium, the latter being the sign of the archbishop's grandeur, was due three times. These fees were 10,000 ducats or 14,000 gulden. The archbishopric was not fully overindebted for that reason alone. Additionally, his region in Erfurt was threatened by Cur Saxony. When the new elections were to be held in 1514, the chapter had to look around for a candidate who had the political and economic backing to master these difficulties. The choice fell on the 24-year-old Albrecht von Brandenburg-Hohenzollern ... As the Archbishop of Magdeburg and the administrator of Halberstadt, Albrecht could not by any means actually accept the vote in Mainz. This was because Canon Law prohibited the accumulation of offices. However, in return for adequate payments, it was certainly possible to receive exemption from this prohibition from the Pope. This also applied to the fact that Albrecht was actually too young to assume the position of a bishop. This became the occasion for Rome to enter into business with Albrecht, since it was clear that because of the payments for the papal confirmation and the exemption from the accumulation of offices, Albrecht, at his young age, was not in a position to come up with 21,000 Ducats or 29,000 Gulden alone. The Fugger bank advanced the amount and mediated the entire transaction. Albrecht was to market the St. Peter's Indulgence throughout his church provinces. Of the revenues, one-half was to be received by Rome, and the other half was to be used to repay Albrecht's debts with the Fuggers. The profit was estimated in advance to be 52,286 Ducats, and the funds were to immediately be handed over to the Fugger representatives after opening the money chests and deducting the costs of doing business ... Pope Leo X's indulgence Bull 'Sacrosancti salvatoris et redemptoris nostri' made the connection between spiritual and financial interests unavoidable. The indulgence was to be marketed for eight years in the Church provinces of Mainz, Magdeburg, and Brandenburg. Objectively, the plenary indulgence was to extend to all sins, save a few exceptions reserved for the Pope. Almost all vows, with the exception of the cloister vows, could be acquired via an indulgence and through a subsequent conversion used as compensation. Almost all offenses, including infidelity and the wrongful acquisition of goods, could be granted dispensation. During the time of the St. Peter's Indulgence, all other indulgences were cancelled. For the benefit of holding indulgence sermons, one refrained from making other sermons. Impeding the indulgence was a punishable offense. However, it took until the beginning of 1517 for the distribution of indulgences to really get underway..."[342]

The papal bull of 1515, which led to detailed instructions such as the executing organ under the leadership of Johann Tetzel[343] and which authorized the archbishop, was not the only significant indulgence bull directly prior to Luther's 95 Theses of 1517. It was also not the only bull with associated financial transactions of this magnitude. Because the French king had debts of one million ducats with collaborators for borrowed soldiers[344], Leo X

---

[342] Martin Brecht. Martin Luther: Sein Weg zur Reformation 1483-1521. Op. cit., pp. 176-177. Brecht adds ibid. p. 177 about Albrecht: "It would be wrong to see in Albrecht von Brandenburg, who was Luther's first adversary in the dispute about indulgences, an unscrupulous church dignitary, even if he does not exactly meet Luther's expectation of a prelate. Albrecht was the son of a leading royal house, aesthetic, musically inclined, and easily influenced. He avoided antagonism and therefore was not the callous opponent of Luther. He was certainly not a great personage. It is repeatedly confirmed that he conscientiously fulfilled his churchly duties such as devotions and confirmation. On the other hand, he was not able to preach. Just as Frederick the Wise, he collected relics, albeit to a greater extent. Thirty-nine million indulgence days could be obtained with his collection in Halle. In many ways Albrecht was a Renaissance prince. He loved church music, acted as a patron of the arts, sought to collect something of a court of muses around himself, and was open for the sciences and humanism. However, this church dignitary understood nothing about theology. His spiritual responsibility and charisma certainly had its limits, and Germany's primates thus played only a subordinate role in the dispute that was beginning."

[343] Comp. the extensive instruction of the Archbishop of Mainz and Magdeburg in Walther Köhler. Dokumente zum Ablassstreit 1517. Tübingen: Mohr, 1934 2nd. ed. pp. 104-124 und in Martin Luther. Sämtliche Schriften. hrsg. von Johann Georg Walch. Bd. 15. Groß Oesingen: Verlag der Lutherischen Buchhandlung, 1987 (1880-1910 reprints 2nd ed.). pp. 301-333, among them also p. 313 with the instructions about how much one had to pay.

[344] Nikolaus Paulus. Geschichte des Ablasses ... Bd. 3. Op. cit., p. 187. Comp also Leo X's 1517 bull Comp. in Martin Luther. Sämtliche Schriften. hrsg. von Johann Georg Walch. Bd. 15. Groß Oesingen: Verlag der Lutherischen Buchhandlung, 1987 (1880-1910 reprint 2nd ed.). pp. 232-245.

The History of Indulgences and Their Theology 87

(1513-1521) issued the 'Salvator noster'[345] bull in 1516 in order to give the French king free disposition over all indulgence moneys.

All these bulls had a tragic antecedent history. In 1506 the laying of the foundation stone of St. Peter's Basilica had taken place. In 1507 two bulls were issued by Pope Julius II (1503-1513), which were to address the financing of the construction of St. Peter's Basilica with indulgences. These bulls were 'Salvator noster' and 'Etsi ex commisso,' whereby the former still required a pilgrimage and the latter allowed funds to simply be deposited Europe-wide. Indulgence revenues began to be collected in all the countries of the western church.[346] The concerns against this activity were so large among the cardinals and in Rome that the Pope who was to be newly chosen in 1513 had to obligate himself before the session (conclave) to rescind the St. Peter's Indulgence![347] This indeed happened, but in the same year the Pope renewed it. **This means that four years prior to the Reformation the cardinals categorically wanted to get rid of the serious deficiency that led to the Reformation, but the Pope prevented it!**

One has to definitely concede to Anton Kurz's statements in his work dated 1900, as well as to other Catholic researchers, that indulgences, both prior to and after Luther, were principally the same theologically and have so remained until today. It was never the case that forgiveness of sins was to be purchased with the money. Rather, it was always that remission of temporal punishment in purgatory alone was to be achieved for those who already had forgiveness.[348] However, Catholic researchers have also indicated that Tetzel himself did not always exactly follow the official line.

Furthermore, among Luther's opponents there were by all means established theologians who agreed with the critique of the business of indulgences, for example, Luther's significant adversary Cardinal Thomas Cajetan. This is seen in Cajetan's writings from 1517-1519. In these writings, Cajetan indicated he was also uncertain about any assured effect of indulgences, in particular for the deceased.[349] Indulgences also exceeded reason-

---

[345] There are several bulls from the time prior to the Reformation with this name.
[346] Nikolaus Paulus. Geschichte des Ablasses ... Bd. 3. Op. cit., p. 147.
[347] Ibid., p. 148.
[348] Anton Kurz. Die katholische Lehre vom Ablass vor und nach dem Auftreten Luthers. Paderborn: Ferdinand Schöningh, 1900, in toto and part. p. 22-35 regarding the years 1470-1517.
[349] Comp. Nikolaus Paulus. Geschichte des Ablasses ... Bd. 3. Op. cit., pp. 74-79 und Nikolaus Paulus. Johann Tetzel, der Ablaßprediger. Mainz: Franz Kirchheim, 1899. pp. 164-165.

able proportions from a Catholic point of view, of all places, in Wittenberg and Halle.[350]

Johann Tetzel was a Dominican and from 1504-1510 a preacher of indulgences for his order in various German states. In 1509 he was an Inquisitor in Poland and in 1517 General Sub-Commissioner of the church province of Magdeburg for the Archbishop of Mainz, Albrecht II. He was a theologian and had a detailed theological and polemic slugfest with Luther that reached considerable proportions – at times book length.[351]

The most significant Catholic researcher on indulgences, Nikolaus Paulus, began his publications on the topic with a biography of Johann Tetzel that is still worth reading. Paulus comes to the conclusion that Tetzel, on the one hand, is not to be seen in the one-sided negative light that has been the case for centuries from the viewpoint of Protestants. On the other hand, Tetzel is not simply inculpable, as the Catholic side often portrays the situation.[352] After all, even the Pope himself was unhappy with Tetzel's sermons.[353] In fact, from a Catholic point of view, Tetzel's teaching on indulgences was basically orthodox,[354] and Tetzel also showed himself in his literary slugfest with Luther[355] to be a full-fledged theologian.

With respect to his view of indulgences for the deceased, Tetzel comes close to the sentence that when in the coffer the coin rings, a soul from purgatory springs.[356] This famous sentence was in fact condemned in 1482 and in 1518 by the Paris Sorbonne, the most significant theological school

---

[350] According to Nikolaus Paulus. Geschichte des Ablasses ... Bd. 3. Op. cit., p. 246.
[351] The discussion between is well summarized in Martin Luther. Sämtliche Schriften. hrsg. von Johann Georg Walch. Bd. 15. Groß Oesingen: Verlag der Lutherischen Buchhandlung, 1986 (1880-1910 reprint 2nd ed.). pp. 71-311 (above all p. 82-101 for two of Tetzel's disputations 1518; p. 100-269 Luther's explanations; pp. 270-275 Luther's 1518 Sermon; pp. 274-295 Tetzel's Answer and p. 296-311 Luther's Answer 1518). Comp. Nikolaus Paulus. Johann Tetzel. Op. cit., pp. 45-69. In Walther Köhler. Dokumente zum Ablassstreit 1517. Tübingen: Mohr, 1934 2nd. ed. pp. 124-127 where there are excerpts of Tetzel's sermons dated 1517, pp. 127-143 Luther's 95 Theses and Antitheses of Wimpina-Tetzel dated 1518 and pp. 146-158 Luther's Sermon on Indulgences and Grace and Tetzel's Refutation dated 1518.
[352] Thus part. in summary manner pp. 165-166. However, it is the assertion at ibid., p. 168, that if Luther had only criticized the abuses, all well-meaning people would have agreed with him, albeit naively. Indeed Luther initially only wanted to criticize the abuses and still met the full force of the papacy and the financial power structures.
[353] Ibid., p. 164.
[354] Depicted in ibid., pp. 84-161.
[355] Thereto ibid., pp. 45-69.
[356] Thus ibid., pp. 166; 138-142.

of that time, but it is no wonder that it came into existence.[357] Luther had, by the way, not attached the financial abuse of indulgences to Tetzel. Rather, and in my opinion completely correctly, he attached it to the big business that the Pope achieved with the sale of dioceses. After all, Tetzel's assignment as General Sub-Commissioner of the Archbishop preceded the papal bull of 1510, which principally made all of that possible.[358]

> According to Luther's own statements, before Tetzel's death in August 1519, Luther let Tetzel know that he was aware that Tetzel was not the actual responsible person but that it was Albrecht from Mainz and the Pope. Luther also expressed words of God's consolation to Tetzel.[359]

4.1.3 The Doctrinal Proclamation of Indulgences of 1518

Pope Leo X (1513-1521) answered Luther's accusation that indulgences had never been doctrinally proclaimed by responding to Cardinal Cajetan's (Thomas de Vio, 1469-1534) wish and spontaneously conveying to Cajetan the 'Cum postquam' bull in 1518. The bull contained a doctrinal proclamation of indulgences, which was presented to a surprised Luther![360] The text of the bull can largely be traced back to Cajetan. "In the meantime, the decree on indulgences directed toward Cajetan and prepared through him appeared on November 9, 1518. It could only be conceived as a doctrinal pronouncement. The bull differentiated sharply between the remission of the guilt of sin in the sacrament of penance and the remission of temporal punishment via indulgences. Only 'members of Christ's body' could par-

---

[357] Ibid., p. 162.
[358] Ibid., pp. 24-44.
[359] Text: Martin Luther. Gesammelte Werke. ed. by Kurt Aland. Digitale Bibliothek Bd. 63. Berlin: Directmedia, 2002 (corresponds to Martin Luther: Luther deutsch. Die Werke Martin Luthers in neuer Auswahl für die Gegenwart. 10 Bde. Göttingen: Vandenhoeck und Ruprecht, 1991). p. 1080 (in the book version vol. 2. p. 18); comp. Martin Brecht. Martin Luther: Sein Weg zur Reformation 1483-1521. Op. cit., p. 180.
[360] Latin and German text: Heinrich Denzinger, Peter Hünermann (ed.). Enchiridion symbolorum ... Op. cit., pp. 486-487, margin no. 1447-1449; Latin text: Walther Köhler. Dokumente zum Ablassstreit 1517. Tübingen: Mohr, 1934 2nd ed. pp. 158-160; Text in Englisch: Paul F. Palmer. Sacraments and Forgiveness. Op. Cit., pp. 360-361. Comp. also in Heinrich Denzinger, Peter Hünermann (ed.). Enchiridion symbolorum ... Op. Cit., p. 487-492, margin no. 1451-1492 the 'Exsurge Domine' bull with a list of Martin Luther's errors, part. no. 17-22 indulgences p. 490, margin no. 1467-1472, mortal sins p. 1520, margin no. 35-36; purgatory p. 1520, margin no. 37-40.

take in indulgences, which come out of the overflowing merits of Christ and the saints (Thesaurus meritorum Jesu Christi et sanctorum). They are conferred (conferre) upon the living and are allocated (per modum suffragii . . . transferre) to poor souls by intercession. The recipient of indulgences is freed not only from canonically imposed temporal punishment for sin but also from temporal punishment attributed to divine justice. This corresponds to the granted and acquired indulgence. At this point, the decree did not follow Cajetan's earlier indulgence tract from 1517, according to which indulgences extended to canonically imposed penance, but rather to the later tract by the same author, dated February 27, 1518. According to the latter tract, indulgences also had validity before the judgment seat of God"[361]

Martin Brecht writes similarly: "At about the same time, Cajetan must have also requested a dogmatic fixing of indulgences via a papal decree in Rome (which there had not been up until that time) and done so by supplying a draft as an addendum. This occurred on November 9, and with it, Luther's excuses that the teaching on indulgences was still a matter of discussion were made baseless. The indulgence decree put the established notion of indulgences on record: The Pope had power of authority regarding indulgences because of the Church keys, and this extended to the deceased in purgatory. The Pope distributed from the treasury of the Church. This had to be held to and preached, and if it were not, there was the threat of being banned. Cajetan was to inform the bishops, and this occurred on December 13 in Linz. Little effort was made with regard to an exegetical justification for indulgences. Luther's enquiries were simply cut off by papal authority, and the indulgence question was decided dogmatically. The dictum of the Church, to which Luther originally wanted to submit, had been supplied."[362]

Catholic researchers on the topic of indulgences have themselves repeatedly confirmed that Luther correctly held that there was no doctrinal confirmation of indulgences. For instance, what Adolf Gottlob wrote in 1906 has, to my knowledge, never been questioned: "A clear conception of what an indulgence actually was and what it meant and achieved for the salvation of a Christian was never provided in this manner. One could say that Innocence III to some degree avoided the question. His successors made continual use of his formula in their crusade bulls. Innocence had even avoided taking up the crusade decrees within the canon of the Lateran

---

[361] Hubert Jedin. Geschichte des Konzils von Trient. Bd. 3. Op. Cit., p. 77-78.
[362] Martin Brecht. Martin Luther: Sein Weg zur Reformation 1483-1521. Op. cit., p. 251.

Council. It stands on its own. The third canon, which was against heretics, only temporarily took things from that time into account and is therefore striking. Can later occasional statements on indulgences, also if they are made by popes, be taken as binding within the Church? In my view, there exists neither a decree by synod nor a papal doctrinal decision with the primary intention of offering a definition of indulgences. There are just as few authoritative statements available which allow the concept of indulgences to be indirectly recognized. We therefore come to the odd result that the first reason for the Reformation was really nothing de jure and that the use of indulgences, as they were practiced at the time of Luther and are still practiced today, was and is a Church custom. One pope thought and wrote one way about indulgences and another pope another way. According to basic Catholic principles, there is not a secure notion of indulgences and therefore no obligatory teaching on indulgences."[363]

4.1.4 John Calvin

John Calvin wrote as clearly as Luther: "All of these indulgences . . . are actually a desecration of the blood of Christ. Then how could one more disgracefully desecrate Christ's blood than by the assertion that it is not sufficient for the forgiveness of sins, for reconciliation and for satisfaction . . . ?"[364] John Calvin dedicates an entire chapter to indulgences in his major work after he refutes the difference between punishment and guilt.[365] His critique of indulgences is even more basic than that of Luther[366] and, by the way, has practically nothing to do with their abuse or their conjunction with financial matters. Calvin's treatment is of a purely theological nature.

This comes out most clearly in Calvin's major work *Institutes of the Christian Religion* (*Institutio*). After he presents the biblical teaching of faith and new birth in detail in Book III, he gives an extensive presentation of the Catholic view of penance, confession, and human merit.[367] In the end, he specifically describes indulgences, the treasury of merit, and purga-

---

[363] Adolf Gottlob. Kreuzablass und Almosenablass. Op. cit., p. 139.
[364] John Calvin. Unterricht in der christlichen Religion: Institutio Religionis Christianae. Neukirchener Verlag: Neukirchen, 1988 5th ed. pp. 432-433.
[365] Ibid., p. 421-441, book 3., chapter 5, sections 1-10 and Book 3, chapter 4, sections 29-39.
[366] So also Gustav Adolf Benrath. "Ablaß". Op. cit., p. 355.
[367] John Calvin. Unterricht in der christlichen Religion. Op. cit., p. 337-432, Book III, chapters 1-4.

tory in detail.[368] With quotes from letters and writings of Pope Leo I (440-461) and Augustine, Calvin documents that the early church did not know of any possibility whereby the good work of a believer or a martyr could be used for the benefit of another person.[369] The question of the financial abuse of indulgences does not arise at all. Rather, basic objections and contradictions within these teachings are addressed using the Scriptures and the experience of the early church.

4.1.5 Protestants Favoring Indulgences? The Example of C. S. Lewis

James Akin refutes the view that the rejection of indulgences and purgatory is characteristic of Protestantism.[370] The only exception that Akin is able to bring, however, is C.S. Lewis. In his *Letters to Malcom*[371] which is often reprinted by Catholic publishers, Lewis presupposes the existence of purgatory (not, however, the existence of indulgences).[372] This exception tends rather to prove the rule, especially since Lewis is in other issues also no classical representative of Protestantism. Rather, Lewis borrows from all confessions and, beyond that, sometimes from other religions. Besides that, Lewis thought that Luther had "good reasons" to "doubt the 'Roman teaching of purgatory' in its form at that time"[373] and massively turned his attention against Dante's 'Purgatorio.' Without a basis in either the Bible or in tradition, Lewis held it to be plainly reasonable to pray for the deceased and believed that the deceased could somehow grow spiritually, which probably includes suffering but surely has no "refinement purpose." In this Lewis rejected the Catholic view of purgatory and put a purgatory of his own making into its place.

---

[368] Ibid., pp. 433-441, book 3, chapter 5, sections 1-10.
[369] Ibid., p. 433, book 3, chapter 5, section 3.
[370] James Akin. "How to Explain Purgatory to Protestants" (13 p.). www.cin.org/users/james/files/how2purg.htm (January 3, 2004), p. 9-10; also www.ewtn.com/library/answers/how2purg.htm, p. 2 (January 3, 2004).
[371] Clive S. Lewis. Briefe an einen Freund, hauptsächlich über das Beten. Einsiedeln: Benziger, 1966; new edition: Du fragst mich, wie ich bete : Briefe an Malcolm. Beten heute 7. Einsiedeln: Johannes-Verlag, 1976; 1978; 1985; Original: Clive S. Lewis. Letters to Malcom: Chiefly on Prayer. London: Bles, 1964; new edition: Prayer : Letters to Malcolm Glasgow : Collins, 1983.
[372] Letter 21, here quoted according to C. S. Lewis. Du fragst mich, wie ich bete : Briefe an Malcolm. Beten heute 7. Einsiedeln: Johannes-Verlag, 1978. p. 115-120, therein pp. 1161-119.
[373] Ibid., p. 117.

4.2 The Council of Trent

What, precisely, was the theological reaction of the Roman Catholic Church to Luther's and the Reformed churches' critiques of indulgences? After the Pope had prevented a council for such a long time – in spite of the repeated requests by the emperor, the Parliament (Reichstag), princes, and church leaders – he finally allowed the Council of Trent (1545-1563) to take place with the sole participation of Roman Catholic bishops and far from the center of the Holy German Empire in Italy in a city under the influence of the Pope. This occurred only after the confessional split in Europe was final and irreversible. The purpose of the Council of Trent was to think about reforms and to compose a defense of the teachings the Protestants had placed in question. "During the session of the Council of Trent in Bologna, on June 19, 1547, the theologians of the Council were presented with seven questions regarding indulgences on the basis of Leo X's (1513-1521) decree. Agreement existed among the theologians only insofar as indulgences were seen as a remission of temporal punishment out of the treasury of the merits of Christ and the saints. Most of the other teachings on indulgences were in dispute and were (along with purgatory) discussed vehemently from June 19 until July 15. This was, above all, the case with the thesis that the jurisdiction of the Pope extended to purgatory (while the contrary thesis, that indulgences for the deceased were effective only per modum suffragii, was called a 'communis fere omnium theologorum sententia'[374]) and with the wording that indulgence absolved 'a culpa et a poena.' The age of indulgences was also a reason for controversy. A text relating to indulgences was not composed in Bologna. By the fall of 1563, the question of indulgences had not been taken any further. On November 15 a working group consisting of five council fathers and five theologians was brought together to develop a decree relating to indulgences. The reading of a draft of the text began on December 2, but it was interrupted because the majority of those present held the actions they were undertaking to be precipitous. On December 4, in Session XXV, the indulgence decree and four other decrees were read and approved without the debate of theologians and council fathers in a fashion resembling the uttermost summary judgment."[375]

That is the answer of the Catholic Church to the abuse of indulgences which the Reformation had caused! And it remained the same in

---

[374] This means the view that the Pope renders intercession for the deceased was considered a disputed notion.
[375] Herbert Vorgrimler. Buße und Krankensalbung. Op. cit., p. 210.

the decades that followed. Basically, indulgences were retained by mere repetition of earlier declarations, while in its details the indulgence was in complete dispute.

The history of the indulgence decree of the Council of Trent as an answer to Luther's and other reformers' critiques is well investigated.[376]

Over the years the Council, as we have seen, had held a theological session regarding the topic of the place of purification and indulgences in Bologna.[377] However, neither the theologians nor the council fathers could come to an agreement. Many of them would have preferred to have remained completely silent on this and other similar subject matters. Thus, at the last minute, a quick text was adopted which contained no theological justification. Rather, it anathematized its opponents. "The controversial teachings upon which the division was ignited, that is, the teaching on indulgences and the veneration of saints, their relics, and pictures, were treated in the end in summary fashion without the otherwise customary debate among theologians and council fathers."[378]

The Council had made no preparations for taking a stand on indulgences whatsoever. "The split in belief began with the dispute over indulgences. Actually it was remarkable that the Council had up until that time not occupied itself with the topic of indulgences . . ."[379] The political pressure from the sides of the emperor and the French king to adopt a decree relating to indulgences was enormous, since this topic had incited a split in the faith. If one remained silent on the issue, there was also the issue of silent acquiescence that the Protestants were correct.[380] Additionally, there was politically no desire to see a condemnation of Protestants. Rather, there was a desire to have some concession toward them. By the way, the intention was for the Council to end as soon as possible. At the same time, all theologians and the council fathers were somehow in favor of indul-

---

[376] Comp. above all Hubert Jedin. Geschichte des Konzils von Trient. Bd. 1: Der Kampf um das Konzil. Freiburg: Herder. 1949, see index under "Ablässe"; Hubert Jedin. Geschichte des Konzils von Trient. Bd. 2: Die erste Trienter Tagungsperiode 1545/47. Freiburg: Herder. 1957, see index under "Ablaß"; Hubert Jedin. Geschichte des Konzils von Trient. Bd. 3: Bologneser Tagung (1547/48) – Zweite Tagungsperiode 1551-/52. Freiburg: Herder. 1970, see index under "Ablaß"; Hubert Jedin. Geschichte des Konzils von Trient. Bd. 4: Dritte Tagungsperiode und Abschluß. Zweiter Halbband. Freiburg: Herder. 1975, see index under "Ablaß".
[377] Hubert Jedin. Geschichte des Konzils von Trient. Bd. 4. Op. cit., p. 180.
[378] Ibid., p. 244.
[379] Hubert Jedin. Geschichte des Konzils von Trient. Bd. 3. Op. cit., p. 76.
[380] Hubert Jedin. Geschichte des Konzils von Trient. Bd. 4. Op. cit., pp. 165-166.

gences, purgatory, and the treasury of merit, but there was an inability to agree upon the definitions and details.[381]

We have already seen that the Pope responded to Luther's allegation that indulgences had never been proclaimed as doctrine by spontaneously proclaiming a papal bull relating to indulgence doctrine in 1518. "Leo X's indulgence decree was the doctrinal basis of the seven questions, which on June 19 were placed to the Council theologians, together with four questions (dubia) regarding purgatory 'in order to occupy' them:

1) Is an indulgence a remission from guilt or punishment?
2) If it is a remission of punishment, is it a remission of eternal or temporal punishment?
3) If it is a remission of temporal punishment, does it extend only to canonical punishment, or does it also extend to punishment imposed according to the righteousness of God?

Question 4 had to do with the treasury of merit: Are the merits of the saints also included? In question 5, a severely contentious problem arose that had to do with the debate regarding justification: If a sinner, on the basis of contrition and confession, is absolved and needs no new application of the righteousness of Christ, how can an indulgence drawing upon the treasury of merit be applied to him? Question 6 is to be understood within the context of the fiscal nature of the late Middle Ages: Does the validity of indulgences depend on a sufficient cause? The seventh and last question was whether and how indulgences were applied to the deceased. What surfaced within these seven questions were the remaining unsolved problems surrounding the teaching on indulgences after Leo X's indulgence decree."[382]

There was also no agreement on the question of purgatory. Thesis 13 of Luther's 95 Theses, according to which death does not cancel imposed punishment for sins, was not taken up in the bull of 1518 and therefore was not denounced. "In turn, as was the case with indulgences, there was agreement among the theologians about foundational truth, that there is a third state between heaven and hell. But in the first answer to the first question, based on available documents, there were significant differences of opinion. The overwhelming majority of theologians believed that they found hints regarding an intermediate state in scriptural passages such as Matthew 12:32; I Corinthians 3:13; I Corinthians 15:1; and John 5:16 among others, and a basis for prayers of intercession for the poor souls in II Maccabees. A minority doubted, more or less, the conclusiveness of the

---

[381] Ibid., p. 180.
[382] Hubert Jedin. Geschichte des Konzils von Trient. Bd. 3. Op. cit., p. 78.

scriptural proofs and moved the tradition of the fathers and the teaching pronouncements into the foreground. The discussion became so embittered that the Augustinian, Gregorius Perfectus, reminded the session that they had come together to find the truth and not to become hostile to each other. A sense of uncertainty surrounding the conclusiveness of the scriptural proofs was also expressed by those theologians who held the teachings as feasible and held to the existence of purgatory as a theological conclusion. Servit Hieronymus from Bologna asked whether eternal life, for the righteous who always lived rightly, will be the same as that for a sinner who converts only at the moment of death. He answered that no one would dare to maintain that such a decree would be reconcilable with the justice of God . . ."[383]

4.3 From the Council of Trent until the Second Vatican Council

"The teachings on indulgences were so exhaustively shaped by the great Scholastics of the thirteenth century that they experienced no significant additions during the time thereafter."[384] From the standpoint of indulgence theology in the middle of the thirteenth century, there was a direct path to the events before and after the Reformation. No significant developments occurred during this time. A true theological reaction to the critique of indulgences in the Reformation did not take place in the sixteenth and seventeenth centuries. If one ignores the time period of 1922-1967, during which theologians tried in vain to renew and alter indulgence theology, one could say there was actually no reaction even up until today. Indulgence theology was itself so disputed among Catholic theologians in its detail that it remained for that reason in its conventional form.

Until the Second Vatican Council, indulgence theology and the practice of indulgences remained practically unchanged. In the twentieth century the theological discussion regarding indulgences began, and that only among theologians. It occurred neither in the Vatican nor among church members. "The theology after Trent and church practice (at times in the seventeenth and nineteenth centuries especially extensive, but receding in

---

[383] Ibid., pp. 84-85.
[384] Nikolaus Paulus. Geschichte des Ablasses ... Bd. 3. Op. cit., p. 1.

the middle of the twentieth century) were not accompanied by any new notable insights."[385]

The expansion among 'Volks Catholicism' did not diminish, since the use of indulgences was the major stimulus for pilgrimages to Rome. The father of pietism, Philipp Jacob Spener, in his book against indulgences in 1750, wrote that he could not see that the business of indulgences had been barred. It was rather the case that indulgences were a 'smokescreen.' "The true cause is actually to make the city of Rome and the papal see richer and more sizable,"[386] also with pilgrimages to the main papal churches in Rome. Precisely this stood in the middle of the resuscitation of indulgences in the jubilee year 2000.

Did not the indulgence fall into oblivion in the nineteenth and in the first half of the twentieth centuries? History proves otherwise. Gustav Adolf Benrath traced the development from the middle of the nineteenth century to the middle of the twentieth century: "Pious IX cherished it particularly highly; he granted numerous new complete indulgences and issued not less than eight Jubilee Indulgences (1846, 1850, 1854, 1857, 1864, 1869, 1871, 1875). He confirmed the privilege of the Franciscan order to obtain innumerable complete and partial indulgences from various churches, basilicas, and all sanctuaries around the world after confession, communion, and praying Psalm 19 and several other prayers (November 22, 1852). While the problems of the theory of indulgences were for the time being not discussed (until there was a decision in favor of them because of Leo XIII's preference for Thomism in the sense of New Scholasticism), the recovery and modification of the practice of indulgences is seen not only in numerous writings for edification and jubilee sermons, but, in particular, in systematic handbooks."[387] "Pious X granted an indulgence of seven years and 280 years for calling the names of 'Jesus, Maria, Joseph,' and even a plenary indulgence for also calling the names daily after confession and communion (I, Nr. 280). Exclaiming 'My Jesus, mercy' received from Pious X 300 instead of 100 days of indulgence, and the prayer calling 'Queen of the holiest rosary, petition for us' received 100 days of indulgence from Benedict XV toties-quoties. It is worth mentioning that in addition to the Lord and Mary festival days that appeared in

---

[385] Herbert Vorgrimler. Buße und Krankensalbung. Op. cit., p. 212. Regarding indulgences in non-Trentine Catholicism comp. Gustav Adolf Benrath. „Ablaß". Op. cit., pp. 355-360.
[386] Philipp Jacob Spener. Der Römischen Kirchen Ablass und Jubel-Jahr. Frankfurt, 1750. p. 67.
[387] Gustav Adolf Benrath. "Ablaß". Op. cit., p. 358.

connection with plenary indulgences in the nineteenth century (Costly Blood of Jesus in 1849; Heart of Jesus Festival in 1856; Festival of the seven pains of Mary in 1814; the Immaculate Conception in 1854), additional ones appeared in the twentieth century: Festival of the Appearance of the Immaculate Virgin Mary at Lourdes (1907); the Festival of the Motherhood of Mary (1931); the Festival of the Immaculate Heart of Mary (1944); the Ascension of Mary (1950); and Queen Mary (1954)."[388] It is out of the question to think that the popes had lost their interest in indulgences and that Pope John Paul II first introduced a revitalization of the practice.

---

[388] Ibid., p. 360.

5 The Reform of the Theology of Indulgences Prior to the Second Vatican Council and Its Failure during the Council and into the Present

5.1 Signs of a Mitigation of Indulgence Theology Prior to 1967

While the practice of indulgences expanded well into the twentieth century, an intra-Catholic discussion began with regard to the theology of indulgences. This is evidenced, above all, by the monumental two-volume work by Nikolaus Paulus in 1922 and 1923[389] and by the works of Bernhard Poschmann in 1948.[390] It is to be noted that Poschmann, who died in 1955, did not only work as a historian but himself was someone who wanted to renew the theology of indulgences. Paulus' efforts were above all to meticulously trace the massive amounts of critique relating to indulgences over the centuries, from the inception of indulgences up to the Reformation as well as into the time of the intra-Catholic discussion.[391] Poschmann, on the other hand, saw indulgences rather critically as an earthly and pastoral action and not as an action with forensic consequences.[392]

---

[389] Nikolaus Paulus. Geschichte des Ablasses im Mittelalter vom Ursprunge bis zur Mitte des 14. Jahrhunderts. Bd. 1. Ferdinand Schöningh: Paderborn, 1922; Nikolaus Paulus. Geschichte des Ablasses im Mittelalter vom Ursprunge bis zur Mitte des 14. Jahrhunderts. Bd. 2. Ferdinand Schöningh: Paderborn, 1923; ders. Geschichte des Ablasses am Ausgang des Mittelalters. ebd. 1923; all three volumes together: Geschichte des Ablasses im Mittelalter. Eingeleitet von Thomas Lentes. Darmstadt: Wissenschaftliche Buchgesellschaft, 2000 2nd ed.; comp. also Nikolaus Paulus. Der Ablaß im Mittelalter als Kulturfaktor. Görres-Gesellschaft ... Erste Vereinsschrift 1920. Köln, J. P. Bachem. 1920.
[390] Bernhard Poschmann. Der Ablass im Licht der Bußgeschichte. Peter Hanstein: Bonn, 1948.
[391] Also Gustav Adolf Benrath. "Ablaß". Op. cit., p. 351.
[392] Also ibid., p. 360. Comp. Bernhard Poschmann. Der Ablass im Licht der Bußgeschichte. Op. cit., pp. 108, 119, 121; Bernhard Poschmann. Buße und letzte Ölung. Op. cit., p. 123. Poschmann dedicated his life's work to the history of penance from the time of the ancient church up to the Reformation, comp. Bernhard Poschmann. Die abendländische Kirchenbuße im Ausgang des christlichen Altertums. Münchener Studien zur historischen Theologie 7. München: Kösel & Pustet,

"A reform of the theology of indulgences came as a consequence of the historical research surrounding penance in the old church. On the basis of Nikolaus Paulus' research, Bernhard Poschmann tried to get beyond the 'newer,' forensic idea of indulgences and to press indulgence teaching ahead in a positive manner."[393] Directly subsequent to Poschmann came Karl Rahner.[394] Rahner wanted a reform of the theology of indulgences. Initially (beginning in 1949) to a slight degree and comprehensively since 1955, Rahner exercised extensive influence up to and including the Second Vatican Council and beyond. However, in spite of the fact that several of Rahner's thoughts were accepted, he was still repudiated by the Pope.

Rahner was interested in the idea that the treasury of merit was not an 'in rem' supply but rather something that derives from a dynamic and personal view.[395] Rahner writes: "The 'treasury of merit' is God's own will for salvation – it is in the end God himself – insofar as God in Christ (as the head) is irrevocably victorious in the world, and who is always desired by God to be 'the firstborn among many brothers,' which is to say with his 'body,' which is the Church. This correct conception of the 'treasury of merit' does not mean that there is something paid quantitatively and in installments out of a store of public wealth which otherwise an individual would have had to pay out of his own wealth. Since this does not occur, the question of whether the treasury of merits can ever be exhausted, because so much has been taken from it and paid, cannot arise in the first place and

---

1928; Bernhard Poschmann. Die abendländische Kirchenbuße im frühen Mittelalter. Breslauer Studien zur historischen Theologie 16. Breslau: Müller, 1930; Bernhard Poschmann. Paenitentia secunda: die kirchliche Buße im ältesten Christentum bis Cyprian und Origenes: Eine dogmengeschichtliche Untersuchung. Theophaneia 1. Bonn: Peter Hanstein, 1940. In the posthumously published lecture: Bernhard Poschmann. Die Lehre von der Kirche: Geschichtlich beleuchtet und dogmatisch dargelegt. ed. by Gerhard Fittkau. Quaestiones non disputate 4. Siegburg: Verlag Franz Schmitt, 2000 begründet Poschmann substantiates in § 9 S. 99-123 the primacy of the Pope, in § 22 S. 240-254 "Die Unfehlbarkeit des kirchlichen Lehramtes", in § 11 S. 139-147 the necessity of the Church for salvation.

[393] Herbert Vorgrimler. Buße und Krankensalbung. Op. cit., p. 212. Comp. Gustav Adolf Benrath. "Ablaß". Op. cit., pp. 361-362.

[394] The primary text dated 1955 can be found in a slightly edited form in Karl Rahner "Kleiner theologischer Traktat über den Ablaß". pp. 472-487 in ders. Schriften zur Theologie. Bd. VIII. Einsiedeln: Benzinger Verlag, 1967; comp. also Karl Rahner "Zur heutigen kirchlichen Ablaßlehre". p. 472-487 in the same Schriften zur Theologie. Bd. VIII. Einsiedeln: Benzinger Verlag, 1967 und Karl Rahner. "Ablaß". p. 46-53 in: Josef Höfer, Karl Rahner (ed.). Lexikon für Theologie und Kirche. Bd. 1. Herder: Freiburg: 1986 (1957 reprint), his own theology therein pp. 51-52.

[395] Comp. also Otto Semmelroth. "Zur Theologie des Ablasses". Op. cit., pp. 58-61.

does not need to be solved by any subtle explanations. It is also clear 'that for that reason God is not' forced to grant such a request for indulgences from temporal punishment for sin, because he can no longer require what he has already (namely, out of the treasury of merit) received. God looks at his own work of grace. Within God's free and unfathomable judgment, and in the harmony he desires, a reason is found for leading one person in one manner and another person in another manner to their respective consummation."[396]

Vorgrimler summarizes Rahner's point of view as follows: "In basic agreement with Poschmann since 1949, Karl Rahner has tried above all to provide an external conception that overcomes a vindictive understanding of the 'punishment of sins.' This punishment is understood by Rahner to be a processing of guilt that is a sorrow producing reaction against man's guilt from the sides of his own nature and from the environment. It derives from the internal nature of sin itself and is not imposed from without. This affliction and processing of residual guilt is not the product of egotism. Rather, it is a necessary exercise by which the Church assists the sinner with its prayers. In this connection the 'treasury of merit' is to be thought of as the complete reality of Jesus Christ's salvation and his life, upon which the Church calls in its prayers. Alternatively, it is nothing other than the will of God for salvation in Jesus Christ. In order to differentiate from every private prayer in the Church, Rahner believes that the prayer of indulgence is an authoritative and official prayer of the Church and, going beyond Poschmann, he sees it as 'opus operatum.' This means that as a result of the promise of Jesus Christ, the answering of the prayer is unfailingly certain and in this sense effectuates the indulgence. In this view an indulgence does not replace penance. Rather, it is an aid to it and achieves its goal only to the degree that a person, under the impulse of the grace of God, truly processes the consequences of his guilt."[397]

In 1961 Paul Anciaux tried to make indulgences more understandable.[398] He seeks to do this by classifying the indulgence historically and systematically with the sacrament of penance.[399] He also wants to get away from the forensic in rem grounds and instead make the community and solidarity of the

---

[396] Karl Rahner "Kleiner theologischer Traktat über den Ablaß". pp. 472-487 in ders. Schriften zur Theologie. Bd. VIII. Einsiedeln: Benzinger Verlag, 1967. p. 482-483 (Original 1955).

[397] Herbert Vorgrimler. Buße und Krankensalbung. Op. cit., p. 213.

[398] Paul Anciaux. Das Sakrament der Buße. Mainz: Matthias-Grünewald-Verlag, 1961. pp. 177-192.

[399] Part. ibid., p. 149 und p. 184.

saints the basis. "It is not enough to emphasize the powers of the Church in connection with the forgiveness of sins. One has to first and foremost highlight the deep meaning of Christian community, by which the believer and the baptized participate in the mystery of Christ in the community of the saints."[400] "The more 'holy' a member of the Church is, the more deeply bound to God, the more profound and fervent his charity or love, the more he will be able to help his brothers and assist them. His prayer and penance, his suffering and his sacrifice will be all the more fruitful for the entire community. Confessors and martyrs were viewed correctly as privileged members of the Church. Were they not the witnesses of Christ par excellence, who, in order to follow him, out of love devoted their lives to him? This is the way one can understand how a penitent can call upon the mediation of these 'saints' in order to be helped in his individual penance by this special love. This is how it came to pass that the advocacy and mediation of these confessors were seen as potent means to diminish imposed penance. Where a penitent could call upon the help of a confessor, he was able to ask for a reduction in the time of penance which had been imposed upon him for reconciliation with the Church and with God."[401]

5.2 The Second Vatican Council

Indulgences are not mentioned once in the documents adopted in the Second Vatican Council. Some people saw in this a positive development and assumed that indulgences no longer played a central role in the Catholic Church. This is not a reflection of the facts, however, and that became evident by 1967 at the latest.

Initially, let us look at the topic of indulgences at the Council itself. "A reform of the character of indulgences was discussed at the Second Vatican Council during the time November 9-13, 1965. Two positions stood in opposition to each other. The one rested upon a 'positio,' which since 1963 had been worked out on behalf of the Apostolic Penitentiary and which was not discussed in detail at the Council. The other group critically viewed the 'positio' to be a way of thinking that had been overcome. The deliberations were broken off because of a lack of time."[402]

Even when Johannes Hüttenbügel also writes that "... the deliberations were broken off due to a lack of time,"[403] such a presentation has to be re-

---

[400] Ibid., p. 186.
[401] Ibid., p. 178.
[402] Herbert Vorgrimler. Buße und Krankensalbung. Op. cit., p. 214.
[403] Johannes Hüttenbügel. Der Ablaß. Zeitfragen 49. Köln: Presseamt des Erzbistums Köln, 1999. p. 9.

futed. The reason that the Second Vatican Council ended without mention of indulgences in any of the texts[404] was that there were two reluctant parties. One took the papal line, which wanted to reform the traditional indulgence teaching but not touch it insofar as its continued existence was concerned. The other wanted a completely new formulation in the spirit of Karl Rahner, which would have not led to an abolishment of indulgences but rather to a mitigation of the teaching and to an ecumenical assimilation. Gustav Adolf Benrath reports on the details: "A number of younger Catholic theologians followed Rahner's thinking. They called for a simplification of the practice of indulgences and for working out theologically, pastoral-theologically, and liturgically a connection between indulgences and the sacrament of penance, and with the active overcoming of the consequences of sin and intercession by the Church. In contrast, representatives of the older generation of Catholic theologians, such as, for example, Johann Brinktrine, held that 'the new teaching on indulgences' abandoned that which was specific to indulgences. They emphasized that what was involved was the jurisdiction of the Church, not only its intercession, that it had to do with the Church's having been given authority, not only mediation, and that it had to do with the treasury of merit that had been assigned to and therefore specific was to the Church, not only a treasury of the saints. Representatives of both positions were pitted against each other during the fourth session of the Second Vatican Council. A 'positio' was submitted that related to the reform of indulgences that had been developed on behalf of the Apostolic Penitentiary since 1963, worked out by Roman theologians and approved by Cardinal Charles Journet of Fribourg (156th-160th General Congregation, November 9-13, 1965). It was never raised for discussion at the Council. While the Polish and many Romanic bishop conferences made favorable statements about the submission, a larger number of North American bishops held the 'positio' to be evidence of a way of thinking that had been resolved by the Council."[405]

There were also voices that wanted to see indulgences abolished completely. This applies in particular to the representatives of the Oriental Catholic Church, for it saw the teaching on indulgences as always having been a matter of the Western Church. "The Melkite Cardinal patriarch Maximos IV. Saigh pointed out that there was an absence of a teaching on indulgences in the first millennium of Christian Church history. An ade-

---

[404] Accordingly in Peter Christoph Düren. Der Ablass in Lehre und Praxis: Die vollkommenen Ablässe der katholischen Kirche. Buttenwiesen: Stella Maris Verlag, 2000². p. 20.

[405] Gustav Adolf Benrath. "Ablaß". Op. cit., pp. 361-362.

quate theological justification was missing, and he criticized the fact that the 'positio' did not do away with a numerical calculation but only simplified it."[406]

New weighty voices were also heard for a new way of thinking that the Pope could simply not ignore. While there was no position taken at the Council, a position was taken after the Council by the Pope alone. Benrath writes: "Cardinal Alfrink (Utrecht) also criticized the continued manner of quantitatively measuring punishment and called for a basic theological examination of the document. Cardinals Franz König (Vienna) and Julius Döpfner (Munich) most extensively pointed out the theological one-sidedness of the 'positio.' They were dictated to some degree by Poschmann's and Rahner's thoughts and supported a revision that would at least provide room for indulgences to be understood as an action of intercession by the Church. Furthermore, it was in their thinking not an in rem mathematical issue but rather a personalistic concept of the punishment for sin and a spiritual interpretation of the treasury of the Church. 'The 'treasury of the Church' is God himself insofar as he . . . receives and responds to the intercession of the Church and the efforts of people with a view to the merits of Christ'."[407]

In their *Journal of the Council* (*Tagebuch des Konzils*), Luitpold A. Dorn and Wolfgang Seibel describe in detail the discussions regarding indulgences and comment on why there was no decree on indulgences.[408] "The draft regarding an indulgence reform, which carried the title 'positio,' goes back to a papal instruction dated July 24, 1963. It was worked out by a commission made up of members and consultors of the Apostolic Penitentiary as well as several Roman theologians. Pope Paul VI had the finished text submitted to the Swiss Cardinal Charles Journet for review. Journet declared he was only able to say that he was 'glad with the profound work' of the participating theologians. Paul VI, however, found it important in this 'difficult and delicate question,' as it was described in a letter from the Cardinal Secretary of State Cicognani, dated June 28, 1965, 'to move ahead with great discretion and not before informing the Episcopacy and asking for their opinion.' It was repeatedly emphasized that one was not dealing here with a Council document but rather with a papal decree, on which only an opinion from the side of the bishops was to be so-

---

[406] Ibid., p. 362.
[407] Ibid., p. 362.
[408] Luitpold A. Dorn, Wolfgang Seibel. Tagebuch des Konzils: Die Arbeit der vierten Session. Nürnberg/Eichstätt: Johann Michael Sailer Verlag, 1966. pp. 233-234, 243-244, 248-253 (and often).

licited. The present draft, which Cardinal Fernando Cento submitted as Head of the Apostolic Penitentiary and which was commented on by the Regent Penitentiary, Msgr. Giovanni Sessolo, included five chapters and a total of 21 subparagraphs. Although the contents had to do with a review of practical norms and not with the theology of indulgences, for which, according to Cardinal Cento's explanation, the Penitentiary was not responsible, the actual text is preceded by an initial section on the theological foundation of indulgences and a brief overview of their history."[409]

According to the draft, the time measure of partial indulgences was to be abolished. In its place there was to be an arrangement that the indulgence should double the dispensation of a good work. The plenary indulgence was to be effected only one time per day. Prior to or after the work of indulgent penance, confession and communion would have been essential; otherwise, only a partial indulgence could be obtained. All in all, "in indulgences the quantitative element is to retire to a position behind the qualitative."[410]

The voices from the Oriental Catholic Churches were devastating for the 'positio.' "The Melkite Cardinal Patriarch Maximos IV Saigh spoke first in the name of his synods. He began by saying that it was undoubtedly the case that the Church could support the prayers and the good works of believers by its intercession. It is as much the case that the Church could acquire remission of temporal punishment of sin from God by its intercession. However, there was no way that one could devise a type of mathematical equation between the works of indulgence and their effects with respect to remission of the punishment for sin. Everything that looks like such an equation would in any event have to disappear from the draft. The practice of indulgences began in the course of the Middle Ages in the Western Church and is as unknown to the entirety of orthodoxy as it was in the first ten centuries of the whole undivided Church. A sufficient theological basis of the practice of indulgences, which led to severe abuses and did the Church immeasurable harm, is missing. In the relevant portion of the draft, one can draw conclusions which go beyond the premises. It would have been better, Maximos declared, if the old practice of penance had not been continued in the form of indulgences. If there was not a desire to simply get rid of the practice of indulgences, then in any case one would have to pay attention to the following aspects; every form of a quantitative calculation of days and years would have to cease to exist, which the draft included. The same applies to any kind of mathematical formula represent-

---

[409] Ibid., pp. 233-234.
[410] Ibid., p. 234.

ing the relationship between the works of indulgence and the remitted punishment of sin; the intended introduction of a type of multiplier in the draft was therefore unacceptable. Also, in the case of a plenary indulgence, any appearance of an automatic effect had to be avoided. If one wants to develop a theology of indulgences, above all a high value has to be set on personal disposition and the personal repentance of the individual. This is the only way that one could slowly bridge the differences with Orthodoxy and the Reformed churches."[411]

The Catholic Church in Egypt sought a declaration on indulgences, since they encumber ecumenism. "The synods of the Coptic Church, represented by the Coptic Cardinal-Patriarch Stephanos I. Sidarouss, basically saw the draft favorably. However, they did not maintain that the handling of the problem was done in an opportune manner, because the agreement with the non-united Coptic Churches would be unnecessarily aggravated."[412] Other national bishop conferences also made similar statements. "Cardinal Lawrence J. Shehan of Baltimore spoke as representative for Cardinal Spellman for the 116 bishops' dioceses from the USA. He emphasized, however, at the end of his statements that a large number of these bishops found a discussion of the problem of indulgences to be unfitting. The matter was not important enough, and, above all, the theology of the draft did not correspond to the theology of the Council. Rather, it reflected a way of thinking that went beyond the Council."[413]

While the bishops' conferences of Catholic countries such as Poland, Spain, and Italy were largely positive, the opinions of the Western European bishops' conferences from completely or partly Protestant countries were negative. "Cardinal Bernard J. Alfrink from Utrecht offered a brief foundational statement and submitted specific remarks. There is a fundamental discrepancy between the practice of indulgences and current indulgence theology. Even in cases where the draft demonstrates progress with respect to abuses and misunderstandings, it in no way abolishes this discrepancy. Cardinal Alfrink views the punishment for sin to always be a type of purely vindictive penalty, which, in part or in whole, could be remitted. For this reason he makes a connection between indulgences and a strongly legal act on the part of the Church. Alfrink still holds to a quantitative assessment of the remission of punishment, while according to the insights of present-day theology, the total has to be seen as a qualitative purification process of the individual. The Dutch bishops' conference,

---

[411] Ibid., pp. 243-244.
[412] Ibid., p. 244.
[413] Ibid.

therefore, wanted a basic review of the 'positio.'"[414] Still clearer were the statements relating to the common opinions of the Austrian and German bishops' conference and made by Cardinal Franz König and Cardinal Julius Döpfner.[415]

5.3 The Abrupt End to Indulgence Theology in 1967

The fact that the Second Vatican Council ended its discussions about indulgences inconclusively enabled the Pope to reformulate and reorder the teaching on and practice of indulgences in 1967 without the Council. In doing so, it was the recommended text of his camp at the Council, as well as his expressed opinions prior to 1967,[416] that contributed considerably to what became the official text of the Catholic Church, and this without having to go into the numerous and fundamental objections from the Council. Gustav Adolf Benrath made it rather clear that the whole lot of theological development on indulgence teaching in the twentieth century was placed to the side: "Without significant changes, the wording of the 1965 positio found its way into the Apostolic Constitution *Indulgentiarum doctrina* addressing the realignment of the character of indulgences. Paul VI's proclamation on January 1, 1967, began the long-awaited reform of the practice of indulgences and sent off any further discussion of the teaching on indulgences to academic circles."[417]

It is safe to say that the Pope took several formulations from Poschmann and Rahner. He partly ended an all too ungainly offset of works of indulgence with times in purgatory, got rid of the differentiation

---

[414] Ibid., p. 249.
[415] Ibid., pp. 249-253.
[416] E.g., Paul VI's Sacrosancta Portiunculae letter, as a source AAS 58 (1966): 633 f, quoted in the Akten Papst Paul VI. Apostolische Konstitution 'Paenitemini'. Trier: Paulinus-Verlag, 1967. p. 105 notation 38 (the following is the translator's rendition of the text): "An indulgence given by the Church to the penitent is a demonstration of that wonderful fellowship of the saints, who in the single bond of the love of Christ and the blessed Virgin Mary and the flock of believers in Christ, as well as those who triumph in heaven or are still in the place of purification or who are still journeying as pilgrims upon the earth, are mysteriously bound together. It is through the indulgence, which the Church conveys, that punishment is reduced or abolished, and by which a person otherwise would be hindered from a closer union with God. For this reason the penitent believer finds an aid in this unique form of ecclesiastical love in order to take off the old man and put on the new 'in the image of its Creator" (Colossians 3:10). '"
[417] Gustav Adolf Benrath. "Ablaß". Op. cit., p. 362.

between personal, real, and local indulgences found in 1917 Canon Law, and tried to create a connection to the teaching of penance in the early church. He also sought to avoid all too forensic language. All in all, however, there was only some change in practical execution, while nothing changed with regard to indulgence theology.

The New Catholic Encyclopedia summarized well what was new in 1967: 1. The times relating to partial indulgences fell away. 2. With partial indulgences, the self-obtained effective time was doubled by the Church. 3. Indulgences were no longer preferentially bound to locations or objects but rather to the completed actions taken there.[418] In my view, this is as many steps forward as back.

Practically all Catholic historians view the actions of the Pope regarding indulgences similarly. Herbert Vorgrimler writes: "Pope Paul VI announced a new general ruling on the character of indulgences on January 1, 1967, in his Apostolic Constitution 'Indulgentiarum Doctrina'.[419] The Pope substantially used the submission worked out for the Council on behalf of the Apostolic Penitentiary. At various places, the influence of Bernhard Poschmann's and Karl Rahner's indulgence theology is recognizable."[420] And Johannes Hüttenbügel writes similarly: "Paul VI announced on January 1, 1967, the Apostolic Constitution 'Indulgentiarum Doctrina' with a new general ruling on the characteristics of indulgences. A theological teaching precedes the 20 norms regarding the practice of indulgences, which substantially reflects the Roman 'positio', but which at points make the influence of the indulgence theology of Poschmann and Rahner recognizable."[421]

In spite of the change in language, there are some examples that stand in opposition and demonstrate that the old spirit of compensation offsets is

---

[418] P. De Letter. "Indulgences". p. 436-444 in: New Catholic Encyclopedia. 2. Aufl. Bd. 7. Detroit u. a.: Thomson Gale, 2003. p. 439.

[419] Papst Paul VI. "Apostolische Konstitution über die Neuordnung des Ablasswesens 1967" (Latin/German). pp. 72-127 in: Akten Papst Paul VI. Apostolische Konstitution 'Paenitemini'. Trier: Paulinus-Verlag, 1967; Handbuch der Ablässe: Normen und Gewährungen. Bonn: Deutsche Bischofskonferenz, 1989. pp. 69-93; on the internet: Papst Paul VI. "Apostolische Konstitution über die Neuordnung des Ablasswesens 1967". http://www.martin-loewenstein.de/unveroef/ablass2.html (1.5.2004); Text extract in: Neuner, Heinrich Roos. Der Glaube der Kirche in den Urkunden der Lehrverkündigung. Op. cit., pp. 435-437.

[420] Johannes Hüttenbügel. Der Ablaß. Zeitfragen 49. Köln: Presseamt des Erzbistums Köln, 1999. p. 9.

[421] Herbert Vorgrimler. Buße und Krankensalbung. Op. cit., p. 212.

more alive than ever. The Church has doubled the reduction in punishment since 1967. This is because the Church, on the one hand, offsets what the believer does, and on the other hand, adds the works out of the treasury of merit as well.[422] It was also communicated more clearly than ever before that indulgences are only valid when accompanied by papal consent, and only such a person who has been provided with this right by the Pope is allowed to distribute an indulgence.

What is decisive above all is that the Pope issues a clear denial of the views of Poschmann and Rahner, among others, that we are only dealing with intercession on the part of the Church and not with a legal act that produces something factual: "When the Church in an indulgence makes use of its power as a servant of the saving work of Christ the Lord, it doesn't only pray. Rather, it authoritatively allocates to the rightly prepared believer the treasury of the satisfaction of Christ and of the saints for remission of temporal punishment."[423]

The Pope begins his Constitution with the words:
"1. The teaching on and practice of indulgences has existed for centuries in the Church. They are based on the divine revelation of God and are therefore based on a firm foundation which, as passed on by the Apostles, 'is advanced by the assistance of the Holy Spirit in the Church' by which 'the Church ... in the course of the centuries continually strives toward the fullness of divine truth until God's Word fulfils itself in such truth.' For the correct understanding of this teaching and of its beneficial use we have to remind ourselves of certain truths which the entire Church, in the light of the divine Word, has always held fast and which the bishops, as successors of the Apostles, and particularly, the popes, as successors of St. Peter, have taught and still teach in pastoral practice as well as in the documents of teaching pronouncements over the course of the centuries.
2. According to the teaching of divine revelation, the results of sin are punishments imposed because of God's holiness and righteousness. They are atoned for in this world through suffering, adversity, and hardship in life and particularly through death, as well as in the future world by fire and torment or by the punishment of purification."[424]

---

[422] Comp. Otto Semmelroth. "Ablaß – vierhundertfünfzig Jahre nach der Reformation". pp. 9-27 in: Karl Rahner, Otto Semmelroth (ed.). Theologische Akademie. Bd. 5. Frankfurt a. M.: Josef Knecht, 1968. p. 17.
[423] Ibid., p. 105.
[424] Papst Paul VI. "Apostolische Konstitution über die Neuordnung des Ablasswesens 1967". Op. cit., pp. 73, 75.

The Pope thereby refers expressly to the Council of Trent.[425] Regarding the treasury of merit the Pope writes the following: "This is the ancient dogma of the community of saints, that after the life of each child of God in Christ and through Christ, the lives of all other Christian brothers are also bound together in the supernatural unity of the mystical body of Christ as in a mystical person in a wonderful assembly. In this there exists the 'treasury of merit.' It is not something like the sum of goods according to the ways of material wealth, which have been accumulated over the course of the centuries. Rather, it consists in the unending and inexhaustible value which Christ the Lord's atonement and merits have with God which were offered so that all of humanity could be free from sin and attain to communion with the Father. The treasury of merit is Christ, the Savior himself, insofar as in him the satisfaction and merits of his saving work have constancy and worth. Furthermore, to this treasury there also belongs the true and immeasurable, inexhaustible, and continually new value which before God the prayers and good works of the blessed virgin Mary and all the saints possess. They follow the traces of Christ the Lord with his grace and complete the work assigned by the Father. In such manner they act upon their own salvation and thus also contribute to the salvation of their brothers in the unity of the mystical body."[426]

Otto Semmelroth writes in his introduction to the German translation of the Apostolic Constitution: "It may be by chance that the Apostolic Constitution's 'Indulgentiarum doctrina' regarding indulgence reform was published on January 1 of the year that in Protestant Christianity is the 450th anniversary of the Reformation."[427] It is even more astonishing that Semmelroth means that through the Constitution Protestant Christians now might have access to receiving indulgences.[428]

---

[425] In ibid., p. 73, notation 1, the following is stated (the following is the translator's rendition): "Comp. the Council of Trent, 25th session. Decree regarding Indulgences: 'Since the Church was given full authority by Christ to issue indulgences and since the Church has made use of this full authority since the earliest days...' (DS [= Denzinger-Schönmetzer] 1835); comp. Matthew 28:18."
[426] Ibid., pp. 85, 89, 91.
[427] Otto Semmelroth. "Zur Theologie des Ablasses". Op. cit., p. 51.
[428] Ibid., p. 51.

5.4 Orthodox Believers' Response to the Pope's 1967 Apostolic Constitution on Indulgences

On behalf of Orthodox churches, Emilianos Timiades, the Metropolitan Bishop of Calabria, submitted the Pope's 1967 Apostolic Constitution to a devastating critique.[429] He writes: "There is hardly another teaching that is so opposed to the biblical and catholic faith as that of the teaching of indulgences. Nowhere in the Bible is it said that given true repentance and atonement, sins remain nonetheless unforgiven unless the sinner subjects himself to an additional type of redeeming punishment. It is rather the case that the Gospels show many examples in which Christ rejoices at a sinner's sincere repentance and does not demand any additional work of satisfaction. Christ's atonement and redemption are effective to free the wrongdoings of all humanity."[430]

Initially the Orthodox theologian refers back to the theological teaching in which indulgences are imbedded. "The basic precondition of the Roman Catholic notion of indulgences rests upon three interconnecting teachings. These are:

a) The teaching of the mystical body in its special form, whereby it receives a treasury of merits that can be administered by the Church.
b) The notion of the confessor as a judge, who is authorized to grant indulgences.
c) An estimation of good works which deviates from the Orthodox view."[431]

Thereafter Timiades addresses the Catholic understanding of sin: "... we have to present the nature and effects of sin. These are threefold:

---

[429] Emilianos Timiades. "Zur apostolischen Konstitution über die Neuordnung der Ablässe". pp. 319-349 in: Damaskinos Papandreou (ed.). Stimmen der Orthodoxie: Zu Grundfragen des II. Vatikanums. Wien/Freiburg: Herder, 1969; similarly Johannes N. Karmiris. "Abriss der dogmatischen Lehre der orthodoxen katholischen Kirche", pp. 15-120 in: Panagiotis Bratsiotis (ed.). Die orthodoxe Kirche in griechischer Sicht. 2 Bde./Teile. 1. Teil. Ev. Verlagswerk, 1959 1st ed.; 1970 2nd ed. (both parts in one vol.). p. 113-117; comp. Andreas Merkt. Das Fegefeuer: Entstehung und Funktion einer Idee. Darmstadt: Wissenschaftliche Buchgesellschaft, 2005. p. 73.
[430] Emilianos Timiades. "Zur apostolischen Konstitution über die Neuordnung der Ablässe". Op. cit., p. 327.
[431] Ibid., p. 321.

a) Sin is misconduct against God, which separates the sinner from God. As a consequence, sin includes guilt, or 'culpa,' which means there is a necessary 'reatus poenae aeternae.'
b) The sinner acts as if there is no God. From this there rises up a 'reatus poenae sensus,' which remains as long as mortal sin itself.
c) Each sin is also an attack on the body which is the Church and is a break from it."[432]

Central for Timiades then is the question of whether a person can bring any merits at all before God: "Eternal life is a gift that is completely outside of all 'merits,' which can be obtained by any person. Good works which we accomplish with the help of divine grace are always truly deserving, insofar as they are vital elements of our spiritual growth and are a demonstration of our ethical suitability for salvation. We will be judged and rewarded according to our deeds, which means according to personal merits to which our works testify."[433]

The early church plays a large role in the Orthodox Church. Timiades, however, observes: "The Greek fathers hold unanimously that the completion of penance is neither an integral part of the sacrament of penance nor can it be strengthened or even replaced by the efforts of others. There is nothing in the early traditions, in the Bible, or in the writings of the fathers that could lend such a novel conception any true support. In contrast, there is the fact that in the Western Church, this idea was completely unknown. It was not until 1343 that Pope Clement VI formally opened the 'treasury of merit' with respect to indulgences, such that this theory became an official part of the teaching of the Roman Catholic Church."[434] If we check the New Testament or the teaching of the early church, we do not find a trace of punishment in a legal sense, nor do we see a hint of a motive of vengeance. In contrast, sinners are treated as children of God and are accepted as such (Romans 6:5; 8,14; James 2:23; Ephesians 2:3). The early Greek fathers refer clearly to the dilemma that would arise from a legalistic standpoint. Clement of Alexandria observed: 'Justice is not brought by laws and the sword and also not by fear or punishment but rather by the love of God.'"[435] "Whatever can be said with respect to the practice of granting indulgences, certain facts remain untouched. Such a practice was completely unknown in the early church. Indulgence theology was really first

---
[432] Ibid., p. 326.
[433] Ibid., p. 347.
[434] Ibid., p. 343.
[435] Ibid., p. 323.

The Reform of the Theology of Indulgences 113

demonstrably developed during the Council of Trent (1545-1563), although the elaboration of such theology had begun earlier in a number of papal decrees, for example in Clement VI's (January 1518) bull 'Unigentius Dei Filius' and in the same Pope's 'Exsurge Domine' bull (June 1520). After Trent, Pious VI developed the theology further in the August 1794 'Auctorem Fidei' bull."[436]

Detailed justification of why the teaching on indulgences from the viewpoint of Orthodox theology contradicts the New Testament will be presented further below.

Purgatory is specifically addressed, which is indeed unknown, but which central problem is seen in the teaching of the deservingness of works before God: The primary discrepancy between the Roman Catholics and us does not have to do with purgatory itself but rather with the erroneous notion that the punishment of the sinner could be reduced by the good works of others. Orthodox believers teach that good works indeed lead to a true 'satisfaction' (onesis) but one without satisfactory effect. Such a thing is impossible and unnecessary, because God has provided complete satisfaction by the one-time sacrifice of his Son. No human work is required, no matter what value it might have. If such works are without relevance in this life, how much truer is this in life after death. After all, the soul of a person who dies impenitently cannot in any manner of speaking automatically and against the will of the individual be purified by a simple fire (pyr), whatever this might mean. A passive improvement is also not thinkable, since there is no possibility of a further development and perfection (satispassio) after death."[437]

"The points of agreement and divergence between the Roman Catholic and the Orthodox Church with respect to our topic can be seen clearly from the following statement by Gennadius, the Patriarch of Constantinople: 'There is no need for the existence of purgatory as the Roman Catholics maintain . . .'"[438]

5.5 Karl Rahner after 1967

Karl Rahner undertook efforts after 1967 to show that his indulgence theology is not in opposition to the 1967 papal teaching. "As already mentioned, there is a difference of opinion about whether 'authoritative' means a jurisdictional act or whether an official intercessory prayer of the Church

---

[436] Ibid., pp. 319-320.
[437] Ibid., p. 340.
[438] Ibid., p. 347.

is to be understood by it. Karl Rahner and others affirm the latter and see no contradiction with the Constitution on indulgences. According to him, such a prayer is authoritative in the sense that it is a prayer of the Church – one offered by the united and mysterious body of Christ and assured of being answered – and thereby is an infallible prayer."[439]

Rahner had written in 1957 that indulgences carried "no jurisdictional power" but rather "consist in being a special prayer of the Church"[440] and are only an intercession of the Church,[441] "according to the Words of Christ an infallibly effective prayer."[442] In 1967[443] he defended the compatibility of Poschmann's and his teaching with Pope Paul VI's Apostolic Constitution, in which he countered the critique "of the 'new' theory of indulgences," which viewed indulgences to be a prayer and no jurisdictional act, and by adding that he naturally believed in the legal meaning of indulgences on the basis of God's conferring 'potestas' on the Church.[444] While many Catholic theologians had held with Rahner until 1967,[445] after 1967 there were only isolated cases where theologians represented an alternative theology on indulgences. The reform of indulgence theology was in principle given up. It also died as an issue on the side of its most important representatives, while thinking moved in favor of the view of papal authorities.

By the way, Rahner came out just as clearly and massively against most intra-Catholic opinions in 1967 relating to certain teaching formulated at Trent and twice again at the Second Vatican Council.[446] The teaching was that the sacrament of penance included reconciliation with the Church. Such voices

---

[439] Johannes Hüttenbügel. Der Ablaß. Zeitfragen 49. Köln: Presseamt des Erzbistums Köln, 1999. p. 16.
[440] Karl Rahner. "Ablaß". Op. cit., pp. 51-52.
[441] Karl Rahner "Kleiner theologischer Traktat über den Ablaß". Op. cit., pp. 484-489.
[442] Ibid., p. 483.
[443] Karl Rahner "Zur heutigen kirchlichen Ablaßlehre". Op. cit.
[444] Ibid., pp. 493-497.
[445] E. g. Max Lackmann. "Überlegungen zur Lehre vom 'Schatz der Kirche'". pp. 75-157 in: Georg Muschalek et al. Gespräch über den Ablaß. Arbeiten zur kirchlichen Wiedervereinigung – Kirchengeschichtliche Reihe 2. Graz: Verlag Styria, 1965. pp. 150-151; Georg Muschalek. "Der Ablaß in der heutigen Praxis und Lehre der katholischen Kirche". p. 13-37 in: Georg Muschalek et al. Gespräch über den Ablaß. Arbeiten zur kirchlichen Wiedervereinigung – Kirchengeschichtliche Reihe 2. Graz: Verlag Styria, 1965. pp. 36-37; Otto Semmelroth. "Zur Theologie des Ablasses". Op. cit.
[446] 'Lumen gentium' Chapter 11 und 'Presbyterorum ordinis' Chapter 5.

saw the teaching as new and harmful.[447] According to Rahner, the teaching had fallen into oblivion in the intervening centuries since Trent and for the first time in 1922 was again represented by B.F. Xiberta.[448] He also criticized important historians of the sacrament of penance, who held this to be new thinking.[449] In reality, on the basis of covenantal ethics in the Old and New Testaments, the teaching was biblical.[450] It arose unavoidably from the teaching of binding and loosing and was taught by the church fathers.[451]

5.6 Schillebeeckx in Light of 1967

Edward Schillebeeckx assumed, in a very insightful article on the history of indulgences in 1964,[452] that Luther turned against the abuse of the church office in dealing with indulgences[453] but not against indulgences as they were originally conceived in the time from the eleventh until the thirteenth centuries. One had long ago returned to the original indulgence concept, and for hundreds of years 'the jurisdictional remission' of ecclesiastical-canonical punishment had lost its content and become hypothetical."[454] Indulgences were simply an intercession on the part of the Church and were therefore no longer a stumbling block for Protestants.

It is ascertainable that Paul VI's 1967 return to classical teaching on indulgences made Schillebeeckx's thought largely obsolete and revealed it to be a pipe dream. Also, viewed from a historical standpoint, it is not possible to agree with him. Indulgences were not associated with financial abuse for the first time in the sixteenth century. This had already occurred at the time they appeared and during their dissemination via the fusing of the notion of crusades with indulgences. A direct decoupling of financial transactions from indulgences was first called for at the Council of Trent, but it was not accomplished until about 100 years later. Furthermore, the core of Luther's indulgence critique was never the financial aspect but rather the denial of the remaining punishment for sin, the treasury of merit, and the

---

[447] Karl Rahner "Das Sakrament der Buße als Wiederversöhnung mit der Kirche". p. 447-471 in ders. Schriften zur Theologie. Bd. VIII. Einsiedeln: Benzinger Verlag, 1967.
[448] Ibid., p. 447.
[449] Ibid., pp. 447-448.
[450] Ibid., pp. 456-457.
[451] Ibid., pp. 459-462; insbesondere Letzteres ist sehr umstritten.
[452] Edward Schillebeeckx. "Der Sinn der katholischen Ablaßpraxis". Lutherische Rundschau 17 (1967): 328-353.
[453] Ibid., p. 328.
[454] Ibid., p. 353.

papal keys of authority over otherworldly destiny. These factors were all present long before the Reformation and were never the subject of revision.

5.7 The Modern View of the Treasury of Merit

It was not until the twentieth century that theologians such as Rahner tried to formulate the teaching of the treasury of merit more precisely and spiritually, as we have above addressed. Basically the new approach failed because of the 1967 papal Constitution.

All the same, the Catholic Church is currently trying to get away from the teaching of the treasury of merit as a calculable measurement. A Catholic theologian writes: "The consequence of this is above all to no longer base the treasury of merit upon the works of saints but rather upon the works of Christ."[455] "The Indulgence Constitution states it more clearly and explicitly: 'The treasury of merit is Christ the Saviour himself, insofar as the satisfaction and merits of his work of redemption have constancy and validity' (Number 5). The new Canon Law of the Church no longer uses the concept of the treasury of merit. It speaks of the treasury of the merits of Christ and of the saints and thereby directs the view away from the mediation of the Church to the origination and the source of the grace of indulgences. In the same way that salvation is a personal and not an in rem reality, so the grace of indulgences is participation in the personal encounter and community of the Son with the Father in the Holy Spirit."[456]

"The Catechism of the Catholic Church indeed tries to adjust the all too material talk of the 'treasury of merit[457] by stating the following: It is 'not the sum total of the material goods which have accumulated during the course of the centuries' (No. 1476);[458] and it describes the work of Christ in a manner that is also acceptable to us: 'The treasury of the Church' is the infinite value that can never be exhausted, which Christ's merits have before God . . . In Christ, the Redeemer himself, the satisfactions and merits of his redemption exist and find their efficacy.' Nevertheless, in the continuation it is completely unacceptable: "This treasury includes as well the prayers and good works of the Blessed Virgin Mary. They are truly immense, unfathomable, and even pristine in their value before God. In the

---

[455] Johannes Hüttenbügel. Der Ablaß. Op. cit., p. 17.
[456] Ibid., p. 17.
[457] A similar example presented in: P. De Letter. "Indulgences". pp. 436-444 in: New Catholic Encyclopedia. Second Edition, vol. 7. Detroit et al.: Thomson Gale, 2003. p. 436.
[458] Available in English at http://www.usccb.org/catechism/text/.

treasury, too, are the prayers and good works of all the saints, all those who have followed in the footsteps of Christ the Lord and by his grace have made their lives holy and carried out the mission the Father entrusted to them. In this way they attained their own salvation (!) and at the same time cooperated in saving their brothers in the unity of the Mystical Body' (No. 1477)."[459]

Does this really reflect the papal line?

In 1989 Zachary Hayes specifically substantiated prayers for the deceased[460] on the basis of the connection between the solidarity of the saints and indulgences but admittedly no more as an alternative to classical indulgence theology.

5.8 The Pope on Indulgences from 1967-2002

The end of the reform of indulgence theology and the revitalization of the view held prior to the Reformation and Trent did not take place from 1998-2000 with Pope Johannes Paul II but rather with Pope Paul VI (1963-1978).

From the 1967 Apostolic Constitution the way goes directly over the then announced new edition of the indulgence handbook 'Enchiridion indulgentiarum' dated June 29, 1968,[461] with all canon and Canon Law details, over intermediate stages in 1975 and 1980, all the way[462] to the 1983 indulgence Codes of Canon Law 992-997[463] which Pope John Paul II released.[464]

---

[459] Theological commission of the society for internal and external missions of the Lutheran Church (Theologischer Ausschuß der Gesellschaft für Innere und Äußere Mission im Sinne der lutherischen Kirche). Ablaß? – Nein danke! Op. cit.
[460] Zachary Hayes. Visions of a Future: A Study of Christian Eschatology. New Theology Series 8. Michael Glazier: Wilmington (DE), 1989. pp. 116-119.
[461] German version: Handbuch der Ablässe: Normen und Gewährungen. Bonn: Deutsche Bischofskonferenz, 1989, part. 19-29 Normen von 1968, p. 30-68 Bewilligungen von 1968.
[462] Rudolf Henseler describes this development. "Ablaß". pp. 707-712 in: Joseph Listl, Hubert Müller, Heribert Schmitz (ed.). Handbuch des katholischen Kirchenrechts, F. Pustet: Regensburg, 1983 1st ed.
[463] Johannes Paul II. Codex Iuris Canonici: Codex des kanonischen Rechtes: Lateinisch-deutsche Ausgabe. Verlag Butzon & Bercker: Kevelaer, 1984². pp. 444-445.
[464] Comp. L. Hödl regarding indulgences in 1917 Roman Catholic Canon Law and before the Second Vatican Council and 1983 Roman Catholic Canon Law following therefrom. "Ablaß V. Kirchenrechtlich". pp. 53-54 in: Josef Höfer, Karl

For those who know the Catholic Church well, Pope John Paul II's Jubilee bull dated November 29, 1998, with its recourse to the bull of 1300 and enormously positive historical references to indulgences, was not a surprise. The Jubilee bull was combined with a worldwide publicity campaign for the 2000 jubilee year that could not be described without including indulgences. Jörg Haustein writes: "The year 2000 will be a 'holy year' for the Roman Catholic Church. It could only be expected that the Bishop of Rome would invite believers into his city with the notification that the visit in Rome would be connected with opportunities for merits and the generous granting of a general indulgence. The November 29, 1998, indulgence bull 'Incarnationis mysterium' could not have been a real surprise. There is not a holy year without an indulgence. Whether the bull could have been more discreet is an open question. In any case, it does not represent an ecumenical step backwards. It is rather a piece of Roman Catholic normalcy."[465] Admittedly, he writes: "Even those who know the Roman Catholic Church well, such as the Waldensians and the other Protestants in Italy, were so irked by the form and content of the bull that they called off all activities that they had planned to have in Italy in 2000. The World Alliance of Reformed Churches also called off all talks with the Roman Catholic Church for the year 2000. One can ask himself whether this reaction was the only right one, but it was a correct one in any event. Whoever wants true progress in ecumenism has to take a step backwards at times."[466]

Rahner (ed.). Lexikon für Theologie und Kirche. Bd. 1. Herder: Freiburg: 1986 (1957 reprint) und Erhard Wagenhäuser (ed.). Ablaßbuch: Neue amtliche Sammlung der von der Kirche mit Ablässen versehenen Gebete und frommen Werke: Einzige von der Pönitentiarie genehmigte vollständige deutsche Ausgabe. Regensburg: Friedrich Pustet, 1952 3rd ed. pp. XI-XVI; Rudolf Henseler. "Ablaß". pp. 707-712 in: Joseph Listl, Hubert Müller, Heribert Schmitz (ed.). Handbuch des katholischen Kirchenrechts, F. Pustet: Regensburg, 1983 1st ed. pp. 707-710. Comp. Rudolf Henseler regarding indulgences in 1983 Roman Catholic Canon Law and later. "Ablaß". Op. cit. 1983 1st ed. und 1999 2nd ed.; Josef Kremsmair. "Ablaß IV. Kirchenrechtlich". Sp. 55-56 in: Walter Kasper (ed.). Lexikon für Theologie und Kirche. Bd. 1. Freiburg: Herder, 1993; Johannes Hüttenbügel. Der Ablaß. Zeitfragen 49. Köln: Presseamt des Erzbistums Köln, 1999. pp. 14-21.

[465] Jörg Haustein. Ökumenischer Lagebericht 99 des Evangelischen Bundes. epd-Dokumentation 41a/1999 (September 27, 1999). Frankfurt: epd, 1999, therein p. 6-8 "Das Jahr 2000 und der Ablaß", here p. 6.

[466] Ibid., p. 7. Ibid., p. 6 correctly adds here: "Bulls and indulgences plan a minor role in Germany, while in other countries, such as in Poland, they are the centre of the holy year."

The Reform of the Theology of Indulgences 119

By the way, the marching direction the Pope took in the direction of a revitalization of indulgences as a central activity of the global Church was official for insiders for eight months prior to the Jubilee bull, when the Pope commented briefly but comprehensively on his indulgence theology on March 20, 1998.[467] Since 1981 the Pope had instructed these authorities annually on questions of indulgences in a similar fashion,[468] and since 1981 the Vatican newspaper *L'Oservatore Romano* often contained reports on the activities of the Pope in this respect.

Parallel to the 1998 bull regarding the jubilee year 2000, the 'Apostolic Penitentiary', the highest court[469] responsible for the sacrament of penance and all indulgences[470] in the Vatican, composed[471] the official canon law handbook on indulgences (Enchiridion indulgentiarum: normae et concessiones) in its fourth version,[472] but it has never been translated out of Latin into another language. In it there are 26 central indulgence norms that are only accessible in Latin ('Normae de Indulgentiis').[473] In addition, there

---

[467] Pope John Paul II. "To the Cardinal Major Penitentiary". 20.3.1998, taken from the English version of L'Osservatore Romano dated April 8, 1998.p. 5. www.ewtn.com/library/papaldoc/jp2penan.htm (May 13, 2004).

[468] Ibid., p. 1-2 (point 2).

[469] Comp. the page of the Apostolic Penitentiary: www.vatican.va/roman_curia/tribunals/apost_penit/index_ge.htm; Lexikon und Ilona Riedel-Spangenberger. "Apostolische Poenitentiarie". Sp. 422-423 in: Bruno Steimer (Red.). Lexikon der Päpste und des Papsttums. Freiburg: Herder, 2001.

[470] There are in addition two other highest courts in the Vatican.

[471] Comp. the difficult translation of the official publishing decree at the beginning of Enchiridion indulgentiarum (see information below): "Decree Fourth edition of the 'Enchiridion Indulgentiarum'". Translated from L'Osservatore Romano vom September 29, 1999, www.catholicculture.rog/docs/doc_view.cfm?recnum=1292 (May 13, 2004); comp. the Zenit press release "Indulgences are not Invention of Medieval Age". Dated September 17, 1999 at www.ewtn.com/library/theology/zindulg.htm (May 13, 2004).

[472] Enchiridion indulgentiarum: normae et concessiones. quarto editur. Vatikanstadt: Libreria editrice vaticana, 1999. 126 pages; accessible officially on the internet as: Paenitentiaria apostolica. "Enchiridion indulgentiarum quarto editur". July 16, 1999. http://www.vatican.va/roman_curia/tribunals/apost_penit/documents/rc_trib_appen_doc_20020826_enchiridion-indulgentiarum_lt.html; am besten zugänglich über die verschlagwortete Internetfassung: Paenitentiaria apostolica. "Enchiridion indulgentiarum". July 16, 1999. www.intratext.com/x/lat0279.htm (not a German translation); comp. the excellent Protestant commentary by Pierre Bühler. Ablass oder Rechtfertigung durch Glauben: Was brauchen wir zum Jubiläumsjahr 2000? Zürich: Pano Verlag, 2000. pp. 1-21.

[473] Ibid., pp. 5-8.

appeared in a shortened version the directive "The Gift of the Indulgence,"[474] which explains to believers how indulgences look in detail.

Furthermore, there were numerous other addresses and texts surrounding the Jubilee year, such as a general audience given by the Pope on indulgences[475] and purgatory[476] and a papal address regarding indulgences in a sitting of the 'Apostolic Penitentiary,'[477] which was directed to its chairman Cardinal William W. Baum.

Also after the Jubilee year 2000, the Vatican remained active on the topic of indulgences with respect to canon law, for example, with the "Decree on Indulgences attached to devotions in honor of Divine Mercy" and the "Decree on the authorization of imparting the annual Papal Blessing with the attendant Plenary Indulgence once a year in the co-cathedral churches," both from 2002.[478]

In the first decree, the Pope declared the second Sunday of Easter to be 'Divine Mercy Sunday' and combined this with the plenary indulgence if in a specific church before the Sacrament one reciteds the Our Father or the *Creed* and "adds a devout prayer to the merciful Lord Jesus (e.g., Merciful Jesus, I trust in you!")."[479] For mariners, the same applies in front of an image of Jesus.[480] For whomever even that is not possible, they may obtain the Plenary Indulgence "if with a spiritual intention they are united with

---

[474] Apostolische Pönitentiarie. "Das Geschenk des Ablasses". January 29, 2000. http://www.vatican.va/roman_curia/tribunals/apost_penit/documents/rc_trib_appen_pro_20000129_indulgence_ge.html.

[475] Johannes Paul II. "Indulgences are Expression of God's Mercy": Generalaudienz September 29, 1999. Translated from L'Osservatore Romano dated October 10, 1999. p. 15, www.ewtn.com/library/papaldoc/jp2indlg.htm.

[476] Johannes Paul II. "Purgatory Is Necessary Purification": Generalaudienz August 4, 1999. Translated from L'Osservatore Romano. http://www.catholicculture.org/docs/doc_view.cfm?recnum=1185.

[477] Pope John Paul II. "Message to Cardinal William W. Baum". April 1, 2000, taken from the English version of L'Osservatore Romano dated April 12, 2000. p. 5. www.ewtn.com/library/papaldoc/jp2baum.htm (May 13, 2004).

[478] At www.vatican.va/roman_curia/tribunals/apost_penit/index_ge.htm are all the official decrees in various languages relating to indulgences, including "Dekret über die Andachtsübungen zu Ehren der Göttlichen Barmherzigkeit mit Ablässen verbunden" (June 29, 2002) and "Dekret über die Berechtigung zum jährlichen Päpstlichen Segen mit verbundenem vollkommenen Ablaß in den einzelnen konkathedralen Kirchen" (June 29, 2002).

[479] Op. cit., p. 2. Available in English at http://www.vatican.va/roman_curia/tribunals/apost_penit/documents/rc_trib_appen_doc_20020629_decree-ii_en.html.

[480] Ibid., pp. 2-3.

those carrying out the prescribed practice for obtaining the indulgence in the usual way."[481]

In the latter, it is declared in great detail in which church buildings and under which circumstances the indulgence can or cannot be granted. Particularly incomprehensible for Protestants are the detailed guidelines that regulate the former cathedral churches where once a year the papal blessing as a plenary indulgence is received through the bishops. This actually applies to all cathedral churches, but here it pertains to churches that at one time were bishop's churches and are no longer such but retain the right of indulgences if the bishop holds a worship service there.

5.9 The Apostolic Penitentiary in 2000

The 'Apostolic Penitentiary,'[482] which is the responsible authority in the Vatican for penance and indulgences, has released a directive relating to the Pope's Jubilee and Indulgence bull entitled "The Gift of the Indulgence."[483] It describes how indulgences look in detail. In that document one finds the following:

"A plenary indulgence can be gained only once a day. In order to obtain it, the faithful must, in addition to being in the state of grace:
– have the interior disposition of complete detachment from sin, even venial sin;
– have sacramentally confessed their sins;
– receive the Holy Eucharist (it is certainly better to receive it while participating in Holy Mass, but for the indulgence, only Holy Communion is required);
– pray for the intentions of the Supreme Pontiff.[484]

"Having fulfilled" these "necessary conditions . . . the faithful may gain the Jubilee indulgence by performing one of the following works, listed here below in three categories":

---

[481] Ibid., p. 3.
[482] See above relating thereto.
[483] Apostolic Penitentiary. "Das Geschenk des Ablasses". January 29, 2000. http://www.vatican.va/roman_curia/tribunals/apost_penit/documents/rc_trib_appen_pro_20000129_indulgence_ge.html.
[484] Ibid. Available in English at http://www.vatican.va/roman_curia/tribunals/apost_penit/documents/rc_trib_appen_pro_20000129_indulgence_en.html.

- "Works of piety or religion
  - Either make a pious pilgrimage to a Jubilee shrine or place (for Rome: one of the four Patriarchal Basilicas — St Peter, St John Lateran, St Mary Major, St Paul —, or to the Basilica of the Holy Cross in Jerusalem, the Basilica of St Laurence in Campo Verano, the Shrine of Our Lady of Divine Love, or one of the Christian Catacombs, and participate there in Holy Mass or another liturgical celebration (Lauds or Vespers) or some pious exercise (the Stations of the Cross, the Rosary, the recitation of the Akathistos Hymn, etc.)
  - or make a pious visit, as a group or individually, to one of these same Jubilee places and spend some time there in Eucharistic adoration and pious meditations, ending with the "Our Father," the profession of faith in any approved form, and prayer to the Blessed Virgin Mary."
- "Works of mercy or charity
  - Either visit their brothers or sisters in need or in difficulty for a suitable time (the sick, the imprisoned, the elderly living alone, the handicapped, etc.), as if making a pilgrimage to Christ present in them;
  - or support by a significant contribution works of a religious or social nature (for the benefit of abandoned children, young people in trouble, the elderly in need, foreigners in various countries seeking better living conditions);
  - or devote a suitable amount of personal free time to activities benefiting the community or other similar forms of personal sacrifice."
- "Acts of penance
  For at least one whole day
  - Either abstain from unnecessary consumption (smoking, alcohol, etc.);
  - or fast,
  - or abstain from meat (or other food according to the specific norms of the Bishops' Conferences), and donate a proportionate sum of money to the poor."

From a Catholic point of view, Christoph Düren writes the following: "The Church is very generous with granting indulgences. This is particularly demonstrated with 'grants that are tied to works, by which the believer – each for himself and on any day of the year – can receive a plenary indulgence . . . The named works are adoration of the most blessed sacrament, at least one-half hour long; the Stations of the Cross; the Rosary, the recitation of the Akathistos Hymn in a church, in a public chapel, in the family, in a religious order, in a religious community, in a Christian association, and generally, if several people come together for an honorable purpose; the meditative reading of the Holy Scripture for at least one-half hour' (EI 1999, S. 49; comp. HA 1989, S. 38, EI 1986, S. 44f)."[485]

Düren summarized well what according to Canon Law and the current state of affairs are the preconditions for indulgences to be considered valid, because it is naturally seen as a caricature that indulgences are effective independent of personal contrition and repentance. First of all, he mentions the necessary components of the characteristics of Catholic penance: "In order to obtain a plenary indulgence, there are generally five conditions that have to be met: 1) sacramental confession, that is to say, freedom from guilt (a confession is sufficient for obtaining several indulgences, about 20 days before or after), 2) a resolute turning away from all sin, that is, the firm resolution to live according to the will of God in all things, 3) receiving the Holy Eucharist, that is, sacramental union with Jesus Christ in the Eucharist, 4) prayer for the intentions of the Holy Father, that is to say, prayers for the representative of Christ on earth who can grant remission of the penalties of sin (e.g., the Our Father and Hail Mary), 5) fulfillment of prescribed works (mostly an indulgence prayer)."[486]

Next to this the basic conditions of Canon Law can be mentioned: "Furthermore, there are, on the basis of Canon Law (c. 996 CIC; comp. EI 1999, No. 17, p. 25) five conditions required for obtaining indulgences: 1) whoever wants to obtain an indulgence has to be a baptized Christian, 2) the person may not be excommunicated, 3) the person has to at least be in a state of grace upon completion of prescribed acts , 4) he or she must have the intention of obtaining indulgences, and 5) he or she must fulfill the imposed acts according to conditions in the set time and in the necessary manner."[487]

---

[485] Peter Christoph Düren. Der Ablass in Lehre und Praxis: Die vollkommenen Ablässe der katholischen Kirche. Buttenwiesen: Stella Maris Verlag, 2000 2nd ed. p. 49 (there as a graphic, here the graphic version on the internet site of the publisher and the author, http://home.t-online.de/home/sabine.dueren/ablass.) Ibid., p. 49 (compare the note to the comment before last).
[486] Ibid., p. 44.
[487] Ibid.

5.10 On the Abolishment of Temporal Assignments Relating to Indulgences

Let us take a look at the history of the temporal assignments that were abolished in 1967. "Thus were indulgences developed upon the foundation of redemption and absolution in the eleventh century, and they were at first sparsely granted by bishops and popes. They comprised a definite and certain effectual promise, and they numerically and clearly circumscribed provisions relating to the remission of temporal punishment imposed by God: a 100-day indulgence exculpated a temporal punishment, for which redemption an earthly service of penance with a duration of 100 days would have been necessary and/or, as was later taught, it shortened the (unknown) entire duration of punishment in purgatory by 100 days. The precondition of the effectiveness was always to be an attitude of penance and an accompanying work of penance of the recipient which at least had a relative correspondence to the indulgence granted (causa proportionata). There were far-reaching consequences now that the subscriber of indulgences could direct the good work of penitent service toward completely specific and beneficially declared goals as defined by him."[488]

Vorgrimler writes: "Initially indulgences consisted of achieving complete remission of imposed penance for a part of confessed grievous sins, or they achieved a reduced punishment for all sins on the basis of a church visit and (often) a financial performance. Later the remission of penance was only expressed in temporal terms (remission of punishment for sin, for which there was a penance of several or many days, from one year or several years and up to many – 1,000, and in the seventeenth century, even 100,000 – years that would have had to be served). In the oldest documents relating to indulgences, there are some clearly disparaging traits in the form of an intercessory absolution for the case where the penitent dies before the expiration of the term of penance.'"[489]

Only in the literature prior to 1967 is it explained how these times are to be understood. An indulgence of about 300 days, according to Gisbert Menge, means that the penitent "thereby expiates that much temporal punishment for sin as he would expiate were he to do strict penance for 300 days of the first Christian time."[490]

---

[488] Gustav Adolf Benrath. "Ablaß". Op. cit., p. 348
[489] Herbert Vorgrimler. Buße und Krankensalbung. Op. cit., p. 205.
[490] Gisbert Menge. Der Ablaß, eine kostbare Frucht der Erlösung. Katholisches Denken 11. Hildesheim: Franz Borgmeyer, 1934. 31 pages. p. 17.

The Reform of the Theology of Indulgences 125

In Pope Paul VI's January 1, 1967, Apostolic Constitution 'Indulgentiarum doctrina,' the earlier common temporal allocations of days, months, and years were abandoned with respect to a 'partial' indulgence, such that there only remained 'partial' indulgences next to 'plenary' indulgences.[491] Indirectly it is admittedly assumed that it is somehow possible to definitively grasp punishment for sin temporally and associate it with an indulgence. Only in this way can it be understood that the Constitution taught for the first time that a partial indulgence doubles one's penitent service of effective satisfaction and shortens purgatory.

In earlier times there used to be comprehensive collections of indulgences[492] that were issued in many languages for believers, which were made up of Canon Law and official statements from the Vatican that expressed which temporal shortenings there were in purgatory for which activities. Even if temporal details have been abolished in the meantime, two examples from the 1952 indulgence collection should be given:

"To the King of Eternity, the Immortal One, invisible, only God be honor and glory in eternity. Amen (from the breviary)
500-day indulgence. Plenary indulgence under usual conditions when one prays the ejaculatory prayer for an entire month each day devoutly (Penitentiary, June 7, 1921, and December 9, 1932)."[493]

Here are two indulgences for the deceased:
"Lord, give them eternal rest, and may the eternal light enlighten them! May they rest in peace! Amen.

---

[491] Pope Paul VI. "Apostolische Konstitution über die Neuordnung des Ablasswesens 1967" (Lateinisch/Deutsch). pp. 72-127 in: Akten Papst Paul VI. Apostolische Konstitution 'Paenitemini'. Trier: Paulinus-Verlag, 1967. Chapter V = pp. 117-119; comp. comment by Semmelroth p. 69-71.

[492] The most important official or semi-official collection of indulgences in German, are, in chronological order: A. Sommer. Gnadenschatz oder Sammlung von Ablässen, welche die römischen Päpste für die Gläubigen beiderlei Geschlechts auf immer verliehen haben. Augsburg: Kollmann, 1843; Erhard Wagenhäuser (ed.). Ablassbuch: Neue amtliche Sammlung der von der Kirche mit Ablässen versehenen Gebete und frommen Werke. Regensburg: Friedrich Pustet, 1939 2nd ed.; Erhard Wagenhäuser (ed.). Ablassbuch: Neue amtliche Sammlung der von der Kirche mit Ablässen versehenen Gebete und frommen Werke: Einzige von der Pönitentiarie genehmigte vollständige deutsche Ausgabe. Regensburg: Friedrich Pustet, 1952 3rd ed.; Peter Christoph Düren. Der Ablass in Lehre und Praxis: Die vollkommenen Ablässe der katholischen Kirche. Buttenwiesen: Stella Maris Verlag, 2000 2nd ed. pp. 17-20 lists over 40 books in German on indulgences from the 16th to the 20th century, p. 18 incorrectly Philipp Jacob Spener. Der Römischen Kirchen Ablass und Jubel-Jahr. Frankfurt, 1750.

[493] Erhard Wagenhäuser (ed.). Ablassbuch. Op. cit., p. 1.

300-day indulgence, only allocable to the deceased (Congregation on Indulgences, February 13, 1908; Point. May 17, 1927)"[494]
"Benevolent Lord Jesus, give the deceased eternal rest!
300-day indulgence, only allocable to the deceased (Holy Officium, March 18, 1909)."

In 1971 and 1989, the German versions of the official indulgence ordinances were published at the German Bishops' Conference in Germany.[495] The current valid version, dated 1999, is not available in German.

At present, there are recommendations of how one can obtain an indulgence on which days, but these are primarily issued privately and then distributed and are not from the German Bishops' Conference. For example, Peter Christoph Düren offers the following recommendations – by calling upon documents from the Vatican – for 2003:[496]

For January 18-25, 2003: "Whoever participates in several activities during the week for the unity of Christians and also participates in the final activity of the week will be granted a plenary indulgence (comp. Enchiridion indulgentiarum, No. 11, § 1, p. 58). Regarding the usual conditions for obtaining a plenary indulgence, see the details above."

For January 1, 2003: "If the hymn 'Come, Creator Spirit' [GL 245] ('Veni, Creator' [GL 240]) is prayed . . . together (publicly) on New Year's Day in order to call upon the power of God for the coming year, a plenary indulgence will be granted (Handbook on Indulgences, No. 61, p. 60; comp. Enchiridion indulgentiarum, No. 26, p. 70). Regarding the usual conditions for obtaining a plenary indulgence, see the details above."

At Pentecost: "A partial indulgence will be granted to that Christian believer, who . . . participated in a publicly held novena, or nine-day prayer, . . . in preparation for Pentecost (Handbook on Indulgences, No. 34, p. 52; comp. Enchiridion indulgentiarum, No. 22, 1, p. 68)."

Similar recommendations are also found in churches which have received the right to indulgences. After John Paul II's pilgrimage to Mari-

---

[494] Ibid., p. 305.
[495] Handbuch der Ablässe: Normen und Bewilligungen. München: Rosenkranz-Verlag, 1971; Handbuch der Ablässe: Normen und Gewährungen. Bonn: Deutsche Bischofskonferenz, 1989.
[496] All from Peter Christoph Düren. "Ablass-Gewinnung im Laufe des Jahres 2003". http://home.t-online.de/home/sabine.dueren/ablass.htm (January 3,2004). There are recommendations found in Peter Christoph Düren that are independent of the year. Der Ablass in Lehre und Praxis: Die vollkommenen Ablässe der katholischen Kirche. Buttenwiesen: Stella Maris Verlag, 2000 2nd ed. pp. 49-234. The book carries the episcopal imprimatur and was ceremonially presented to the Pope and was endorsed by the Pope (see the mentioned website).

azell on September 13, 1983, the following can be found on the entry door there[497]: "Up until April 22, 1984, you can also obtain the Jubilee Indulgence under the following conditions:
1. Visit the basilica (personal viewing).
2. Sacramental Confession.
3. Receive the Holy Eucharist.
Prayer (Creed, Our Father, Hail Mary) for the intentions of the Holy Father."

Canon Law specialist Rudolf Henseler gives a brief summary of which types of indulgences there currently are.[498]
1) The use of holy objects of devotion – as a partial indulgence if they were consecrated by a priest and as a plenary indulgence if they were consecrated by someone in the position of a bishop up to the Pope;
2) Plenary indulgence by visiting a church and praying certain prayers, that is, either on January 2 at specific times or February 2 anywhere, for the deceased, on All Souls Day (November 2) or March 2, twice a year in every parish church – for example, mostly on the day of celebration of the church's founding and on the name day of the eponym,
3) The indulgence granted prior to death within the last rites as a plenary indulgence, whereby the Church otherwise also automatically gives the indulgence at the hour of death if the dying person sees to it to regularly pray.

One can receive the plenary indulgence by radio or television if one hears the papal blessing from Rome 'in devotion' and has a sensible reason not to go to mass and beforehand has participated in confession and has received the Holy Eucharist.[499]

---

[497] Privately owned photograph.
[498] Rudolf Henseler. "Ablaß". pp. 707-712 in: Joseph Listl, Hubert Müller, Heribert Schmitz (ed.). Handbuch des katholischen Kirchenrechts, F. Pustet: Regensburg, 1983 1st ed.; Rudolf Henseler. "Ablaß". pp. 857-862 in: Joseph Listl, Hubert Müller, Heribert Schmitz (ed.). Handbuch des katholischen Kirchenrechts, F. Pustet: Regensburg, 1999 2nd ed.
[499] "Ablaß per Fernsehen". Die Welt dated December 19, 1985.

6 The Dogmatic Debate: Questions and Biblical Justification

6.1 Catholic and Protestant Questions

Regarding indulgences there are numerous unanswered questions. Why does the treasury of merit only expiate temporal punishment of sin? Why not also all the consequences of sin? Where in the Holy Scriptures, in the church fathers, or in tradition can the thought be found that the good works of Christ and the saints are not appropriate for guilt and punishment but rather only for temporal punishment of sin? And vice versa: If the work of Christ not only extinguishes temporal punishment for sin but also the entire guilt and punishment – which is also the Catholic teaching – why does something have to be undertaken to impute Christ's good works with respect to temporal punishment that does not have anything to do with forgiveness on the basis of the work of Christ? Luther asked the question of how we know whether souls in purgatory want to be saved in Thesis 29 of his 95 Theses.[500]

The Catholic researcher Anton Kurz wrote the following in 1900 in a section entitled "Of What Do Indulgences Consist?"[501]: "There are various opinions among theologians on this issue."[502] It has been especially often discussed whether an indulgence is a judicial absolution by the Pope, a payment, or a sheer intercession.

The following is what should occupy us here: There are a number of questions, misgivings, and unsatisfying arguments from Catholic authors. The Catholic Bishop Gerhard Ludwig Müller has stated: "Current theology finds in its historical theological study an abundant mixture of theological reflection with regard to indulgences"[503]

---

[500] Martin Luther. Gesammelte Werke. Digitale Bibliothek. Op. cit., p. 1145: 29. These "Wer weiß denn, ob alle Seelen, die im Fegefeuer sind, den Wunsch haben, daraus losgekauft zu werden?"
[501] Martin Luther. Gesammelte Werke. Digitale Bibliothek. Op. cit., p. 1145: 29. These "Wer weiß denn, ob alle Seelen, die im Fegefeuer sind, den Wunsch haben, daraus losgekauft zu werden?"
[502] Ibid., p. 19.
[503] Gerhard Ludwig Müller. "Ablaß I.-III.". Sp. 51-55 in: Walter Kasper (ed.). Lexikon für Theologie und Kirche. Bd. 1. Freiburg: Herder, 1993. Sp. 54 (abbreviations written out fully).

For example, Bernhard Poschmann writes: "It is precisely the theory of a treasury of merit that makes the Church's teaching on indulgences embarrassing, even offensive ... The misgivings are actually not without reason. The theory carries the complexion of the time from which it originates."[504]

In the same way, Poschmann asks why a person always has to obtain new plenary indulgences. Because so many are given, one cannot be assured of their effectiveness![505]

The Catholic theologian Otto Semmelroth asks in his theology on indulgences how one can even conceive of a plenary indulgence and, in addition to that, how its efficacy can be seen in advance.[506] If the temporal punishment for sin is an earthly and temporal consequence of concrete sins, how could these consequences 1) be removed in advance; and 2) how can they be removed during the time of earthly life?

Let us specifically single out an often-posed question from the Middle Ages and from Luther's time: **Why do not all Christians receive a temporal indulgence from the Pope?**

Helmut Echternach asks the question of what sense at all the temporal punishment for sin has, especially in light of the fact that it can be absolved for every Catholic via a plenary indulgence at any time.[507]

We have seen that Zachary Hayes, as do many others, bases the indulgence on the solidarity of the saints.[508] Admittedly, there is for me at this point a critical objection: If this were the case and my membership in the body of Christ is assured, why is the indulgence not automatically valid with membership in the body of Christ? Why is the body of Christ, represented by the Pope, allowed to give or deny indulgences and lay down precisely under which circumstances I receive an indulgence and under which circumstances I do not? That the Church can proceed so generously demonstrates the fact that the plenary indulgence is automatically valid for all

---

[504] Bernhard Poschmann. Der Ablass im Licht der Bußgeschichte. Peter Hanstein: Bonn, 1948. p. 104.
[505] Bernhard Poschmann. Der Ablass im Licht der Bußgeschichte. Op. cit., p. 114.
[506] Otto Semmelroth. "Zur Theologie des Ablasses". p. 51-72 in: Akten Papst Paul VI. Apostolische Konstitution 'Paenitemini'. Trier: Paulinus-Verlag, 1967. p. 70.
[507] Helmut Echternach. "Korreferat". S. 39-51 in: Georg Muschalek et al. Gespräch über den Ablaß. Arbeiten zur kirchlichen Wiedervereinigung – Kirchengeschichtliche Reihe 2. Graz: Verlag Styria, 1965. p. 47.
[508] Zachary Hayes. Visions of a Future: A Study of Christian Eschatology. New Theology Series 8. Michael Glazier: Wilmington (DE), 1989. pp. 116-119.

pious, dying Catholics if they no longer have time for the Eucharist or for extreme unction.[509]

The question of why the Pope does not simply absolve their punishment for sin has been discussed in Catholic circles for centuries. "If the Church has the source to expunge all temporal punishment, why does it not do it?"[510] James Akin answers this question as follows: 1) because God does not desire it; and 2) so that it depends on the person's disposition.[511] But 1) God would want this if the Pope decrees it; and 2) the Pope could decree that every person who demonstrates penance will receive absolution of the punishment of sin. That he could do that has been known and thought since mediaeval Scholasticism. Otto Semmelroth, for example, answers as follows: the main reason is personal dignity, which takes the responsibility of the sinner seriously.[512] Of course, there is one thing, and that is that de facto the sinner does nothing at all. He indeed should have to do something, but he has it done for him and is thereby absolved.

Bernhard Poschmann asks the question more with respect to history: Why has the remission of the punishment for sin developed in such a complicated manner and demanded at the beginning the difficult dimension of the teaching of the treasury of the Church? According to Poschmann, this can only be seen in light of the history of the sacrament of penance, in which it was originally stated: "Through one's own works of penance can misdoings be cleared away."[513] Thus the complicated construction arose that after forgiveness the believer actually would have had to do something, but now he doesn't have to, since others do it for him.

---

[509] Comp. above to practical use of indulgences.
[510] James Akin. "A Primer on Indulgences" (1996). www.cin.org/users/james/files/indulgen.htm, p. 4 (January 3, 2004).
[511] Ibid.
[512] Otto Semmelroth. "Ablaß – vierhundertfünfzig Jahre nach der Reformation". pp. 9-27 in: Karl Rahner, Otto Semmelroth (ed.). Theologische Akademie. Bd. 5. Frankfurt a. M.: Josef Knecht, 1968. p. 27.
[513] Bernhard Poschmann. Der Ablass im Licht der Bußgeschichte. Peter Hanstein: Bonn, 1948. p. 101.

6.2 Biblical Justification?

6.2.1 The Orthodox Church's View of the Contradiction between the New Testament and the Teaching of Indulgences

We have already seen above that the Orthodox representative Emilianos Timiades holds the teaching of indulgences as something fully foreign to Scripture. Let us look at the reasons in detail: "Even if various passages differentiated sin and guilt from absolution and guiltiness (as in Romans 5:15 and 8:32), these sections know no justification by works. It is rather confirmed that the blood of Christ washes away all sin. And if in the case of forgiveness in the Old Testament (Moses, Aaron, David) and occasionally in the New Testament (comp. Matthew 3:8; 4:17; Luke 14:47; Acts 2:38; and Romans 6:19) there are certain external works that are required as preconditions, it is only for the educational reasons of reform in the sinner. Whoever requires a punishment of the repentant sinner as satisfaction of divine justice and as a condition for the forgiveness of sins beyond contrition and repentance underestimates the power of salvation through Christ. Christ's blood is, according to 1 John 1:7, wholly effective. For this reason, good works and penalties of affliction cannot be considered as valid parts of the required satisfaction for sin. Rather, they are only a convincing proof and fruit of demonstrative repentance. Wherever the Bible speaks of punishment ('timoria', 'thlipsis', 'paideia'), this may not be understood in any legal sense. It would be a contradiction in God's actions if one wants to say that he calls the sinner to serious and expeditious repentance, since the doors of his mercy are always open, and at the same time requires from weak people a substitute or satisfaction in the form of a hard and heavy punishment that would conform to his justice."[514]

The New Testament teaching of complete salvation in Christ cannot be reconciled with the teaching of indulgences, according to which human satisfaction pays for some aspect of sin. "Our Lord brought, once and for all, a full and complete satisfaction of divine justice. He paid the debt for the sins of all sinners in order to free them from their wrongdoings, as Isaiah clearly said. He has therefore become our eternal High Priest, the one and only sacrifice and at the same time the Advocate who lives and intercedes

---

[514] Emilianos Timiades. "Zur apostolischen Konstitution über die Neuordnung der Ablässe". p. 319-349 in: Damaskinos Papandreou (ed.). Stimmen der Orthodoxie: Zu Grundfragen des II. Vatikanums. Wien/Freiburg: Herder, 1969. p. 328.

for us eternally (Hebrews 7:25). Every sin, whether committed before or after baptism, is forgiven in the unending mercy and atonement of the Lord and never on the basis of human good works in themselves. All relevant Bible passages demonstrate that man is not justified by good works but rather that these good works are only external conditions or visible signs of reconciliation. The requirement for satisfaction from the side of the penitent can easily awaken the impression that either Christ himself and the satisfaction he brought on the cross for sin is in God's eyes insufficient, and God therefore requires additional punishment from sinners, or that belief and remorse of the penitent, which are both necessary dispositions, are incomplete. Most quotes from the early Latin Church teachers, which present imposed penitence ('epitimia') as 'satisfactiones,' emphasize the fact that they do not have a value toward salvation but are rather signs of fatherly chastisement in order to shake up the sinner. All writers who directly or indirectly refer to the necessity of good works should be so understood to mean that these works are visible expressions of an inner remorse, which changes the life of the sinner. If Christ's crucifixion were insufficient for our salvation, that would mean that God's glory requires punishment and retribution as expressions of repentance for salvation of the soul. Then it could not be accepted why all sinners do not receive the same chastisement for the same misdeeds. Therefore, we further maintain that penance is in actuality a corrective disciplinary measure..."[515]

At this point, the teaching of the treasury of merit is downright symptomatic. "This use of the teaching of the transferability of the merits of the saints is unacceptable. The merits – however great they may be – could never be viewed as supererogatory or superabundant or as serving as payment for the misdeeds of others. Good works, also those good works of the saints, cannot be overvalued in such a manner and seen as perfect, because they were done completely with the help of God and are rooted in his grace. All glory and grandeur therefore appertain to him. 'To all perfection I see a limit; but your commands are boundless' (Psalm 119:96), because the end and the measure are not human, but rather God himself (Matthew 5:48). For this reason, even Paul does not hesitate to admit that he is unworthy and to belittle his true worth. It is rather the case that he holds onto his imperfection (Philippians 3:13). The same can be said for every pioneer of the faith."[516]

---

[515] Ibid., p. 328-329.
[516] Ibid., p. 336.

6.2.2 Individual Biblical Texts and Topics

In the USA there is a group of Evangelicals who have converted to Catholicism and have missional webpages attempting to prove to their former Evangelical friends that all Catholic teaching can be traced back to Holy Scripture. They are particularly active in the defense of the teaching of purgatory.[517] Which texts from the New Testament do they present in favor of purgatory?[518]

After noting that the tradition primarily relies on 2 Maccabees 12:38-46; Matthew 5:26; 12:32; and I Corinthians 3:11-15, the American Catholic author Zachary Hayes writes in his defense of the teaching of purgatory that it does not contradict the Bible:[519] "While there are no proof texts that contradict the teaching of purgatory, the biblical basis for the teaching remains unclear."[520]

The Catholic Bishop Gerhard Ludwig Müller writes at the beginning of his article in the *Lexicon of Theology and the Church* (*Lexikon für Theologie und Kirche*): "Indulgences have in practice and in their theological jus-

---

[517] E. g. James Akin. "How to Explain Purgatory to Protestants" (13 pages). www.cin.org/users/james/files/how2purg.htm (3.1.2004), p. 2; also www.ewtn.com/library/answers/how2purg.htm, p. 2 (January 3, 2004) ; Basil Cole. "Devotion to the Poor and Rich Souls in Purgator". Homiletic & Pastoral Review (199): 29-46. www.catholicculture.org/docs/doc_view.cfm?recnum=1210 (January 3, 2004); Fr. James Buckley. Most Reasonable Doctrine". Homiletic & Pastoral Review (199): 29-46. www.catholicculture.org/docs/doc_view.cfm?recnum=4683 (January 3, 2004); James Akin. "Purgatory" (1996). www.ewtn.com/library/answers/purgatory.htm (January 3, 2004); James Akin. "Purgatory" (1996). www.ewtn.com/library/answers/purgatory.htm (January 3, 2004); Brent Arias. "Purgatory". www.catholicsource.net/articles/purgatory.htm (January 3, 2004). Comp. Additionally www.catholiclinks.org/lastthingsenglish. htm; www.salvationhistory.com/library/apologetics/purgind.cfm; http://home pages.paradise.net.nz/mischedj/ct1_purgatory.html; http://cr.ashlux.com/apologetics/salvation/purgatory/.

[518] Well compiled in John C. Keenan. "On Indulgences". 6 pages. www.integrityonline.com/homes/mgross/keenan_indulg.html (April 3, 2004) p. 3-5. The best discussion of the arguments of which I am aware are found in Norman L. Geisler, Ralph E. MacKenzie. Roman Catholics and Evangelicals: Agreements and Differences. Baker Books, 1998 (1995). p. 333-337. A German language website, which similarly argues for indulgences and purgatory with Bible texts is www.fegefeuer.ch/page49.html through ... page51.html.

[519] Zachary Hayes. Visions of a Future: A Study of Christian Eschatology. New Theology Series 8. Michael Glazier: Wilmington (DE), 1989. pp. 111-116; comp. 116-121.

[520] Ibid., p. 112.

The Dogmatic Debate: Questions and Biblical Justification 135

tification no exemplar in the New Testament and in the public church of the first century."[521]

6.2.2.1 2 Maccabees 12:41-46

In Luther's time[522] and up until the current day,[523] 2 Maccabees 12:41-46 was believed to be the primary witness to and proof of purgatory. An Orthodox theologian writes the following about the Catholic conception: "The teaching that virtues produce merit is often seen by Roman Catholic theologians in connection with sacrifices brought by Maccabeus for the dead warriors of his army."[524] In the Catechism of the Catholic Church,[525] it is stated as follows: "This teaching is also based on the practice of prayer for the dead, already mentioned in sacred Scripture: 'Therefore [Judas Maccabeus] made atonement for the dead, that they might be delivered from their sin' (2 Maccabees 12:46). "

In 2 Maccabees 12:43-44, funds are collected for the fallen in order to bring a sin offering. Prayers for the deceased are mentioned in 2 Maccabees 12:44, 46: "And making a gathering, he sent twelve thousand drachmas of silver to Jerusalem for sacrifice to be offered for the sins of the dead, thinking well and religiously concerning the resurrection. (For if he had not hoped that they that were slain should rise again, it would have seemed superfluous and vain to pray for the dead), and because he considered that they who had fallen asleep with godliness, had great grace laid up for them. It is therefore a holy and wholesome thought to pray for the dead, that they may be loosed from sins" (2 Maccabees 12:43-46).

---

[521] Gerhard Ludwig Müller. "Ablaß I.-III.". Sp. 51-55 in: Walter Kasper (ed.). Lexikon für Theologie und Kirche. Bd. 1. Freiburg: Herder, 1993. Sp. 52 (abbreviations written out fully).

[522] See Jacques Le Goff. Die Geburt des Fegefeuers: Vom Wandel des Weltbildes im Mittelalter. München: dtv, 1990. pp. 59-60.

[523] E. g. James Akin. "How to Explain Purgatory to Protestants" (13 pages). www.cin.org/users/james/files/how2purg.htm (January 3, 2004). p. 1, 2-3; also www.ewtn.com/library/answers/how2purg.htm (January 3, 2004) "Purgatory: What the Bible Says". http://www.religioustolerance.org/purgatory2.htm (May 1, 2004). p. 1.

[524] Emilianos Timiades. "Zur apostolischen Konstitution über die Neuordnung der Ablässe". pp. 319-349 in: Damaskinos Papandreou (ed.). Stimmen der Orthodoxie: Zu Grundfragen des II. Vatikanums. Wien/Freiburg: Herder, 1969. p. 339.

[525] Katechismus der katholischen Kirche. Oldenbourg: München, 1993. p. 294, No. 1030. Available in English at http://www.usccb.org/catechism/text/pt1sect 2chpt3art12.htm.

Completely disregarding the fact that for Protestants this text does not belong to the Holy Scriptures,[526] and that the modus operandi is also an isolated case in Judaism, the text also does not prove what it is supposed to prove even if we were to count it as part of God's Word. What we are dealing with here is to be seen as sin offerings for fallen soldiers within the framework of the Jewish and Old Testament system of sacrifice. If it has to do with anything, it has to do with forgiveness; and also, according to the Catholic conception in the New Testament era, it is not an indulgence but rather repentance and forgiveness that are proper in this regard. That one can effect the forgiveness of sins of the deceased is also an idea that is clearly rejected by the Catholic Church. Indulgences can only be received for those who have received forgiveness prior to their deaths and are freed from eternal punishment. This is, however, not mentioned anywhere in 2 Maccabees.

6.2.2.2 I Corinthians 3

As mentioned already, 1 Corinthians 3:10-15, in particular verse 15, has historically been the classical text mentioned, in addition to 2 Maccabees 12:41-46, as evidence for purgatory (not, however, for indulgences), even though nowadays the text is only rarely referred to in this connection[527] and is no longer mentioned by more recent Catholic commentators with regard to purgatory.[528]

After presenting Paul and Apollos as workers who are building God's building and church, which has Jesus Christ as its foundation, we read the following in 1 Corinthians 3:14-15: "If what he has built survives, he will receive his reward. If it is burned up, he will suffer loss; he himself will be

---

[526] Comp. arguments in Norman L. Geisler, Ralph E. MacKenzie. Roman Catholics and Evangelicals: Agreements and Differences. Baker Books, 1998 (1995). pp. 333-335 in my book Die Apokryphen. VTR: Nürnberg, 2005.

[527] E.g., http://www.americancatholictruthsociety.com/jrw/jw_1cor3.htm: Antworten von Scott Windsor (kath.) auf den dort abgedruckten Artikel des evangelischen Autors James White. "1 Cor 3:10-15: Exegesis and Rebuttal of Roman Catholic Misuse".

[528] Comp. e.g., Hans-Josef Klauck. 1. Korintherbrief. Die neue Echter Bibel 7. Würzburg: Echter, 1984. p. 7, which understands the expression "as one escaping through the flames" to be a figure of speech meaning "by the skin of one's teeth" and not as a description of a true or conveyed fire; additional arguments can be found in Wolfgang Schrage. Der erste Brief an die Korinther. 1. Teilband. EKK 7,1. Zürich: Benzinger & Neukirchen-Vluyn: Neukirchener Verlag, 1991. pp. 302-304.

saved, but only as one escaping through the flames." Paul is thus treating the question of whether the church, which we build, has spiritual constancy or not. Whether someone has built Jesus' church in a way that has constancy or whether it only has the appearance of Jesus' church, which under pressure and in judgment does not have constancy, is a determinant with regard to his wages but not to his salvation. The workers of God do not burn up in the fire, but rather their earthly works do. By no stretch of the imagination is there mention of purgatory or a time of purification that can make up for earthly failings.

Joachim Gnilka has shown in his book on the history of the interpretation of 1 Corinthians 3:10-15 that this text was the most often quoted text of the early church,[529] of which there were a number of interpretations. These interpretations can be grouped according to whether one viewed the Day of Judgment as Judgment Day, the day of death, or the time of tribulation. The view initially prevailed that fire meant a fire of testing, and Origen held the notion that it was a fire of purification, because that could better explain why the righteous had to go through a fire.[530] Gnilka writes: "This reinterpretation is only possible with a very loose treatment of the biblical text,"[531] because the testing applies not to the person of the teacher and also not, above all, to the building but rather to the work.[532] The development of an understanding of purgatory is found only in the Latin Church and not in the Greek Church. The Catholic Bishop Artur Michael Landgraf has documented in detail that the discussion of purgatory in 1 Corinthians and in the entire discussion in the early church and in the Middle Ages does not have to do with exegesis.[533] So it was perhaps Augustine's vague view in the direction of a fire of purification that became determinative, although Augustine never firmly committed himself one way or another.[534]

---

[529] Joachim Gnilka. Ist 1 Kor 3,10-15 ein Schriftzeugnis für das Fegefeuer? Eine exegetisch-historische Untersuchung. Düsseldorf: Michael Triltsch Verlag, 1955, p. 115.
[530] See part. ibid., p. 117.
[531] Ibid., p. 117-118.
[532] Ibid., p. 123; comp. Gnilkas treffende und gründliche Exegese p. 118-130.
[533] Artur Michael Landgraf. "1 Cor 3, 10-17 bei den lateinischen Vätern und in der Frühscholastik". Biblica (Rom) 5 (1924): 140-172.
[534] According to ibid., p. 148.

6.2.2.3 Remaining Consequences of Forgiven Sins (Including 2 Samuel 12)?

As a justification of the continuation of "temporal punishment" in spite of forgiveness, reference is often made to the temporal consequences of sin, and in particular to 1) necessary recompense, 2) the consequences of sin, and 3) the visible punishment by God that arises in spite of forgiveness.

With respect to 1): The thief had to render compensation in spite of forgiveness, and other offenses also had as a consequence that damages were retrieved. We are first of all dealing here with punishment by the state, which, according to the Bible, is in all cases invariably prescribed. It does not have to do with ecclesiastical punishments, which the church on its own authority varyingly sets down in a variable manner and which, by the way, could not simply be decreed. And secondly, it has to do with making good the damage that has been done to another and not with a punishment relating to oneself. For this reason, it could not simply be absolved.

With respect to 2): The remaining earthly consequences of sin, for example, that the victim of a murder is dead or that a divorce has occurred, are, despite forgiveness, not able to be undone. No action on the part of the guilty person – including an indulgence – can change this.

With respect to 3): God has, in particularly severe cases, partially exercised an earthly, visible punishment in spite of forgiveness. Here, also, there is no action on the part of the guilty party – including an indulgence – that can change anything. This is, least of all, so in the case of death.

The most celebrated example used from the side of Catholics[535] is David, whose adultery and murder (2 Samuel 11), in spite of repentance and forgiveness (Psalm 51; 2 Samuel 12:1-13, particularly 12:13), are punished by the death of the child arising from the adulterous relationship (2 Samuel 12:14-25): "The LORD has taken away your sin. You are not going to die. But because by doing this you have made the enemies of the LORD show utter contempt, the son born to you will die" (2 Samuel 12:13b-14). This death had nothing to do with working off guilt[536] and could not have been avoided by anything. Nowhere can it be seen that the prophet Nathan (or later the Church) would have had authority and power to suspend such consequences.

---

[535] "Purgatory: What the Bible Says". http://www.religioustolerance.org/purgatory2.htm (May 1, 2004) und James Akin. "A Primer on Indulgences" (1996). www.cin.org/users/james/files/indulgen.htm, pp. 2-3 (January 3, 2004).

[536] Comp. Philipp Jacob Spener. Der Römischen Kirchen Ablass und Jubel-Jahr. Frankfurt, 1750. pp. 29-30.

Would the church have been able to simply absolve the consequences of David's actions?[537]

Moses is mentioned in addition to David;[538] according to Exodus 32:32, he was not allowed to enter the Promised Land although he had been forgiven.[539] In Exodus 32:32 Moses is ready to give up his salvation for that of the children of Israel, but the deciding factor is that this is not accepted by God. By the way, if what we are dealing with here is salvation, we deal with eternal guilt and not with temporal punishment or the treasury of merit. "When Moses and Paul declare that they are willing to be deprived of God's kingdom in order for the people to be saved (Exodus 32:32; Romans 9:3), then they do not do this in order to apply their virtue to others. The lapses of a person cannot be forgiven on the basis of supererogated merits of another. The servants of the church have no right to forgive by virtue of the 'superabundant' merits of the saints."[540]

6.2.2.4 Matthew 5:26; 12:32

Texts from the New Testament that are sometimes mentioned as counter examples (Matthew 5:6; 12:32; 18:34; 2 Timothy 1:16-18) do not appear to me to be evidence that people can obtain forgiveness of sins after death if they did not receive forgiveness prior to death. Matthew 18:34 and 5:6 appear in parables which refer to our lives prior to death. In Matthew 12:32, one sees that there are sins that are forgiven neither in this life nor in the afterlife. However, one does not see that there are sins that are not forgiven here and yet are forgiven there. In 2 Timothy 1:16-18, it is unclear to me why Onesiphorus should have been thought to have died. Should one conclude from the mention of the "household of Onesiphorus" that the father is no longer living? He could just as well be included or just not have been in Crete at the time.

In Matthew 5:26, it is written: "I tell you the truth, you will not get out until you have paid the last penny." It is not the future of the believer, who

---

[537] Also according to Helmut Echternach. "Korreferat". pp. 39-51 in: Georg Muschalek et al. Gespräch über den Ablaß. Arbeiten zur kirchlichen Wiedervereinigung – Kirchengeschichtliche Reihe 2. Graz: Verlag Styria, 1965. p. 66.

[538] E.g., "Purgatory: What the Bible Says". http://www.religioustolerance.org/purgatory2.htm (May 1, 2004) and James Akin. "A Primer on Indulgences" (1996). www.cin.org/users/james/files/indulgen.htm, p. 2-3 (January 3, 2004).

[539] Comp. Philipp Jacob Spener. Der Römischen Kirchen Ablass und Jubel-Jahr. Frankfurt, 1750. pp. 28-29.

[540] Ibid., p. 336.

basically has had his guilt removed but who now still has to pay off some small amounts, that is being described here. Rather, it is the future of that person who does not accept the pure grace of forgiveness of guilt and wants to tally up the bill. If I want to transfer the image, then the unrelenting payoff of debt is a picture of hell and not of purgatory.

Matthew 12:32 reads as follows: "Anyone who speaks a word against the Son of Man will be forgiven, but anyone who speaks against the Holy Spirit will not be forgiven, either in this age or in the age to come." In this verse, it is the lost state of man and 'hell' that are being described. Jesus does not want to say, in addition, that whoever does not receive forgiveness in this life can receive it in the next. Rather, it is just the opposite, that whoever does not receive forgiveness here cannot expect it there.

6.2.2.5 The Perfection of Forgiveness

From a Protestant point of view, the Scriptures teach that forgiveness is complete for him who repents from the heart and believes in what Jesus did for him[541]: "Therefore, there is now no condemnation for those who are in Christ Jesus" (Romans 8:1a). All sins are removed (Psalm 103:12; Isaiah 43:25; 44:22; Micah 7:19; Jeremiah 50:20), and nothing hints at the fact that this only applies to a certain segment of sins, or that between guilt and punishment or between temporal and eternal punishment there are differentiations to be made. It is a teaching of the Old Testament that it is the Messiah, the "Prince of Peace," who is at the same time "Everlasting Father" and "Mighty God" (Isaiah 9:6), who not only pays the debt, but who also is punished in our place (Isaiah 53:4) so that we can have peace with God: "... the punishment that brought us peace was upon him..." (Isaiah 53:5b).

Believers Find Nothing Missing before God
Revelation 14:13: "Then I heard a voice from heaven say, 'Write: Blessed are the dead who die in the Lord from now on.' 'Yes,' says the Spirit, 'they will rest from their labor, for their deeds will follow them."   Colossians 1:22: "But now he has reconciled you by Christ's physical body through death to present you holy in his sight, without blemish and free from accusation."

---

[541] Comp. part. Philipp Jacob Spener. Der Römischen Kirchen Ablass und Jubel-Jahr. Frankfurt, 1750. pp. 22-31.

> Hebrews 10:10: "And by that will, we have been made holy through the sacrifice of the body of Jesus Christ once for all."
> Hebrews 10:14: "Because by one sacrifice he has made perfect forever those who are being made holy."
> Romans 8:1: "Therefore, there is now no condemnation for those who are in Christ Jesus."
> Ezekiel 33:12: "Therefore, son of man, say to your countrymen, 'The righteousness of the righteous man will not save him when he disobeys, and the wickedness of the wicked man will not cause him to fall when he turns from it. The righteous man, if he sins, will not be allowed to live because of his former righteousness."

The spirit of Christians, according to the admittedly less than comprehensive and guarded witness of the New Testament, goes directly to Jesus even if it does not receive a new body until the resurrection. This is how the thief on the cross receives the promise that on the same day he will be together with Jesus in paradise (Luke 23:43). Paul says he would prefer to die and "be with Christ" (Philippians 1:23). The martyrs are immediately carried away to be with Christ, according to Revelation 6:9-10, as was Enoch, according to Hebrews 11:5. If one guardedly takes the parable of the rich man and poor Lazarus as an image for a dogmatic statement, since it is not taught elsewhere in the Scriptures, Jesus assumes at that point that hell begins for the unbeliever as immediately after death as Lazarus' time at Abraham's side begins (Luke 16:22-24). In Hebrews 9:27, one finds the following: "Just as man is destined to die once, and after that to face judgment . . . (Hebrews 9:27).

While the Scripture is the sole basis for the believer as the foundation for reconciliation with God 'here and now' and 'then and there,' according to the Catholic understanding, complete grace can only be achieved through baptism, the Pope, priests, confession, sacraments, reconciliation with the Church, satisfaction, and with various other things. The Christian who is continually threatened by mortal sin finds himself lost again through mortal sin, and he has to be saved again.

A Catholic author expresses the point well: "Protestantism has to reject the Catholic teaching of penance, because according to it, the individual participates in the saving work of God and is responsible for his action. In Protestantism there is only faith on the part of the powerless and sin-bound believer in the Savior, who for us is responsible for tendering satisfaction. Penance is just to be made conscious of this fact."[542]

---

[542] P. Thomas Jentzsch. Grundfragen der Ökumene. Op. cit., p. 120.

An additional point is to be made, using words of a Catholic author. "For the sake of historical appreciation, the indulgence can be best placed in connection with its ecclesiastical counterpart, excommunication. Both institutions, the one with a positive nature and the other with a negative nature, have worked together to basically change the position of the Church in the business of salvation. Instead of being a mediator of grace and a helper to the Christian on the sacred journey to God, as it was initially, the Church of the late Middle Ages became the absolute lord of salvation. The Church closed and opened heaven, depending on the political ambitions of the central government and the greater or lesser devotion of the individual to these same ambitions. As long as the Church held complete power, therein lay the innermost reason for moral decline, the source of everything that was elevated to serious conflict, and the cause of the continual call for reform."[543]

---

[543] Adolf Gottlob. Kreuzablass und Almosenablass. Op. cit., p. 298.

7 Appendix: The Development of the Papacy and the Final Disempowerment of the Council

"All statements relating to the authority of the Church as the representative of Christ and God are subsumed, according to Roman Catholic teaching, in the office of the so-called representative of Jesus Christ on earth, the Pope, and find their culmination in him. This finds its blatant expression in connection with indulgences. It is principally the Pope's position to grant and proclaim indulgences. For this reason, it is so solemnly stated in the bull: 'As I lean on these teachings and interpret the maternal sense of the Church, I decree that all believers, insofar as they are adequately prepared, can come during the entire Jubilee Year for the rich enjoyment of the gift of indulgence in a manner relating to the instructions attached to this bull' (IM, No.10, p. 14). The indulgence only becomes valid via this decree of the Pope, and he, therefore, alone has this right to determine the manner in which it is implemented."[544]

Whether the indulgence shortens or completely does away with temporal punishment for sin finally has to do with a decree and decision of the Pope. The effectiveness of the indulgence "is also not based upon the devotion and zeal with which these works are conducted, but rather the cause and extent of the remission of punishment is solely the will of him who grants the indulgence. It is at his discretion whether and how much temporal punishment he chooses to remit to the performer of certain works."[545]

Therefore, we will take a look at the development of the office of the Pope in recent times.

The papacy was extended over the course of the centuries. At the same time, one sees that the relationship of the Pope to the assemblies of bishops, the Council, has always been a significant point of contention. Since only the Pope was able to call a Council, and the Council could decide infallibly in its teaching pronouncements and stood on an equal footing with the Pope, the next step was undertaken in the nineteenth century: in 1870, "ex cathedra" teaching pronouncements made by the Pope were declared infallible. As the Catholic historian August Bernhard Hasler has shown, the

---

[544] Theologischer Ausschuß der Gesellschaft für Innere und Äußere Mission im Sinne der lutherischen Kirche. Ablaß? – Nein danke! Op. cit.
[545] Leopold Kopler. Bußsakrament und Ablaß. Op. cit., p. 216.

Pope did not enforce this dogma in a very transparent and spiritual manner vis-à-vis the Council.[546]

However, the new dogma remained largely theory after this showdown, because the Council and the Pope were in agreement with respect to the questions at hand and no "ex cathedra" decisions were made. It was not until 80 years later[547] that the papacy took the next step by exercising the dogma of papal infallibility: the Pope proclaimed, without the Council and without even referring to an existing historical church tradition, the dogma of the ascension of Maria. Hasler writes: "For the first time after the Vatican Council, he [the Pope] made an infallible cathedral decision, when in the 'Munificentissmus Deus' Apostolic Constitution, dated November 1, 1950, he declared as dogma that 'the immaculate mother of God and eternal virgin Maria was taken body and soul into heaven."[548] "Pious IX himself believed to have had a vision of the Virgin that assured him of the infallibility of this teaching."[549]

This move was an additional step of 'progress' toward placing full power in the Pope, and preparation of the next step could be made: the judicial disempowerment of the Council. The Council was at that time still on an equal footing with the Pope and could also make infallible decisions.

---

[546] August Bernhard Hasler. Wie der Papst unfehlbar wurde: Macht und Ohnmacht eines Dogmas. München: Piper:, 1979; Ullstein: Frankfurt, 1981^Tb; comp. in more detail August Bernhard Hasler. Pius IX. (1846-1878), päpstliche Unfehlbarkeit und 1. Vatikanisches Konzil: Dogmatisierung und Durchsetzung einer Ideologie. Päpste und Papsttum 12. 2 Bde. Stuttgart: A. Hiersemann; Comp. comp. also Hans Küng. Unfehlbar? Eine Anfrage, Frankfurt: Frankfurt: Ullstein, 1980 (part. the historical details); Urs Baumann. "Christ sein auf dem Weg: Ein theologisches Lebensprogramm". pp. 27-62 in: in Hermann Häring, Karl-Josef Kuschel (ed.). Hans Küng: Neue Horizonte des Glaubens und Denkens: Ein Arbeitsbuch. München: Piper, 1993, p. 39-42 [Zusammenfassung von Unfehlbar?]; Otto Hermann Pesch. "Die Unfehlbarkeit des päpstlichen Lehramtes: Unerledigte Probleme und zukünftige Prespektiven". pp. 88-128 in: Hermann Häring, Karl-Josef Kuschel (ed.). Hans Küng: Neue Horizonte des Glaubens und Denkens: Ein Arbeitsbuch. München: Piper, 1993.

[547] Comp. to the more recent papal history and to the extension of papal claims in Hubert Kirchner. Die römisch-katholische Kirche vom II. Vatikanischen Konzil bis zur Gegenwart. Kirchengeschichte in Einzeldarstellungen IV/1. Leipzig: Ev. Verlagsanstalt, 1996 und Gottfried Herrmann. "Römisch-katholische Kirche – damals und heute". Theologische Handreichung und Information für Lehre und Praxis der lutherischen Kirche 17 (1999) 3 (July): 2-8.

[548] August Bernhard Hasler. Wie der Papst unfehlbar wurde. Op. cit., p. 222.

[549] Ibid., p. 79.

Appendix: The Development of the Papacy

The Extension of Papal Power in Modern Times		
1983	Canon Law	The Council is not infallible without the Pope.
1950	Marian Dogma	The Pope is infallible without the Council.
1870	Papal Dogma	The Pope is infallible, as is the Council.
Prior to 1870		The Council is infallible.

This final disempowerment of the Council took place tacitly and covertly with new Canon Law[550] in 1983 (particularly Can. 749 §2). The nice word "collegiality" cannot hide the fact. This tension is clear in Can. 333 §2, which explains the absolute power of the Pope over the Church and particular churches described in Can. 333 §1: "In fulfilling the office of supreme pastor of the Church, the Roman Pontiff is always joined in communion with the other bishops and with the universal Church. He nevertheless has the right, according to the needs of the Church, to determine the manner, whether personal or collegial, of exercising this office."[551]

According to these paragraphs, the Pope works collegially as long as it appears good to him. An appeal to the Council against the Pope is forbidden (Can. 1372). The Council is now only "together with its head and never without this head... the subject of supreme and full power of the universal Church" (Can. 336). For this reason, the decrees of the Council are only valid with the assent of the Pope (Can. 341 §1)! All of Canon Law rests upon the authority of the Pope (CIC XVII/XXV). Repeatedly, his paramount authority is recognized: he is the supreme judge, who cannot be taken before court (Can. 1404-1405), and without him, no Council can decide upon matters, and no Council can take place (Can. 336-341). He is infallible in his decisions regarding teaching (Can. 749 §1, comp. §2). In Can. 331, one reads: "The bishop of the Roman Church, in whom continues the office given by the Lord uniquely to Peter, the first of the Apostles, and to be transmitted to his successors, is the head of the college of bishops, the Vicar of Christ, and the pastor of the universal Church on earth. By virtue of his office, he possesses supreme, full, immediate, and universal ordinary power in the Church, which he is always able to exercise freely."

---

[550] John Paul II. Codex Iuris Canonici: Codex des kanonischen Rechtes: Lateinisch-deutsche Ausgabe. Verlag Butzon & Bercker: Kevelaer, 1984 2nd ed.
[551] Available in English at http://www.vatican.va/archive/ENG1104/__P16.HTM.

The title "Vicar of Christ" had indeed been used before, but now, for the first time, it is anchored in Canon Law. Can. 330-336 greatly strengthen the office of the Pope, and it is left to him "to determine the manner, whether personal or collegial, of exercising this office" (Can. 333 §2). Speaking out of the college of bishops is a mere formality, since Council and the Synod of Bishops are both disempowered.

Additional quotes from new Canon Law document the fact that little can be added to the authority of the Pope: "No appeal or recourse is permitted against a sentence or decree of the Roman Pontiff" (Can. 333 §3). "The Roman Pontiff is the supreme judge for the entire Catholic world; he renders judicial decisions personally, through the ordinary tribunals of the Apostolic See or through judges he has delegated" (Can. 1442). "Students are so to be formed that, imbued with love of the Church of Christ, they are bound by humble and filial charity to the Roman Pontiff, the successor of Peter ... [and] are attached to their own bishop as faithful co-workers ... (Can. 245 §2). "Clerics are bound by a special obligation to show reverence and obedience to the Supreme Pontiff and their own ordinary"(Can. 273). "With respect to the universal Church, the function of proclaiming the gospel has been entrusted principally to the Roman Pontiff and the college of bishops" (Can. 756 §1).

One generally gets the impression, in large measure, that the new Canon Law is actually papal law. In all significant chapters, the absolute primacy of the Pope is emphasized, whether it has to do with pastoral care, evangelization, the wealth of the church, adjudication, or legislation. All functions of the Church are actually only by order of and in representation of the Pope, and this is how they derive their authority.[552]

One sees that with respect to the Catechism of the Catholic Church, what became a completely normal part of teaching had been in part decreed for the first time in Canon Law one and one-half decades earlier. Regarding the Pope, one reads the following: "The Roman Pontiff, as the successor of Peter, is the 'perpetual and visible principle and foundation of unity of both the bishops and of the faithful.' (LG 23). "In virtue of his office, that is, as Vicar of Christ and pastor of the whole Church, the Roman

---

[552] Additional instances of the paramount role of the Pope: Can. 204 §2 (leadership of the people of God); 377 §1-3 (election of bishops); 782 §1 (leadership of all missions); 1256 (authority over all financial assets); 1273 (administration of all church property); additional examples in the list found in the table.

Pontiff has full, supreme, and universal power over the Church. And he is always free to exercise this power" (LG 22).[553]

"'But the *college* or *body of bishops* has no authority unless it is understood together with the Roman Pontiff, the successor of Peter as its head.' Under this condition, the order of bishops 'is also the subject of supreme and full power over the universal Church . . . This power can be exercised only with the consent of the Roman Pontiff'" (LG 22).[554]

Just how much the new Canon Law can be seen as a further development of the papal supremacy is shown by the critiques coming from the pens of Catholic scholars.[555] The journal *Diakonia* dedicated an issue to the topic of "The Bishop." In that issue Heinz Schuster lamented "the covert disempowerment of bishops."[556] Regarding Canon Law, he writes: "A further indication of disempowerment has been signaled for quite a while. It is disguised by a term that is completely innocuous and sounds absolutely conciliar – that is to say, in the sense of the Second Vatican Council: collegiality. That this term has to be spelled out anew, above all, in the light of that which the new Codex Iuris Canonici (CIC) has set down regarding the college of bishops, will be made clear in another article in this issue."[557]

This other article attacks the new Canon Law rather strongly with the title "Collegiality of the Bishops without Roman Centralism?"[558] The Catholic Canon Law specialist Knut Walf assumes that in post-Council development what the term *collegiality* promised has not come to pass. He writes, for example: "If there is anything in the foreseeable future that is an insurmountable barrier in the way of leading to a relaxation between the primate and the episcopacy, it is the new 'Codex Iuris Canonici' from 1983. It cannot be repeated often enough: In its constitutional part, the new Codex does not ex-

---

[553] Katechismus der katholischen Kirche. Oldenbourg: München, 1993. p. 261, No. 882. Available in English at http://www.vatican.va/archive/hist_councils/ii_vati can_council/documents/vat-ii_const_19641121_lumen-gentium_en.html.
[554] Ibid., p. 261, No. 883.
[555] Information in the following; comp. with similar criticism in issues 13 (1982) 4 and 17 (1986) 2. This admittedly does not prevent the conservative Catholic author Georg May. "Kirchenrechtsquellen I. Katholische". Op. cit., p. 36 from writing the following regarding 1983 Canon Law: "The weakening of the primate is unmistakable. The bishops in each category are significantly 'enhanced' . . ." One would have expected a more sophisticated statement from an protestant dictionary.
[556] Heinz Schuster. "Die heimliche Entmachtung der Bischöfe". Diakonia: Internationale Zeitschrift für die Praxis der Kirche 17 (1986) 3: 145-148.
[557] Ibid., pp. 146-147.
[558] Knut Walf. "Kollegialität der Bischöfe ohne römischen Zentralismus?". Diakonia: Internationale Zeitschrift für die Praxis der Kirche 17 (1986) 3: 167-179, here pp. 167-173.

ude the spirit of collegiality. Rather it petrifies the papal position of primacy in such a way that was even foreign to the 1917 Codex. Due to space limitations, this will be made clear using three examples from the new Codex.[559]

Walf mentions as examples:
- the shift of emphasis toward a greater position of power of the Pope in Can. 331: "in a manner that cannot be exceeded, the position of power held by the Pope in the Church and, in particular, within the college of bishops is newly defined"[560], whereby Walf refers to the "modest formulation of the earlier Codex;"[561]
- taking up use of the title "Vicar of Christ" in Can. 331;[562]
- taking up the title for the emperor in the Roman Empire "principatus" in Can. 333 §1 and with it, the associated extension of legal power over the entire Church; furthermore, "ordinary power" that deals not only with the Church but rather extends "over all particular churches and groups of them"[563] (Can. 331 §1);
- the "relativization" of the Ecumenical Council. As Walf sees it, "in the new Codex, the Council is methodically pushed off into a corner in a legally systematic manner."[564] While the old Canon Law treated the Pope and the Council on equal footing in a few sections, in the new Canon Law, the differences are blurred. The Council is integrated in the section about the Pope, and the collegiality of bishops can take place under the leadership of the Pope in a Council by letters and in other ways not heretofore known.[565]

A similar critique of the new position of power of the Pope vis-à-vis the Council can be found among numerous Catholic authors. The international Concilium Foundation[566] dedicated one issue of its journal *Concilium*, which appears in seven languages, to the meaning of the Ecumenical Council.[567] In

---

[559] Ibid., pp. 171-172; comp. the entire text of examples pp. 172-173.
[560] Ibid., p. 172.
[561] Ibid.
[562] Ibid.
[563] Ibid., pp. 172-173.
[564] Ibid., p. 173.
[565] Ibid.
[566] For an official Catholic critique of the Concilium Foundation position comp. Joseph Listl et al. (ed.). Handbuch des katholischen Kirchenrechts. Op. cit., p. 21. Comp. also Rene Metz. "Der Papst" (§ 26). pps. 252-266 in: ibid., which comments on the paragraphs on the Pope of the new church law from an official point of view.
[567] Concilium Foundation. "Das ökumenische Konzil: Seine Bedeutung für die Verfassung der Kirche". Themenheft Kirchenordnung. Concilium (German edition) 19 (1983) 8/9: 499-586.

his contribution, the Italian Church legal scholar Giorgio Feliciani[568] criticized the commission which prepared the ordinances for new Canon Law regarding the college of bishops, because it simply dropped the central role of the Council without any closer attention to providing substantiation of the direction it took. The American theology professor Joseph Komonchak[569] demonstrates that the new Canon Law distorts the provisions of the Second Vatican Council in favor of new papal dominance. He fears that, in the end, the bishops will become servants of the Pope and will no longer have their own authority.

Most clear , however, is the "Statement of the Concilium Foundation on the New Codex of Canon Law" entitled "Anxiety about the Council."[570] The foundation laments the serious changes in the provisions regarding the Ecumenical Council. It compares new Canon Law with the old Canon Law, in which the Pope and the Council stood next to each other on an equal footing in their respective sections. "In the new Codex there is no individual chapter that is especially dedicated to the Ecumenical Council. Instead, the provisions for the Council were taken up in the second part of the chapter that had to do with the Pope and the college of bishops."[571] Furthermore, it is criticized that the Pope has received a line of new titles, for example, that of "Vicar of Christ," while, at the same time, a list of similar titles for the Council has been dropped.[572] The foundation sees in this course of action a development that has been some time in preparation and that leads to a neutralization of the Ecumenical Council.' The Council "is now no longer its own legal institute of the Catholic Church sufficiently distanced from the primate. On the contrary, there is now the danger that the Council will be absorbed by the papal primate."[573]

Needless to say, I am not concerned with saving the Ecumenical Council. I am only trying to make the following clear: If there is to be any 'progress' in new Canon Law, it has to be 'progress' in a definite direction. There is no progress seen in opening to simple biblical truth or to evangelical teaching but rather a further expansion of papal power. This development is even encountering strong criticism within the Catholic Church, and it is furthermore actually being seen by many as a break with Catholic tradition.

---

[568] Giorgio Feliciani. "Der Prozeß der Kodifizierung". Concilium (deutsche Ausgabe) 19 (1983) 8/9: 526-530.
[569] Joseph Kommonchak. "Das ökumenische Konzil im neuen Kirchenrechtskodex". Concilium (German edition) 19 (1983) 8/9: 574-579.
[570] Concilium Foundation. "Sorge um das Konzil: Eine Erklärung der Stiftung Concilium zum neuen Codex Iuris Canonici". Concilium (German edition) 19 (1983) 8/9: 585-586.
[571] Ibid., p. 585.
[572] Ibid.
[573] Ibid., p. 586.

8 Important Literature Regarding Indulgences

This book originally was written in German and mainly used German as well as Latin sources. The debate over indulgences started up between Germany and 'Rome' in the 16th century and the center of the debate always stayed between this axes. Most major works on the history or theology of indulgences from Protestant, Catholic and secular authors were written in German or Latin. Therefore the literature given below (starting with 'Sources') *is the literature given in the German original.*

Here are some further studies in English, which were used for the research, but not listed in the German original:
Kenneth Walter Cameron. The Pardoner and His Pardons: Indulgences Circulating in England on the Eve of the Reformation. Hartford: Transcendental Books, 1965
Joseph Edward Campbell. Indulgences: The Ordinary Power of Prelates Inferior to the Pope to Grant Indulgences. Universitas Catholica Ottaviensis 19. Ottawa (CAN): University of Ottawa Press, 1953
The Handbook of Indulgences: Norms and Grants. National Conference of Bishops. New York: Catholic Book Publ., 1991
Henry Charles Lea. A History of Auricular Confession and Indulgences in the Latin Church. Vol III. Indulgences. Elibron Clasics: Marston Gate (GB), Reprint von Swan Sonnenschein: London, 1896
Alexius M. Lépicier. Indulgences, their Origin, Nature, and Development. Paul, Trench, Trübner: London, 1906[2]
Robert W. Shaffern. The Penitent's Treasury: Indulgences in Latin Christendom, 1175-1375. University of Scranton Press: Chicago, 2007
R. N. Swanson (ed.). Promissory Notes on the Treasury of Merits: Indulgences in Late Medieval Europe. Brill's Companion to the Christian Tradition 5. Leiden: Brill, 2006

The following books are used in the German or Latin original, but have been translated into English:
Catechism of the Catholic Church. Liguori (Italy): Liguori Publ., 1994; London: Burnes & Oates, 2004
Nikolaus Paulus. Indulgences as a Social Factor in the Middle Ages. New York: Devin-Adair, 1922

Hubert Jedin. A History of Council of Trent. 2 vols. Freiburg: Herder, 1961

Bernhard Poschmann. Penance and the Anointing of the Sick. Freiburg: Herder, 1964

An interesting comment published only recently, but proving some of my statements to be right, can be found under: Bonnie Rochman. "Why Catholic Indulgences Are Maling a Comeback". Time. www.time.com/time/printout/0,8816,1881152,00.html, 22.2.2009

8.1.1 Sources

Akten Papst Paul VI. Apostolische Konstitution 'Paenitemini'. Trier: Paulinus-Verlag, 1967

Heinrich Denzinger, Peter Hünermann (ed.). Enchiridion symbolorum definitionum et declarationum de rebus fidei et morum: Kompendium der Glaubensbekenntnisse und kirchlichen Lehrentscheidungen: Lateinisch-Deutsch. Herder: Freiburg, 1991 37th ed. Texte Reg. S. 1621, K10b Fegefeuer S. 1645-1646, M1b (letzte 2 Abs.)

Handbuch der Ablässe: Normen und Gewährungen. Bonn: Deutsche Bischofskonferenz, 1989

Wilfried Joest. Die katholische Lehre von der Rechtfertigung und von der Gnade. Quellen zur Konfessionskunde, Reihe A: Römisch-katholische Quellen, Heft 2. Heliand-Verlag: Lüneburg, 1954

Walther Köhler. Dokumente zum Ablassstreit 1517. Tübingen: Mohr, 1934 2nd ed.

Martin Luther. Gesammelte Werke. ed. by von Kurt Aland. Digitale Bibliothek Bd. 63. Berlin: Directmedia, 2002 (entspricht Martin Luther: Luther deutsch. Die Werke Martin Luthers in neuer Auswahl für die Gegenwart. 10 Bde. Göttingen: Vandenhoeck und Ruprecht, 1991)

Paul F. Palmer. Sacraments and Forgiveness: History and Doctrinal Development of Penance, Extreme Unction and Indulgences. Sources of Christian Theology 2. Westminster (MD): The Newman Press & London: Darton, Longman & Todd, 1960

8.1.2 Catholic Literature Prior to the Second Vatican Council (chronologically)

Al. Bendel. Der kirchliche Ablaß in seiner historischen Entwicklung, dogmatischen Auffassung und practischen Anwendung nebst einem

Anhang über das Jubiläum. Rottweil a. N.: Verlag der J. P. Setzerschen Buchhandlung, 1847
W. H. Kent. "Indulgences". Catholic Encyclopedia (1908). www.newadvent.org/cathen/07783a.htm (3.1.2004) (aus Charles G. Herbermann [ed.]. The Catholic Encyclopedia. 15 Bd. New York: Appleton, 1907-1912)
Leopold Kopler. Bußsakrament und Ablaß. Linz: Verlag des katholischen Preßvereins, 1931. S. 210-222
Gisbert Menge. Der Ablaß, eine kostbare Frucht der Erlösung. Katholisches Denken 11. Hildesheim: Franz Borgmeyer, 1934. 31 S.
Bernhard Poschmann. Der Ablass im Licht der Bußgeschichte. Peter Hanstein: Bonn, 1948
Bernhard Poschmann. Buße und letzte Ölung. Handbuch der Dogmengeschichte. Bd. IV Sakramente und Eschatologie. Faszikel 3. Freiburg: Herder, 1951
Paul Anciaux. Das Sakrament der Buße. Mainz: Matthias-Grünewald-Verlag, 1961. S. 177-192
Edward Schillebeeckx. "Der Sinn der katholischen Ablaßpraxis". Lutherische Rundschau 17 (1967): 328-353

8.1.3 Catholic Literature Since the Second Vatican Council (alphabetical)

Peter Christoph Düren. Der Ablass in Lehre und Praxis: Die vollkommenen Ablässe der katholischen Kirche. Buttenwiesen: Stella Maris Verlag, 2000 2nd ed. S. 13-43
Gisbert Greshake (ed.). Ungewisses Jenseits? Himmel – Hölle – Fegefeuer. Schriften der katholischen Akademie in Bayern 121. Düsseldorf: Patmos, 1986
P. Andreas Hönisch. Liebe Freunde von Pfadfinder Mariens. Katholische Pfadfinderschaft Europas: Meckenheim, 2001. S. 134-141
Johannes Hüttenbügel. Der Ablaß. Zeitfragen 49. Köln: Presseamt des Erzbistums Köln, 1999. bes. S. 14-21
P. De Letter. "Indulgences". S. 436-444 in: New Catholic Encyclopedia. 2. Aufl. Bd. 7. Detroit u. a.: Thomson Gale, 2003
Otto Semmelroth. "Zur Theologie des Ablasses". S. 51-72 in: Akten Papst Paul VI. Apostolische Konstitution 'Paenitemini'. Trier: Paulinus-Verlag, 1967
Otto Semmelroth. "Ablaß – vierhundertfünfzig Jahre nach der Reformation". S. 9-27 in: Karl Rahner, Otto Semmelroth (ed.). Theologische Akademie. Bd. 5. Frankfurt a. M.: Josef Knecht, 1968

8.1.4 Protestant Writings against Indulgences (chronologically and excluding the Reformation)

Philipp Jacob Spener. Der Römischen Kirchen Ablass und Jubel-Jahr. Frankfurt, 1750

Heinrich Eberhard Gottlob Paulus. Geschichtliche und rechtliche Prüfung des Jubeljahr-Ablasses enthaltend zwei Jubeljahrs- und Ablaß-Bullen ... 4 Bücher. Heidelberg/Leipzig: Neue akademische Buchh. von Karl Groos, 1824 (Bd. 1-2) und 1825 (Bd. 3-4)

Helmut Echternach. "Korreferat". S. 39-51 in: Georg Muschalek u. a. Gespräch über den Ablaß. Arbeiten zur kirchlichen Wiedervereinigung – Kirchengeschichtliche Reihe 2. Graz: Verlag Styria, 1965

Norman L. Geisler, Ralph E. MacKenzie. Roman Catholics and Evangelicals: Agreements and Differences. Baker Books, 1998 (1995). S. 331-355

Pierre Bühler. Ablass oder Rechtfertigung durch Glauben: Was brauchen wir zum Jubiläumsjahr 2000? Zürich: Pano Verlag, 2000

Theologischer Ausschuß der Gesellschaft für Innere und Äußere Mission im Sinne der lutherischen Kirche. Ablaß – was ist das? Evangelische Anmerkungen zu der päpstlichen Bulle "Incarnationis mysterium" (IM) vom 29.11.1998. Lutherische Nachrichten 20 (2000) 3: 33-48; jetzt als Faltblatt und unter www.ekir.de/lutherkonvent/Archiv/Aufs%C3%A4tze/Ablass.htm (3.1.2004) = Theologischer Ausschuß der Gesellschaft für Innere und Äußere Mission im Sinne der lutherischen Kirche. Ablaß? – Nein danke! Neuendettelsau: Gesellschaft für Innere und Äußere Mission, (Faltblatt 8 S.)

8.1.5 Historical Presentation from the Pens of Catholics and Protestants (chronological)

Anton Kurz. Die katholische Lehre vom Ablass vor und nach dem Auftreten Luthers. Paderborn: Ferdinand Schöningh, 1900

Adolf Gottlob. Kreuzablass und Almosenablass: Eine Studie über die Frühzeit des Ablasswesens. Stuttgart: Ferdinand Enke, 1906; Nachdruck: Amsterdam: P. Schippers, 1965

Nikolaus Paulus. Geschichte des Ablasses im Mittelalter vom Ursprunge bis zur Mitte des 14. Jh.s. Bd. 1. Ferdinand Schöningh: Paderborn, 1922 (now vol 1 of ed. 2000)

Nikolaus Paulus. Geschichte des Ablasses im Mittelalter vom Ursprunge bis zur Mitte des 14. Jh.s. Bd. 2. Ferdinand Schöningh: Paderborn, 1922 (now vol 2 of ed. 2000)

Important Literature Regarding Indulgences

Nikolaus Paulus. Geschichte des Ablasses am Ausgang des Mittelalters. Ferdinand Schöningh: Paderborn, 1923 (now vol 3 of ed. 2000)

Nikolaus Paulus. Geschichte des Ablasses im Mittelalter. Eingeleitet von Thomas Lentes. 3 Bde. Darmstadt: Wissenschaftliche Buchgesellschaft, 2000 2nd ed. (Reprint of 1st ed. plus an extra introduction)

Bernhard Poschmann. Der Ablass im Licht der Bußgeschichte. Peter Hanstein: Bonn, 1948

Bernhard Poschmann. Buße und letzte Ölung. Handbuch der Dogmengeschichte. Bd. IV Sakramente und Eschatologie. Faszikel 3. Freiburg: Herder, 1951. S. 112-124

Ludwig Hödl. Die Geschichte der scholastischen Literatur und der Theologie der Schlüsselgewalt. 1. Teil. Beiträge zur Geschichte der Philosophie und Theologie des Mittelalters XXXVIII/4. Münster: Aschendorffsche Verlagsbuchhandlung, 1960

Edward Schillebeeckx. "Der Sinn der katholischen Ablaßpraxis". Lutherische Rundschau 17 (1967): 328-353

Karlheinz Frankl. "Papstschisma und Frömmigkeit: Die 'ad instar-Ablässe'". Römische Quartalschrift für christliche Altertumskunde und Kirchengeschichte 72 (1977): 57-124; 184-247

Gustav Adolf Benrath. "Ablaß". S. 347-364 in: Gerhard Krause, Gerhard Müller (ed.). Theologische Realenzyklopädie. Bd. 1. Berlin: Walter de Gruyter, 1977 = 1993 (Studienausgabe)

Herbert Vorgrimler. Buße und Krankensalbung. Handbuch der Dogmengeschichte. Bd. IV, Faszikel 3. Herder: Freiburg, 1978 1st ed.; 1978 2nd ed. S. 203-214

Martin Brecht. Martin Luther: Sein Weg zur Reformation 1483-1521. Stuttgart: Calwer Verlag, 1983 2nd ed.

Kurt Aland. Die 95 Thesen Martin Luthers und die Anfänge der Reformation. Gütersloh: Gütersloher Verlagshaus, 1983

Bernd Moeller. "Die letzten Ablaßkampagnen: Der Widerspruch Luthers gegen den Ablaß in seinem geschichtlichen Zusammenhang". S. 539-567 in: Hartmut Boockmann, Bernd Moeller, Karl Stackmann (ed.). Lebenslehren und Weltentwürfe im Übergang vom Mittelalter zur Neuzeit. Abhandlungen der Akademie der Wissenschaften zu Göttingen. Phil.-hist. Klasse 3, Folge 179. Göttingen: Vandenhoeck & Ruprecht, 1989 = Bernd Moeller. "Die letzten Ablaßkampagnen: Der Widerspruch Luthers gegen den Ablaß in seinem geschichtlichen Zusammenhang". S. 53-72 in: ders. Die Reformation und das Mittelalter: Kirchenhistorische Aufsätze. Göttingen: Vandenhoeck & Ruprecht, 1991

Christine Neuhausen. Das Ablasswesen der Stadt Köln vom 13. bis zum 16. Jahrhundert. Kölner Schriften zu Geschichte und Kultur 21. Köln: Janus, 1994

Wilhelm Ernst Winterhager. "Ablaßkritik als Indikator historischen Wandels". Archiv für Reformationsgeschichte 90 (1999): 6-69

Thomas Lentes. "Einleitung zur 2. Auflage: Nikolaus Paulus (1853-1930) und die 'Geschichte des Ablasses im Mittelalter'". S. VII-LXXVIII in: Nikolaus Paulus. Geschichte des Ablasses im Mittelalter. 3 Bde. Bd. 1. Darmstadt: Wissenschaftliche Buchgesellschaft, 2000 2nd. ed.

Andreas Merkt. Das Fegefeuer: Entstehung und Funktion einer Idee. Darmstadt: Wissenschaftliche Buchgesellschaft, 2005

9 Chronology of Indulgences

From 6th cent.	The tariff penance combined with confession comes from Ireland and instigates the discipline of penance in the ancient church.
Around 1000	A change occurs from the tariff penance to the shrift. Absolution and reconciliation with the Church is no longer dependent on personal service of penance but rather prior thereto.
1029	The oldest known but unpreserved indulgence
1035	The oldest preserved letter of indulgence
1063	Pope Alexander II proclaims a plenary indulgence for all combatants in the crusade against the Saracens in Spain, giving a new impetus to the notion of crusades.
1063	Pope Alexander II proclaims, in this connection, the first plenary indulgence.
1095	Pope Urban II proclaims a plenary indulgence for all participants in the crusade against Muslims at the Council of Clermont.
1125/1138	Peter Abelard is the first theologian to discuss indulgences. He basically rejects them as the first among a line of theologians in the twelfth century.
1145	Pope Eugene III grants in a crusade indulgence a remission of the punishment for sin that is also clearly identifiable with purgatory.
1145/1146	Pope Eugene III authorizes crusade orders (initially the Knights Templar) to collect for indulgences.
1150-1230	Gradual systematic expansion of theretofore absent indulgence theology
From 1170	First example of theologians who argue for purgatory
1187	Pope Gregory VIII proclaims a plenary indulgence for all participants in crusades and for all those who make significant financing available.
Prior to 1197	Cantor is the first theologian to teach purgatory.
1199	Pope Innocent III decrees in a bull that collection boxes be placed in all churches in Europe for crusade indulgences.
1215	The Fourth Lateran Council confirms crusade indul-

	gences. It seeks to end the abuse of indulgences and to reduce their frequency but is ultimately unsuccessful.
1215	The Fourth Lateran Council enacts 'private penance' and the shrift as an obligatory condition for forgiveness.
After 1215	Albert the Great becomes the first theologian to argue for the difference between eternal and temporal punishment.
1230	Hugo of St. Cher becomes the first theologian to formulate the teaching of the treasury of merit.
1231/1254/1274	Ecclesiastical decisions are made to reject the Eastern churches, since they do not teach purgatory.
1248/1249	Albert the Great becomes the first theologian to argue for indulgences, and St. Bonaventure follows shortly thereafter.
1253-1255	St. Thomas Aquinas (1225-1274) for the first time classically formulates indulgence theology in a form that stands until today. He separates indulgences from the process of penance and sees indulgences as assigned to the jurisdiction of the Pope.
Middle 13th cent.	Time of the first known example of indulgences for the deceased, which, however, are rejected by theologians
Appr. 1280	While recipients of indulgences up to this point have primarily been needy churches and monasteries, now all parish churches, monasteries, and foundations are recipients.
1300	Pope Boniface VIII proclaims the first jubilee indulgence. With this, the teaching of indulgences and purgatory fuses for the first time.
1343	Pope Clement IV mentions the treasury of merit in his bull relating to the jubilee year for the first time as grounds for indulgences.
From 1350	There is an increased proliferation of indulgences for the deceased.
1418	The Council of Constance tries in vain to radically reform indulgences.
1439	The Council of Florence promulgates purgatory.
1457	The first known papal indulgence for the deceased occurs. Up until that time such an indulgence has been strongly debated among theologians.
1475	Because the jubilee indulgence of 1475 is used for the crusade against the Turks, the clear separation in the

	meaning between crusade and Jubilee indulgences becomes blurred.
1475	For the first time, with the invention of printing, the jubilee indulgence of 1475, papal indulgence bulls and shrift letters can be distributed in large numbers in Europe. Single-page printing (flyers) brings dissemination of the notion of indulgences in an unprecedented manner.
1476	Sixtus IV uses indulgences for the deceased as a papal teaching for the first time.
1506	Builders lay the cornerstone for St. Peter's Cathedral in Rome; it is predominantly built with funds from indulgences. Beginning in 1507, papal bulls relating to St. Peter's appear.
1510	Proclamation of the St. Peter's indulgence for all of Europe
1513	Cardinals obligate the Pope to be newly chosen to retract the St. Peter's indulgence. In the end, the new Pope, Pope Leo X, rejects this commitment and issues even more extensive indulgences.
1517	Luther sends his 95 Theses to the Archbishop of Magdeburg et al. and to other Church leaders and later turns them over for academic discussion.
1518	Popo Leo X's bull is drafted by von Cajetan for discussion with Luther. What Luther has determined to be a missing official proclamation for indulgences is also submitted in the bull.
1520	Pope Leo X issues a bull banning Luther, which also condemns his rejection of indulgences and purgatory.
1536	In the first edition of his major work, John Calvin makes a detailed rejection of indulgences.
1547	The Council of Bologna discusses indulgences but cannot come to basic agreement or to agreement in many detailed questions and therefore abstains from producing a text.
1563	Without articulation, at the last minute, the Council of Trent produces a short indulgence decree. Without going into the discussion of the Council fathers or the Protestant critique, pre-Reformation indulgences are confirmed.
1794	Pope Pious VI condemns the rejection of the teaching of the treasury of merit as heresy.

1922/1923	Nicholaus Paulus publishes his monumental work on the history of indulgences.
1948	Bernhard Poschmann publishes a history of indulgences and a draft of a new indulgence theology. A request begins for a new indulgence theology, which sees indulgences only as intercession and not as a forensic act.
1949/1955	Karl Rahner, the primary representative of a new indulgence theology, produces writings up until the Second Vatican Council, in which he participates as a Council theologian.
1965	Intense discussion takes place regarding indulgences at the Second Vatican Council between advocates of Karl Rahner's line and the attempt of the Pope to codify traditional teaching on indulgences in a 'Positio.' Because of the objections of the German speaking bishops' conferences, the discussion is broken off, and indulgences are not mentioned in any of the Council documents.
1967	Pope Paul VI issues an Apostolic Constitution regarding indulgences, which essentially adopts the 'Positio' and signifies the end of all attempts to reform indulgences.
1967	The exact times attached to partial indulgences are abolished.
1968	A new papal handbook on indulgences, 'Enchiridion indulgentiarum,' is published, which governs the receipt of indulgences.
1981	Pope John Paul II holds an annual address before authorities in the Vatican responsible for indulgences, in which he confirms classical indulgence theology and announces the expansion of the practice of indulgences.
1983	An extraordinary jubilee year is declared in Rome.
1998	Pope John Paul II publishes an encyclical for the time of the Jubilee year 2000 which, particularly in predominantly Catholic countries, leads to a renewed extension of indulgences.
2000	Jubilee year and jubilee indulgence
2002	Numerous papal decrees are issued that address details of indulgences.

www.ingramcontent.com/pod-product-compliance
Lightning Source LLC
Chambersburg PA
CBHW071506150426
43191CB00009B/1438